Sergei Nechaev

Sergei Nechaev

Philip Pomper

Rutgers University Press
New Brunswick, New Jersey

Frontispiece. One of the few known photographs of Nechaev, taken sometime before his arrest in Switzerland in 1872. *Courtesy Staatsarchiv Zürich*

Library of Congress Cataloging in Publication Data

Pomper, Philip.
Sergei Nechaev.

Bibliography: p.
Includes index.
1. Nechaev, Sergei Gennadievich, 1847–1882.
2. Revolutionists—Russia—Biography.
3. Anarchism and anarchists—Russia—Biography.
DK219.6.N4P65 322.4′2′0924 [B] 79-9983
ISBN 0-8135-0867-3

Manufactured in the United States of America

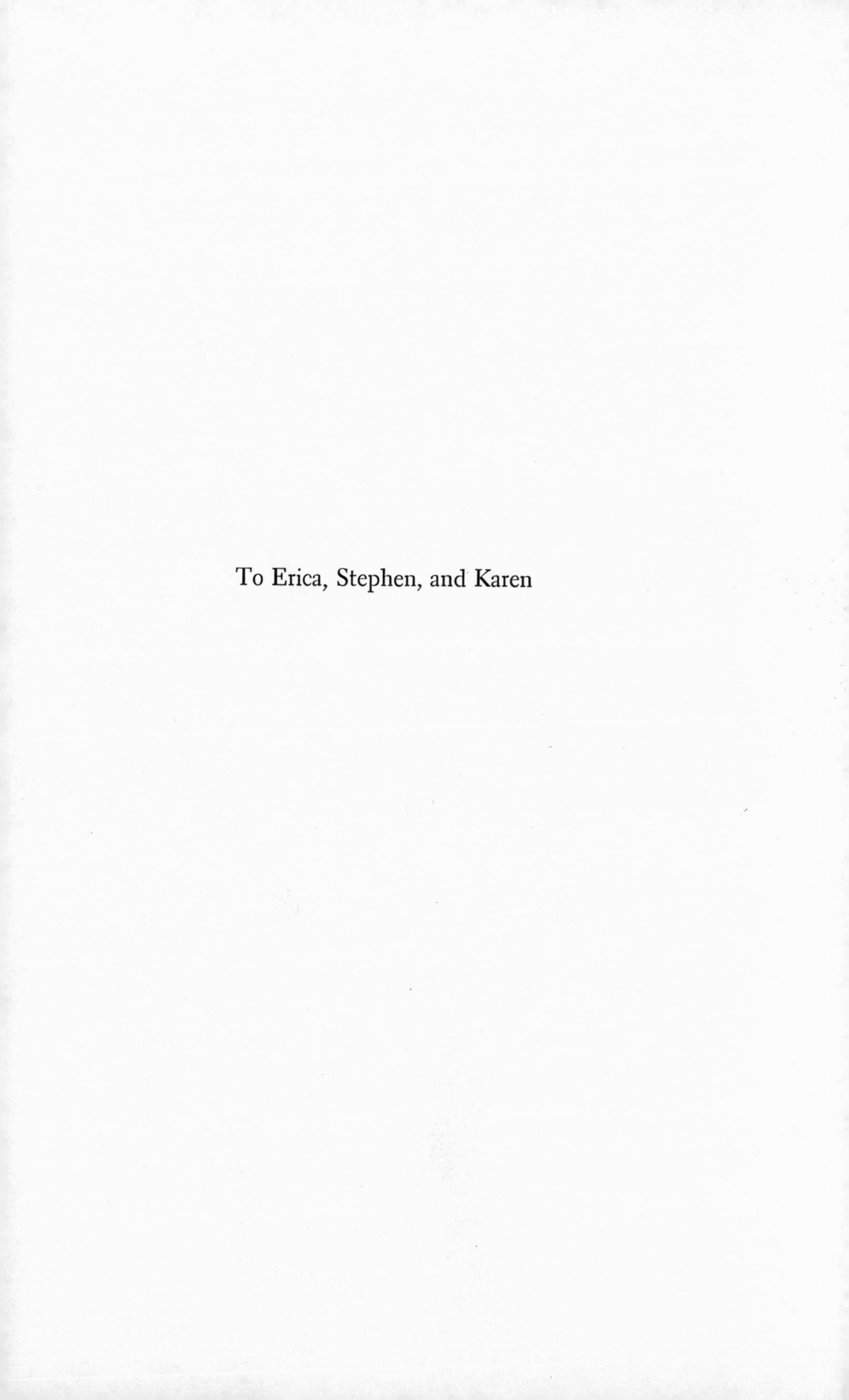

To Erica, Stephen, and Karen

Contents

Preface

This study of Nechaev owes a great deal to the pioneering work of B. P. Koz'min and P. E. Shchegolev. The best recent Nechaev scholarship deals with his relationship to other revolutionaries rather than with Nechaev himself. The work of Arthur Lehning, Michael Confino, and Stephen Cochrane on the Bakunin-Ogarev-Nechaev collaboration and split deserves special mention, as does that of V. Ia. Grosul, K. A. Poglubko, and Woodford McClellan on Nechaev's ties with Balkan revolutionaries—an aspect of his career to which I have devoted relatively little space in this study. I have concentrated on the phenomenon of Nechaevism in the Russian revolutionary movement and have attempted to explore the psychology of Nechaevism.

The research for this book was made possible by a grant from the International Research and Exchanges Board for a trip to the Soviet Union in 1973. Wesleyan University provided a sabbatical and leave as well as research funds without which the project would have been of smaller scope.

I am grateful to M. G. Sedov for his advice and help in the Soviet Union and to the staffs of the Central State Archive of the October Revolution in Moscow and the Central State Historical Archive in Leningrad for theirs. Boris Sapir and Jaap Kloosterman assisted me in my work at the International Institute of Social History in Amsterdam. My special thanks go to Claire Reade for her work with the material in the Staatsarchiv in Zurich. Anna Mikhailovna Bourguina generously shared her vast knowledge about Nechaev and gave me access to her own collection of materials, as well as to the documents of the Nicolaevsky Archive in the Hoover Institution for War, Revolution, and Peace in Stanford, California. In addition, I would like to thank the staff of the Hoover Institution for their kind assistance.

Dorothy Hay, Edna Haran, and Jane Tosto helped in the preparation of the manuscript; Richard Johnson tabulated some of the material on Nechaev's followers; and as in every project that I have undertaken, my wife Alice has helped at every stage of the work in ways too numerous to mention.

I would like to thank Charles Schlacks, Jr., editor of *Canadian-American Slavic Studies,* for permission to use my translation of the "Catechism of a Revolutionary," and Michael Confino for permission to use excerpts from the translations in his book, *Daughter of a Revolutionary.* All other translations are my own unless otherwise indicated. In addition, I am grateful to the Staatsarchiv in Zurich for permission to use the photograph of Nechaev appearing as the frontispiece.

Finally, I would like to thank a group of friends in the Soviet Union without whose warmth and comradeship life there would have been bleak. I shall never forget their hospitality.

Middletown, Connecticut
June 1978

Introduction

The best surviving photograph of Nechaev confirms the descriptions of memoirists and police agents. The photograph shows the convulsively compressed lips described by one of Nechaev's former comrades; the sparse beard and moustache; the studiedly penetrating glance, which had seemed eagle-eyed to some and hypnotic or terrifying to others, but which might best be described as sinister—generally, a youthful face taut with aggression. Below the neck the effect fades. Nechaev wears a cravat, an ill-fitting jacket, and striped trousers. He holds a light-colored, broad-brimmed hat in one hand. His feet are turned at an angle to each other and the half-boots look worn. The comic element which Dostoevsky had perceived in the character who became Peter Verkhovenskii in *The Devils* is definitely present. The staginess of the portrait overwhelms the sinister power in the gaze—it loses cogency—yet a similar kind of theatricality appears in the portraits of dictators of our century.

Nechaev was indeed a dangerous man. Rage and an urge to violent action permeated his being. He wore a red shirt and high boots and carried a cudgel while walking the streets of St. Petersburg. Later, he added a revolver and a knife, and he probably experimented with explosives. One of his disguises was as a Russian Imperial Communications Engineer. The uniform's psychological impact was similar to that produced by an airline pilot's uniform today, for the railroad was to that era what the jet plane is to ours—a symbol of modernity and dynamism. Somehow, he convinced a great many people that weapons and disguises were necessary to his revolutionary activity; and he convinced others that deception, murder, and blackmail were appropriate revolutionary methods. On November 21, 1869, with the help of four members of his conspiratorial organization, The People's Revenge, he murdered another member of the organization, a young man named Ivan Ivanov. Like everything else about Nechaev, the murder had an air of cheap theatricality. Shortly thereafter, the Tsarist police discovered the body and, connecting it with other discoveries made coincidentally, rounded up Nechaev's organization and tried his followers. The lurid story of the murder appeared in the stenographic account of the trial published during the summer of 1871. Dostoevsky's elevation of the story of the conspiracy and murder to art in *The Devils* (1871–1872) secured the young terrorist a place in history.

Even before the appearance of Dostoevsky's novel, Nechaev had become notorious in Russia and Europe by virtue of his original interpretation of the role of revolutionary. But by the time people realized what he was really like, he had caused harm to a substantial number in the still nascent revolutionary movement in Russia and to the community of revolutionary émigrés as well. He paraded as a just avenger, the righteous executioner of a traitor to the cause, and regaled the prominent émigré revolutionaries Michael Bakunin and Nicholas Ogarev with stories of his suffering at the hands of the police and his miraculous escapes from their clutches. The middle-aged émigrés were enchanted. He represented to them a new breed of revolutionary—a fanatic, to be sure—but just what was needed to revive the movement. Not only that, he claimed that behind him stood a substantial army. Bakunin's credulousness is a complicated question, which we will discuss later. Whether Bakunin really believed Nechaev or not, he placed at his disposal the prestige of an international reputation, connected him with revolutionaries of several nations, and helped him acquire substantial sums of money. Bakunin and Ogarev placed their pens in the service of Nechaev's "Committee," which was largely a figment of the young man's imagination. Nechaev served as a quasi-disciple to the émigré revolutionaries during his first stay in Switzerland in 1869. During his second stay abroad in 1870, he revealed his true intentions: He sought complete domination of the movement and its resources and the conversion of everyone, including Bakunin and Ogarev, into his obedient instruments.

Nechaev was unmasked within a few months of his second flight abroad, but instead of withdrawing from the movement he played his role to the bitter end. By the summer of 1871, when the full story of the murder of Ivanov appeared, he had relatively few allies left in the Swiss colony of revolutionary émigrés. In August 1872, one of the émigrés betrayed him to the Russian secret police, and he was arrested in Zurich. The Swiss government arranged an extradition agreement with Russia. They handed him over on the condition that he be tried as a common murderer and not as a political criminal. Though the Russian government complied with this aspect of the treaty in January 1873, instead of carrying out the verdict handed down by the court—twenty years of penal servitude in Siberia followed by permanent settlement there—they spirited him away to a cell in the Peter and Paul Fortress in St. Petersburg. After eight years of secret confinement Nechaev reestablished contact with the revolutionary underground. In one of the most extraordinary episodes in revolutionary history, he began to organize his escape with the help of prison guards whom he had converted to the revolutionary cause. Nechaev's life in prison and this last impressive achievement helped him recoup some of his losses in the eyes of fellow revolutionaries, but the terrorists of the Executive Committee of The People's Will recognized in him a dangerous breed of revolutionary. They soon discovered that Nechaev remained an unrepentant Nechaevist and fended off his last attempts to apply his unscrupulous methods to the revolutionary situation of 1880–1881. The People's Will planned and carried out one of Nechaev's longstanding goals, the assassination of Alexander II in March 1881, but they did not issue the false manifestoes and proclamations that Nechaev designed for them. Within a short time the collapse of the Executive Committee and the discovery of his accomplices among the prison guards ended Nechaev's hopes for escape from the fortress. He died in prison on November 21, 1882, at the age of thirty-five.

The tone of this introduction no doubt reveals that I have not tried to write a clinically detached account of Nechaev and Nechaevism. I believe that Nechaev's career provides an unusually clear example of a type of leadership that human groups, from tiny conspiratorial circles to large nation states, can ill afford. Although even a brief outline of Nechaev's career makes the conclusion seem obvious, the story of his life may add to our understanding of an all too familiar phenomenon in radical movements, whether of the left or the right.

Chapter I

From Ivanovo to St. Petersburg

Sergei Gennad'evich Nechaev was born on September 20, 1847, in the town of Ivanovo, 350 kilometers northeast of Moscow.[1] He was the eldest of three children born to Praskov'ia Petrovna (née Litvinova) and Gennadii Nechaev. Praskov'ia Petrovna's origins are more easily established than Gennadii Nechaev's. She was born in Kostroma province in 1826 to Petr Ivanovich and Fedosiia Maksimovna Litvinov, former serfs who had redeemed themselves and become small shopkeepers and craftsmen, or *meshchane*, as they were called in prerevolutionary Russia.[2] Petr Litvinov set up a painting and decorating shop in Ivanovo in which he employed his son-in-law and a few workers. He must have been quite a heavy drinker, for, given the Russian penchant for alcohol, it is otherwise difficult to understand why his drinking habits should have been noted by a memoirist.[3] Custom and circumstance also suggest that Petr Litvinov reigned as patriarch in the three-room flat he occupied with his wife, his workers, and his daughter and son-in-law and their children. One room of the flat served as a workshop, one as a bedroom for Sergei's two sisters (Fioniia and Anna, the former two years younger than he, the latter four), and one as their parents' room. Sergei slept in a screened-off portion of his parents' room, while the grandparents slept on *polati*—berths fixed between the ceiling and stove—in the kitchen, which also served as the dining room and bedroom for Petr Litvinov's workers.[4]

Both before and after her marriage to Gennadii Nechaev in 1846, Praskov'ia Petrovna worked as a seamstress. According to her daughter, she was a good-looking woman. But she was tubercular and, her condition complicated by a pregnancy, Praskov'ia died at about the age of thirty. It is impossible to establish the precise year, but Sergei was only about eight at the time.[5] Presumably, his grandmother provided maternal care and his grandfather paternal guidance after that, for Gennadii left Ivanovo to work in the neighboring town of Shuia soon after Praskov'ia's death.[6]

Although Gennadii Nechaev's origins are obscure, his biography is both longer and fuller than Praskov'ia's, thanks to his daughter's worshipful memoirs and the wary attentions of police authorities after his son became involved in revolutionary activity. He was born out of wedlock in 1822 to Faina Alekseeva, a domestic serf who was freed shortly afterward. In the census of 1834, he appears as a *meshchanin* of Shuia. The town records for 1830–1840 sometimes list his surname as Pavlov and sometimes as Nechaev. They also list his occupation as calico-printer for that period, and it would appear that Gennadii worked in the textile mills during part of his childhood and adolescence. However, he abandoned the mills some time before his marriage in 1846 and became a waiter in one of the taverns of Ivanovo.[7] Even after he started to work in his father-in-law's paint shop, he continued to work as a waiter and caterer in Ivanovo and, following his wife's death in the mid-1850s, in Shuia.

Fioniia Gennad'evna's memoirs portray a man of conflicting traits—a man both strict and generous, restrained and violent, intellectually inclined and suspicious of booklearning; a model to his son and an example of failure against which Sergei had to rebel; a domineering father who coerced his son yet generously helped him find his own path. These contradictions are all inferred from Fioniia's revealing oral testimony, and there is little independent testimony by which to corroborate or dispute the picture she draws. The comment, "They raised the children strictly,"[8] no doubt applies as much to the grandparents as the parents. Fioniia claims that Gennadii did not beat his children yet describes an important episode in which he birches Sergei; she characterizes him as well read, a freethinker who liked to quarrel with local priests. His signature, preserved in official documents, suggests more than bare literacy.[9] Gennadii was probably a talented but deprived man whose struggle for respectability often failed, causing him to vent his resentment occasionally in explosive acts of defiance and rage.

Although he evidently wanted Sergei to realize fully his own talents, at times Gennadii acted as if he wanted nothing more than a new edition of himself—someone who worked in the mills and taverns of Shuia and Ivanovo and fought for lower-middle-class respectability.

Thus, he took his boy with him to the banquet halls and dining rooms of Ivanovo and Shuia, where they waited tables together; enrolled him as an office boy in one of the largest textile mills in Ivanovo; and worked with him in Petr Litvinov's shop, where he taught him how to paint signs.[10] Sergei had to fight for the privilege of becoming a full-time student, but once the father became convinced of the son's commitment and talent, he supported him as generously as the family's circumstances permitted.

Perhaps the most significant change in their relationship occurred when Sergei (and his sisters) fell under the influence of V. A. Dement'ev, who taught in Ivanovo between 1859 and 1862. Through Dement'ev, the Nechaev family came into contact with the local intelligentsia, some of whom had already become *narodniki* (populists)—most notably Filip Diomidovich Nefedov. While Dement'ev played the role of a protective and encouraging uncle, Nefedov, only nine years Sergei's senior, was like an older brother—a more accessible model. Dement'ev, a talented but dissipated man who came to Ivanovo from Moscow, quickly recognized the boy's talents. The young teacher taught and lived at the corner near the Litvinov house, and Sergei frequently visited him.[11]

Gennadii had taught Sergei how to play the flute, although the boy never became the accomplished musician that his father was; he had taught him how to paint signs, and the young revolutionary later boasted that he had painted most of the signs in Ivanovo; and Gennadii had himself helped to decorate the sets for the amateur spectacles which Dement'ev organized for the children in the neighborhood and in which Sergei excelled.[12] But nothing that Gennadii had taught or could teach would bridge the distance created between father and son by the appearance of Dement'ev and Nefedov. Ties of affection and mutual striving—weakened by Gennadii's long absences after Praskov'ia's death, all but sundered by the father's intermittent insistence upon subjecting the boy to his will, strengthened at times by his kindness to his children and efforts to help them in their schooling—ultimately failed to bind the father and son.

Sergei was only one of many talented young provincials who lost their sense of family and were lured, instead, by the ideals and way of life of the intelligentsia. What happened in Ivanovo was happening all over Russia, and Sergei would meet in a few years other young men and women—some noble, some common—who had broken away from their parents' way of life.

It is not certain that Gennadii ever understood what Sergei stood for.

The local police discovered a taint of political unreliability in the father, who zealously delivered into their hands his son's letters to the family. On May 25, 1873, Gennadii attended a drama presented in the house of Count Sheremet'ev, whose family had owned the village of Ivanovo as a *votchina* (patrimony) since 1743. At the end of the spectacle, the audience was invited to sing "God Save the Tsar" to commemorate the sixth anniversary of Alexander II's survival of an assassination attempt at the hands of a Polish revolutionary. Instead of joining in the singing, Gennadii Nechaev crumpled up his program, threw it across the audience, and remained seated, muttering abusive language while the Imperial monogram was displayed.[13] A police report based upon secret surveillance for the years 1876–1877, after noting that the son was a famous political criminal, said of Gennadii that he "is not completely trustworthy in political matters . . . and because of this untrustworthiness does not merit the confidence to permit him to join this *artel'*."[14] The report refers to a cooperative association of waiters and cooks which Gennadii wanted to join; (at the age of fifty-five, he still worked at waiting and catering in addition to painting.) But there is no indication of other subversive activity. Gennadii's outburst of May 1873 remains an isolated and puzzling incident, the only evidence that he was less than a loyal subject of Alexander II. Perhaps his son's trial with its sentence of penal servitude in Siberia[15] four months earlier lay behind this defiant gesture, but its very inarticulateness is revealing. It suggests that intense, pent-up rage against authority existed side by side with equally powerful respect for authority, the latter responsible at times for Gennadii's extravagantly cruel gestures in its behalf.[16] Whatever the reason for this seeming contradiction in Gennadii's behavior—the strains of upward mobility, deep psychosocial or psychocultural pressures—what is important for this study is that Sergei later found a way to forgive Gennadii and to resolve the ambivalence presumably created in him by his father's fluctuating kindness and cruelty, ambitious striving and obsequiousness, generosity and deceit.

Sergei at first was wholly his father's son. Like his father, he served as lackey to the rich merchants of Ivanovo, whose lavish entertainments he later mentioned in letters to his friend Nefedov. Gennadii was evidently not just a waiter, but often acted as head waiter or caterer at wedding banquets and balls or at buffets, where he served snacks and tea. The little boy used to remove the gold and silver labels from the abundant vodka and wine bottles and pretend they were money. At some point, the boy began to resent his father's position. Fioniia reports that he didn't like his father being a lackey to the rich. Sergei also worked for his grandfather. In addition to gilding icons and decorating churches, Petr Litvinov and his helpers polished floors, painted signs, and embellished with crimson flowers the wooden shaftbows used by peasants to support the shafts and collar in their harnesses. Evidently, the grandfather's heavy drinking strained the family finances so that they all had to work extra hard to make ends meet.[17]

Sergei did not attend a formal school, but this was not a sign of unusual poverty. Most of the children of Ivanovo, whether rich or poor, were educated informally by tutors in small groups. There were only three formal schools with five teachers and 175 pupils in Ivanovo in 1855.[18] Sergei was at first educated at home by one Pavel Prokof'evich, who probably instructed him in letters and Bible reading,[19] and in 1859–1860 he began studying with Dement'ev. Dement'ev, himself of humble birth (the son of a deacon), had made some small mark as a fiction writer and journalist in Moscow but had expended most of his energy on popular enlightenment and all of his modest income on drink. After his brief stay in Ivanovo, he returned to Moscow, became secretary and assistant to the prominent conservative historian, M. P. Pogodin, and by 1871 had evidently drunk himself to death.[20] While teaching in Ivanovo, Dement'ev gathered around him a small group of talented young men with literary aspirations, including Nefedov, V. A. Riazantsev, and N. M. Bogomolov.[21] These young men embodied two of the main concerns of the Russian intelligentsia of the late 1850s and early 1860s—popular enlightenment and fear of proletarianization of the peasants.

Only Nefedov realized these aspirations. Riazantsev died young, while Bogomolov abandoned his attempt at a literary career and returned to Ivanovo, where he assumed Dement'ev's former position in a progymnasium.[22] Nefedov's family had been serfs, his father belonging to the Sheremet'ev family. Like so many of the industrious *obrok*-paying peasants of the area, Nefedov's father had started a small industrial enterprise—a quilting factory. After a try at his father's business and a career as auditor in the historical-philological faculty of Moscow University, Nefedov, although barely out of his teens, began to write tales about peasant life for several journals. He did not become prominent, however, until his descriptions of factory life appeared in *Moskovskie vedomosti* (*The Moscow Gazette*) in 1872. They were among the first exposés of the brutal conditions in the textile factories of Ivanovo, which he called the "Russian Manchester." Nefedov spent much of his later life in ethnographic study, trying to recapture the dignity and beauty of Russian peasant culture. Despite his contribution to the literature of *narodnichestvo* and his condemnation of the world of the factory, he cannot be counted as a member of the revolutionary populist movement. In some ways, he was closer to Slavophilism than to *narodnichestvo*.[23] Most important here, his critical, and sometimes satirical, vision of the expansive capitalism of the growing industrial town and his powerful, though often sentimental, vision of the suffering masses contributed greatly to the adolescent Nechaev's world view.

Ivanovo, which had passed from Ivan the Dread to the Princes Cherkasskii in 1561, to the Counts Sheremet'ev in 1743, and then to the bourgeoisie in the second half of the nineteenth century, was not yet a modern factory town during Nechaev's childhood and early adolescence. Much of the local economy depended on cottage industry, and the mill owners continued to give out yarn for domestic spinning long after Iakov Garelin, one of the local industrial magnates, installed the first machine looms in 1853.[24] Ivanovo was, however, a distinctly proletarian mill town, with a long history of commercial and industrial enterprise. The town's industrial character had changed definitively during the early nineteenth century when the local leaders of the cloth-printing industry began to import English cotton yarn. After the burning of Moscow in 1812, Ivanovo became the most important textile manufacturing town in Russia. In 1868 the railroad arrived, and by 1871 there were almost 15,000 factory workers, 1,283 individuals engaged in commerce, and only 859 peasant homeowners.[25] It was the first city to have a Soviet in 1905, although this fact is often obscured by the far greater significance of the St. Petersburg Soviet. Ivanovo had a sister mill town (technically, a *posad*), Voznesensk, to the west of the river Uvoda (from whence derived Nefedov's pen name, Uvodin). It was merged with Ivanovo officially in 1873 to form Ivanovo-Voznesensk. Pot-houses in Ivanovo-Voznesensk outnumbered churches by a ratio of more than ten to one in the 1880s,[26] which suggests that Marx missed the mark in his well-known comment about the opiate of the masses. Gennadii Nechaev had therefore lived at the very center of the people's life—the cloth-printing factories and the taverns—and his son later exploited this connection with the people in his revolutionary tracts. Finally, one should take into account the regional religious outlook. The stubborn fanaticism of the Old Believers somehow survived their transformation into merchants, mill owners, and proletarians, and perhaps their defiant outlook can be detected in the young revolutionary, Sergei Nechaev.

These facts and figures do not present the true face of Ivanovo-Voznesensk with any vividness. Perhaps it is best to let the writer Nefedov present it:

> From a long way off, there unfolds before you a fine city with stone buildings, a multitude of tall smokestacks and still taller bell towers and splendid churches whose gilded cupolas dazzle one's sight. But this impression is instantly replaced by another when the locomotive rapidly deposits you at the railroad station and you find yourself face to face with the Russian Manchester. Where did the beautiful city that had delighted you a few minutes earlier disappear to? Not a bit of it remains—all vanished! Instead of the beautiful city you can already detect a dense mass of wooden structures, black with decay, spread out over a space of six *versty*, though occasionally it is punctuated by the stone houses of the merchants and long factory buildings. Everywhere you see the thatch and boards covering the shacks and dwellings of the manchesterites. The churches alone, topped by their gilded domes and red chimneys, remain in all of their beauty and somehow sharply distinguish themselves from the surrounding mass of squalor and shocking poverty.
>
> The Voznesensk *posad*, comprising, so to speak, a suburb of the Russian Manchester, but at the same time appearing as a kind of independent entity, a separate municipium, also striking at first glance, devolves into an ordinary town: the usual smudgy huts and shanties covered with thatch and boards, the usual pot-houses and homes, the usual tavern with a monstrously swollen samovar on its signboard; then some vacant lots, and finally the center, where one finds the trading rows, quite empty to be sure, a church and Aleksandrovskaia, the main street, reminiscent of a street in a district town.
>
> Ivanovo itself startles the unhabituated eye of the capital dweller: pitted with ravines, it consists of a multiude of crooked and badly arranged streets intersected by narrow sidestreets; the structures are mainly wooden, entire streets comprised of nothing but blackened huts, and only occasionally does one encounter—usually alongside some decrepit peasant shack—a huge factory with panting steam engines or the big stone house of a rich factory owner with damask drapes covering the windows. Add to all of this a market square with trading shops, pot-houses and countless taverns—which one encounters at every step—and you have the entire externality of the Russian Manchester.[27]

This was the physical environment in which Sergei Gennad'evich developed. He evinced quite early extraordinary traits of character that persisted beyond his childhood and early adolescence. Already embittered in childhood, he pursued his adolescent goals with passionate stubbornness. His sister and early companions note his unusual strength of will.[28] Sergei's marked capacity for systematic effort and self-education permitted him to outstrip most of his peers. He was not, however, a precocious, hothouse student detached from his environment. That was not possible, given the demands made upon him by his father and grandfather. Indeed, like most boys, he played with cardboard soldiers—the Russians against the Turks—and learned with a friend the jargon used by the peddlers of Ivanovo to hide their trade secrets from outsiders.[29] His persistent but vain efforts to master the flute drove his grandfather to despair. But Sergei had a special talent for acting, and when Dement'ev, the organizer of the childrens' plays, noticed it (according to Fioniia), he was alarmed lest his star pupil become sidetracked into a theatrical career.[30] Sergei's sister claims that he possessed a magnetic personality and that, even as a boy, he had sufficient moral conviction to face down his father in family disputes.[31] Upon this claim hangs a tale—the closest thing to a birth-of-a-hero story in Fioniia's memoirs.

The usual problems of a seventy-two-year-old memory trying to reconstruct events that are not much younger complicate her tale. According to Fioniia, Gennadii got Sergei a job as office messenger in Iakov Garelin's mill. He was only nine or ten, she claims, but internal evidence indicates that he was at least eleven.[32] (In her story the boy turns to Dement'ev for advice, and since most accounts do not place Dement'ev in Ivanovo before 1859, chances are Sergei was eleven or older when the events occurred.) One week after the boy began work there, Garelin entrusted him with a business letter to be delivered to the manager of the mill. Sergei had to walk a long way in a snowstorm, and he lost the letter. When Gennadii learned about it, he beat his son with birch switches—an extraordinary sentence according to Fioniia.[33] But did he really lose the letter? Fioniia recalled that Sergei hated the job and on another occasion, had shouted: "I won't wipe the boots of those devils."[34] Gogol has immortalized the meanness of the petty office hierarchs of St. Petersburg. One can imagine the hazing to which an initiate in a factory office in the provinces was subjected and conjecture that the "lost" letter was a protest. Furthermore, it is likely that this incident was one of many, a moment in the boy's continuing attempts to remove himself from his father's authority. In Fioniia's account, after the birching Sergei told Gennadii that he didn't want to work in an office—he wanted to study.[35] The incident apparently provoked Sergei's declaration of independence and forced him to assert his choice of a better path than the one chosen for him by his father. It was roughly at this time that he elicited Dement'ev's intervention, although it is not clear how long after the incident, or how long Sergei continued to work in Garelin's office. Fioniia transmits Dement'ev's essential message, distilled from several conversations: "Just look how you run around in circles here and get beaten by your father for it. You'll be better off studying."[36] Sergei became Dement'ev's protegé and ceased to see his future through his father's eyes. Furthermore, at about the time that Sergei was shifting his loyalties to his intelligentsia teachers, Gennadii found himself a new wife, Anna Afanas'evna (a seamstress, as Praskov'ia Petrovna had been), and brought her into the household in 1862. She quickly bore him a son, Vladimir, and eventually another, Leonid.[37] The fact that Nefedov was a witness at Gennadii's second marriage in 1862[38] suggests that Gennadii had reconciled himself to Sergei's calling and embraced his friends and teachers. The marriage and expansion of the family complicated Sergei's life and probably heightened his self-reliance. By the age of fourteen he had reached the major turning point in his foreshortened career. He would be a student.

Sergei's passion for reading evidently dates from the period of his relationship with Dement'ev and Nefedov. They supplied him with books, advised him how to continue his education in their absence, and even treated him as a younger colleague in their educational ventures: the creation of a Sunday school and library for the mill workers and their families. The Sunday school movement of 1859–1862 was the first systematic effort of the intelligentsia to educate the urban factory workers. It achieved significant dimensions mainly in St. Petersburg, but even there did not flourish. A handful of teachers and pupils, who tried to convert what was primarily an attempt to bring literacy to the factory population into a social and political movement, gave the government an excuse to close down the entire system in June 1862. The Ivanovo Sunday school opened on March 12, 1861, in the estate office of Count Sheremet'ev. By April, seventy-six students had enrolled in the school, most of them textile workers.[39] During its short life about 200 students, both adult textile workers and their children, had enrolled in the school, but (as in other Sunday schools) attendance had been sporadic.[40] In addition to the classes, Nefedov, Dement'ev, and four helpers ran a lending library comprised of 370 volumes and four journals. In an article about the Sunday school appearing in the *Moscow Gazette* in 1862, Nefedov listed S. G. Nechaev among the five permanent instructors. An investigation prompted by the article determined that Nechaev had functioned mainly as the librarian.[41]

The closing of the Sunday school probably precipitated the permanent departure of several members of Dement'ev's circle—including Dement'ev himself and Nefedov. But during its brief existence it had accustomed Sergei to the notion that he was somebody. He, the fourteen-year-old son of a part-time lackey and sign painter, had seen his name in a Moscow newspaper. Sergei's precocious entry into the circle of provincial *intelligenty* who conducted their experiment in popular enlightenment in the face of government opposition and who abandoned Ivanovo for Moscow provided him with a link to the outside world. Nefedov began to publish satirical articles about Ivanovo soon after his departure, and Sergei imitated his tone in several letters to him written between 1863 and 1865.[42] Without Dement'ev and Nefedov life in Ivanovo became increasingly intolerable for Sergei. The small circle of youths who had been influenced by Dement'ev could not sustain him. His extraordinary capacity for systematic effort carried him beyond his peers in Ivanovo. One of them, who knew Sergei during his teens, claims that he could work twelve hours a day at his studies. Like other commentators, he uses the adjective *nastoichivyi* (pertinacious or stubborn) to describe the adolescent Nechaev.[43]

The most important source on Nechaev's adolescence, the letters to Nefedov noted above, contain little forewarning of the strange career to come. Two constant refrains thread through them: a powerful desire for higher education and the need to escape from the "devil's swamp"—a phrase borrowed from one of Nefedov's stories about Ivanovo. Bitterness and disillusionment come through as well, though it is impossible to infer their cause from the letters. Nechaev's anguished (though ironic) cries from the provinces are so typical of the Russian intelligentsia, ripe or green, that one can say young Sergei already exhibited a distinguishing trait of the species. However, he reacted to his plight both realistically and aggressively, which distinguished him from his peers. To be sure, an observer who is one hundred years removed and accustomed to adolescent idleness, vacillation, and lack of will, may tend to see as precocious maturity what was in reality an appropriate and common form of adaptation for an ambitious young *meshchanin* of that period. But later testimony reinforces the impression created by the witnesses already cited that Nechaev was unusually willful and energetic, even in a generation of Russian adolescents, many of whom began careers as writers or revolutionaries in their late teens or early twenties. Although he expresses both resentment and contempt for wealth and privilege in his letters, they do not prepare us for the demonic resentment and explosive rage of the twenty-year-old revolutionary. Brief anecdotes about the talented child actor do not foretell the archdeceiver, the conspirator of myriad disguises, nor do testimonials to his determination prophesy the obsessive revolutionary. Only retrospectively can we discover in the child and adolescent the obsessiveness that distinguished Nechaev as a revolutionary.

In several of the fourteen letters to Nefedov (only four were fully dated, but most were evidently written in 1864), Sergei regaled his idol with commentaries on life in Ivanovo. He confirms what we know from the economic history of those years—that the cessation of shipments of American cotton because of the Civil War had depressed Ivanovo's textile industry, and that poverty had increased.[44] Barbed accounts of failures to deal with the poor and hungry alternate with acerbic tales of the local social lions—or "aces," in the slang of that time. In all, one gains the impression of an in-the-know adolescent with literary ambitions. Sergei related with glee the impotent fury of the local bigwigs over Nefedov's satirical descriptions of them, and offered his own:

> A happy Lenten season! I wish you health, not knowing how it is with you in Moscow, but here in Ivanovo, that is, in the devil's swamp, I would say: dreadfully boring, the snow is melting, the streets are full of puddles, everything is flowing, trickling, dripping; not a single soul is visible, instead the animal kingdom occupies every back street, each species disporting itself according to its kind: the pigs wallow in the puddles, the chickens scrabble away at the muck, the dogs run about in packs, and only the cows promenade with the punctiliousness and self-importance characteristic of the merchants of Ivanovo.[45]

Although he sometimes used archaic spellings (*estli* for *esli, Genvaria* for *Ianvaria*), he inserted phrases in French and German, and in general strove for urbanity when not studiedly using slang. He bombarded Nefedov with requests for books in almost every letter.

The later correspondence is punctuated by both bitterness and self-confidence:

> I'm studying assiduously, and there's no other way: the bumpy road I travel knocks me about unbelievably.
>
> Reality very indelicately grabs at me with its clumsy paws and forces me to make enormous leaps. Ah! The sooner I can climb out of this place the better.
>
> Anyway, this acquaintance with reality is useful, because it doesn't permit me to sink into apathy and contemplate the world's charms;

constant analysis of my surroundings gives me a true understanding of my own strength.[46]

Exactly what he meant by "reality" is not too difficult to say. He was an intellectually inclined adolescent living in a crowded family during a depression. Someone who spent much of his time reading Granovskii and Buckle was an economic burden as well as a scholar. In one of the last surviving letters to Nefedov, dated January 8, 1865, Sergei wrote that his family regarded him as a "drone," and that out of pride he could no longer live in the household.[47] (Enormous pride should be added to the list of character traits discussed above.) Evidently Gennadii encouraged his son to leave home to find his own way, and Sergei's decision was only semivoluntary. The letter also reveals that he was depressed and felt both isolated and anxious to get away.

Rather than try to prepare for the university—that would have required an additional year at home without adequate instruction—he hoped to enroll in the sixth class of a gymnasium and therefore asked Nefedov for information about the gymnasium curriculum and enrollment procedures. Nechaev also provided Nefedov with a broad inventory of his academic achievements: knowledge of Russian history (mainly to Peter I); European history (ancient and medieval); rhetoric; geography; algebra (his poorest subject); geometry; Latin (all of the first course and half of the second); French (modest ability to translate); German (quite poor); Russian literature; classical poetry through the Roman epos; and physics, which he had begun but had set aside until his algebra improved.[48] At the age of eighteen he was already a member of a marginal group in Russian society, a growing intellectual proletariat whose existence provoked the imagination of revolutionary publicists and nervous gendarmes alike.

The facts of Nechaev's adolescence refute later myths (largely inspired by him) that he was a barely literate former serf—a creature from another world to the educated youth of the capitals. To be sure, he had to alter his plans to enroll in a gymnasium in order to get a teaching certificate and earn a living. But he was not so much a man of the people in the usual sense as a kind of populist by his late teens—that is, he was closer to and more readily identified himself with the intelligentsia teachers who brought knowledge to the people through the Sunday schools than with the students themselves. Only later did he try to exploit (and sometimes falsified by exaggeration) his origins. His sufferings were not physical; he grew up tough and wiry. His sufferings, in fact, were mainly psychological (in this he differed little from the rest of humanity)—his mother's premature death, his demanding father's intermittent care and guidance, the usual humiliations of a sensitive youth in a rough environment, a sense of being crowded out by Gennadii's new family. Most generally, he suffered from the twofold alienation of the young intellectual in an urban family torn from the soil and village life, a family surviving by petty crafts and semiservile employment and forcing its young to find some place in life as quickly as possible. Although Sergei was not yet eighteen when he finally left home, he had been made to feel like a parasite during much of his adolescence. All of this gives us clues to the self-image he cultivated—but in a dramatically exaggerated form—five years later:

> We are the children of fathers, hungry and crushed by deprivations, of mothers, driven to dullness and idiocy.
>
> We grew up in the midst of filth and ignorance, amid insults and humiliations; despised from the cradle and oppressed by every possible kind of scoundrel, supported happily by the existing state of affairs.
>
> We, for whom the family was preparation for forced labor, for whom the best period of youth passed in a struggle with poverty and hunger, the time for love, the time for amusements in the painful quest for a morsel of bread.[49]

The central idea of Nechaev's self-image is martyrdom—not merely his martyrdom, or his family's martyrdom, but the martyrdom of an entire social class. As we shall see, Nechaev found a way to justify and forgive his family by embracing a social theory that permitted him to fix all blame elsewhere and to cultivate as well a bloody vengefulness. Not merely a sense of martyrdom and a desire for revenge, but the determined pursuit of both martyrdom and revenge, distinguish his career as a revolutionary. One must emphasize these traits, lest Nechaev's behavior be dismissed as that of a sociopath or psychopath—which at times it resembled. The psychological links between martyrdom and conscience are well established. Ultimately, none of the foregoing facts or the conjectures based upon them adequately explains either Nechaev's complex character or his choice of a revolutionary career. However, they do permit us to suggest an explanation for the way in which he played his revolutionary role.

While it is impossible at a century's distance to locate precisely the origins of Nechaev's pathology of conscience, at the very least one may outline the symptoms—symptoms that gave form to Nechaev's revolutionary behavior, but that might have easily expressed themselves in other kinds of activity and other roles. Many of Dostoevsky's portrayals of young men with pathological consciences—for example, Raskolnikov in *Crime and Punishment* and Arkadii Dolgorukii in *A Raw Youth*—had greater psychological verisimilitude than that of Peter Verkhovenskii in *The Devils*. Sickened by a failure of the metabolism of generations, to borrow Erik Erikson's phrase, these young men seemed to want to create themselves anew, whether through revolutionary socialist doctrines, Napoleonic dreams, or inflated bourgeois ambitions. The combination of abject humiliation and vaulting pride might as easily result in crimes of violence, revolutionary conspiracies, or the pursuit of wealth. Most notably, however, the chemistry of humiliation and pride in Russian youth of the 1860s and 1870s created both revolutionary martyrs and vengeful power seekers. The revolutionaries of that era pursued both martyrdom and power in the name of the suffering mass of people—the *narod*—and Nechaev was one of the first to identify his humiliation and suffering and his claims to revolutionary leadership and power with the people's own aspirations—with the people's revenge.

The psychology of identification is an important key to Nechaev's complex behavior, and helps to explain both his successes as a revolutionary and his ultimate failure. He communicated his deeply felt identification with the victimized *narod* to the more privileged youths in the student milieu, while at the same time he concealed from himself his own sense of separation from the *narod* and the accompanying feelings of guilt. Having vaulted out of the "swamp," Nechaev carried with him a burden of guilt for having left his family behind—a burden he may have felt more deeply for having been a drone during his last years in Ivanovo and his brief stay in Moscow. He felt victimized by his family's circumstances and both proud and guilty because he had risen above those circumstances. But there was still another dimension to Nechaev's puzzling character: He later exhibited in particularly extreme form an ego-defensive strategy that Anna Freud has called "identification with the aggressor."[50] She described identification with the aggressor as an intermediate stage in the development of paranoia under certain circumstances. While common and normal in children, in adults it signifies a form of arrested superego development and is the outcome of a fairly complicated combination of the defense mechanisms of identification and projection. On the one hand, the subject identifies himself with a dread, anxiety-producing external object by introjecting and actively—perhaps furiously—imitating some aspect of it. In a sense, he transforms himself into the aggressor and confronts the threatening object with a caricature of itself. On the other hand, the actor projects his own inner guilt over forbidden impulses and desires, which he knows are unacceptable and will be punished, upon the feared object, thereby adding righteous indignation to the attack. These defensive strategies commonly precede the full development of superego and permit an immature subject to criticize vehemently a dread figure—perhaps a parent or teacher—without subjecting himself to the same measure of self-criticism. Despite the distortions of reality involved, as long as this peculiar strategy is employed against appropriate objects—genuinely threatening ones, such as punitive authority figures—it does not necessarily assume a functionally pathological character, even in adults. However, when the projections associated with it are turned against inappropriate objects—spouses, associates, dependents—it becomes functionally pathological.

To put it in simplest terms, Nechaev suffered from both too little and too much superego, leading him now to a sadistic, now to a masochistic ego-defensive strategy. Not only Dostoevsky, but members of the revolutionary subculture themselves sometimes showed remarkable sensitivity to the psychological strategies of their comrades. Rosa Luxemburg, though writing at a later moment in revolutionary history, wryly observed:

> It is amusing to note the strange somersaults that the respectable human "ego" has had to perform in recent Russian history. Knocked to the ground, almost reduced to dust, by Russian absolutism, the "ego" takes revenge by turning to revolutionary activity. In the shape of a committee of conspirators, in the name of a nonexistent Will of the People, it seats itself on a kind of throne and proclaims it is all-powerful. But the "object" proves to be the stronger. The knout is triumphant, for tsarist might seem to be the "legitimate" expression of history.
>
> In time we see appear on the scene an even more "legitimate" child of history—the Russian labor movement. For the first time, bases for the formation of a real "people's will" are laid in Russian soil.
>
> But here is the "ego" of the Russian revolutionary again! Pirouetting on its head, it once more proclaims itself to be the all-powerful director of history—this time with the title of His Excellency the Central Committee of the Social Democratic Party of Russia.[51]

Luxemburg, of course, was referring to The People's Will, which she saw as a forerunner of Bolshevism, but her observations are far truer of Nechaev's organization, The People's Revenge. With equal astuteness, Luxemburg noted the pathology of conscience that leads to martyrdom:

> [T]he utopian or opportunist dreams of the Russian intellectual who has joined the socialist movement tend to nourish themselves on theo-

> retic formulae in which the "ego" is not exalted but humiliated, in which the morality of renunciation, expiation, is the dominant principle.[52]

Literally hundreds of examples can be drawn from memoirs of the revolutionary movement testifying to the relative dominance of the ego strategy of self-sacrifice, or self-chosen redemptive suffering for the *narod*. There were indeed self-punishing egos as well as vengeful, power-seeking ones—and there were painfully conflicted ones, simultaneously pursuing martyrdom and vengeance. In Nechaev, a powerful martyr identification existed alongside his identification with the aggressor and fatally modified his criminality and power seeking. Much of Nechaev's career revolved around ultimately self-fulfilling prophesies about his being captured, beaten, tortured, and killed by the Tsarist authorities. His urge for power and revenge was offset by a desire for punishment. The mistakes he made as a conspirator call to mind Dostoevsky's Raskolnikov rather than the demonic Verkhovenskii—Nechaev was a "pale criminal" in the Nietzschean sense. The circumstances of his imprisonment and death suggest a quest for martyrdom no less powerful than that of the seventeenth-century Russian sectarians. The Russian Orthodox philosopher, Nicholas Berdiaev, believed that the revolutionaries of the 1860s perpetuated the spirit of Orthodoxy and that Nechaevism was a "grim degree of Orthodox asceticism turned inside out and mixed with Jesuitism."[53] Later evidence reveals that Nechaev and his comrades consciously identified themselves with earlier fanatic sectarians, but the unconscious, deep background for Nechaev's career had been created during his childhood and adolescence in Ivanovo.

During the era of the development of the revolutionary subculture, tens of thousands of rebellious Russian youths confronted in their daily lives centuries-old cultural and psychological adaptations transmitted through the medium of the family. In Erik Erikson's illuminating essay, "The Legend of Maxim Gorky's Youth,"[54] the child Alyosha (Gorky) successfully struggles toward the creation of a new Russian identity, despite a multitude of psychological perils and temptations in his family milieu. In reality, however, many young rebels, like Nechaev, failed to fend off traditional Russian modes of adaptation and the psychological strategies associated with them. To be sure, individual and subcultural values and roles assumed extreme and superficially novel forms, but cultural myths and symbols are not easily overcome, and even the Western-oriented revolutionary subculture took on a distinctively Russian cast. For example, in no other nation did Christian symbolism get so thoroughly mixed into the mystiques of the rulers and the nation, or the self-image of the self-chosen saviors of the people—the revolutionary intelligentsia. The image of Christ's redemptive suffering now transfigured the rulers in the eyes of the people, now the land itself and the people in the eyes of the intelligentsia. Finally, the intelligentsia, in its heroic effort to merge with the *narod* and to pay back the vast debt owed to the exploited peasants, created its own myth about itself. A student of Russian national myths and symbols put it this way:

> In the modern and final period [of Russian history, P.P.] the history of the myth of the ruler and the myth of the people was also the history of the myth of the intelligentsia. . . . But because for the intelligentsia the myths were involved in the search for individual identity, they acquired the colorings of all the individual inclinations and differentiations.[55]

The nihilist movement of the 1860s was a conscious, consistent effort to negate traditional Russian culture, but deeply internalized national myths and symbols affected interpretations of the doctrines associated with the movement. Furthermore, revolutionary strategies and roles associated with nihilism (and later, with *narodism* and Marxism) assumed typical forms, which reflected the influence of individual psychological strategies commonly employed in the search for a new identity in a Russian cultural context. The effects of a brutal patriarchal culture and Christian values often manifested themselves in individual psyches as self-martyrdom, in which the young revolutionaries, often of the more privileged social strata, identified themselves with the victims of autocratic power and shared the people's suffering. Still other Russian youths devised strategies to bring down the autocratic power, although they themselves did not seek power. Only a handful sought power for themselves, and among these there appeared, now and again, aspiring leaders like Nechaev, who (whether consciously or unconsciously) identified themselves with the power they sought to overthrow. In view of the revolutionaries' rejection of autocratic power, it might seem odd that leaders of a dictatorial bent should emerge within the movement, but a number of factors, which will be examined below in greater detail, favored their success. Those who were the most vehement in their attacks upon the old order and authorities, the most sanguine about the prospects for revolution, and the most concrete and practical in their plans for a revolutionary upheaval were sometimes able to attract a following, despite otherwise unattractive personal qualities. Extremism is a virtue in revolutionary subcultures, and extreme rhetoric, which might in individual cases be symptomatic of a paranoid tendency and an abnormal desire for power, might not be recognized as pathological. It might be difficult to distinguish paranoid projections—such as those associated with the ego-defensive strategy of identification with the aggressor—from legitimate revolutionary unmasking of the old regime. Finally, it seems undeniable that there were revolutionaries who were attracted to autocratic forms of leadership and who did not submit to centralized authoritarian parties out of strategic revolutionary considerations alone.

All of these features issued from the interaction of the revolutionary movement with traditional Russian culture. The struggle took the form of cultural and political conflicts, and the conflicts both shaped and were shaped by the search for new identities conducted by the thousands of young people who entered the movement during the 1860s and 1870s. Nechaev was one of many, but the psychological strategies underlying his interpretation of the role of revolutionary had profound significance for the revolutionary movement both during his short career and after it.

In August 1865, Sergei applied to the town council of Shuia, where Gennadii was registered as a *meshchanin*, for permission to move to Moscow.[56] Unfortunately, we know very little about the crucial months in Moscow. He clearly did not achieve what he set out to do, abandoning his plans to enter a gymnasium and instead preparing himself to take an examination for the position of either tutor (*domashnyi uchitel'*) or district teacher (*uezdnyi uchitel'*). At some point, he moved into a furnished room in Dmitrovka, the poor student section of the city, P. I. Makhin, a university student, took Nechaev as a roommate at Nefedov's request. During part of his stay in Moscow, Nechaev worked as copyist for the historian Pogodin, a position he obtained through Dement'ev, and evidently received room and board in Pogodin's pension by way of compensation.[57] For at least a short time in Moscow, then, Nechaev maintained connections with his former teachers and more or less followed the course set by them. Why he left Pogodin's pension is unknown, but it is known that he parted company with Makhin on bad terms after having lived with him for five or six months.[58] Since he could not have lived in Moscow for more than eight or nine months altogether (August 1865–April 1866), it appears that he spent most of his time in Dmitrovka.

Nechaev probably left Moscow for St. Petersburg for practical reasons. He had not passed the teacher's examination in Moscow, and perhaps he had been told that it was easier to obtain a certificate in St. Petersburg. All the while he lived mainly on funds given him by his father. Fioniia in her memoirs emphasizes Gennadii's efforts to set up Sergei properly for his career as a student but obviously resources were limited. In any case, the move proved beneficial, for he passed the examination in St. Petersburg in good time and obtained his first steady work in the autumn of 1866 in the Andreevskii school.[59] Evidently, he had also worked as a tutor (exactly when is not known) for the children of one Baron Vol'f, but had demanded such high wages that the irate baron dismissed him. More important, he had returned to Ivanovo in the summer of 1866.

When Nechaev arrived in Ivanovo he found his sister Fioniia married and with babe in arms. Fioniia tells us that Sergei always stood by her in quarrels with the adults in the family about her marriage. Gennadii and their stepmother, Anna Afanas'evna, had wanted to marry her off as quickly as possible to a local peasant, Ia. G. Postnikov, whose family had long been close to the Nechaev family and who would not demand a dowry. She had persistently refused until Gennadii told her that he had received a letter from Sergei telling them that she should marry. Gennadii had lied. When Sergei saw her with a baby he cried: "My God—Fotia, Fotia, what have you done?"[60] Because he had been a drain on the family resources he was indirectly responsible for Fioniia's position. Once established, Sergei would undoubtedly have called both sisters to St. Petersburg. Now he decided to take Anna with him (although not immediately) to preserve her from Fioniia's fate.

What impact did his sister's misfortune have on Sergei? After presenting the family, Fioniia had said simply: "Sergei Gennad'evich loved me."[61] Perhaps sibling relationships in families where the younger generation had to ward off arbitrary and coercive treatment were particularly close. The generations, so to speak, conspired against each other. But perhaps it is best to read Dostoevsky's *Crime and Punishment*, which appeared that very year (1866), and reflect on the striking similarities between Nechaev-Fotia and Raskolnikov-Dunia. In both cases, resolve or violent action appears to have been triggered in the young students by the news that their sisters had been forced to marry, and in both cases, the sister's fate had been determined by the scheming of a parent or parents. It is also notable that young men in the nihilist subculture often assumed the role of protector (older brother) to young women trying to escape parental domination and the traditional woman's role. In reality, as well as in fiction—Chernyshevskii's novel, *What Is to Be Done?* is an example—the role of protector sometimes prefaced a sexual relationship, and one wonders if an unconscious incestuous element was involved in Nechaev's case. Still, it is possible that an unusually highly developed sense of sibling solidarity existed and that older male siblings felt responsible for the fate of younger siblings. The overt conflict of generations in the 1860s no doubt heightened what was already a tendency in Russian culture.

Whatever the deeper psychological background, the summer of 1866 was probably another turning point in a life of increasingly bitter disappointments. If there were other turning points in the period 1866–1867, it is impossible to say what they were. Family history in this instance is more complete than the history of Nechaev's interaction with the larger world.

The events of the larger historical world in 1866 were violent and full of meaning for Nechaev's later career, although we do not know how they affected him at that time. On April 4, 1866, a student named Dmitrii Karakozov tried to assassinate Alexander II but failed in the attempt, unleashing a government reaction so extreme that it was called the "White Terror." Rumors circulated in the city about Karakozov, the brutality of the police, and who would be arrested next. This was the lurid atmosphere in St. Petersburg when Nechaev arrived.

Once secure in his position in the Andreevskii school, Nechaev encouraged his friend Aleksei Kapatsinskii to move to the capital and room with him. Kapatsinskii had studied with Sergei in Ivanovo, although like the other students in their circle, Kapatsinskii had fallen behind his friend. According to a deposition he gave to the police in May 1869, Kapatsinskii arrived early in 1867. He found a changed person—too formal, given their past relationship, and shut up in himself. Nechaev either worked alone in his room or left the apartment without a word to his friend. Although he had promised to find Kapatsinskii work (the latter too had little money), nothing materialized, and Kapatsinskii continued to prepare himself to teach. He had to pawn his overcoat to survive. Meanwhile, Nechaev found a better position in the Sergievskii parochial school, where he taught Bible. It appears that he finally confronted Kapatsinskii over finances—the latter had not been able to contribute anything to living expenses—and they split up in October 1867.[62] However, they evidently maintained at least indirect ties through Vladimir Orlov and Evlampii Ametistov, two of Nechaev's close collaborators in the first period of his revolutionary career. Furthermore, Kapatsinskii received a letter from Nechaev himself early in May 1869, which indicated that he was involved—though he never admitted it—with Nechaev's circle.[63]

It is not clear from Kapatsinskii's deposition to the police (the letter from Nechaev had been intercepted, leading to Kapatsinskii's arrest in May 1869) precisely when Nechaev expressed the radical ideas described there. He claimed that he had seen Nechaev only once or twice after October 1867, but not on a friendly basis. All of this implicitly contradicts much of the substance of the deposition, which provides a striking picture of Nechaev's personality and at least an outline of his ideas. Although the picture seems accurate, coinciding with everything we know about Nechaev from other sources, it is, if anything, exaggerated in order to put Nechaev (who, after all, was at large) in the worst possible light and to make Kapatsinskii appear an innocent bystander. Numerous depositions and trial testimonies duplicate this strategy, but at least Kapatsinskii, when asked by the secret police to serve as an agent provocateur and help them trap Nechaev abroad, staunchly refused—and paid the price for his refusal.[64] Kapatsinskii was not released until June 1870, at which time he was sent to a little town in Khar'kov province in the Ukraine, where he lived under police surveillance until his death in 1875.

In any case Kapatsinskii's character sketch remains one of the best sources on Nechaev for the period 1867–1868:

> The first impression Nechaev makes is unpleasant yet actually seductive. He is pathologically touchy—and one feels this at first contact, although Nechaev tries to restrain himself. He reads a great deal . . . especially books of historical and sociological content, and thus knows a great deal, although when he cites various authors he is sometimes quite careless. In debate he will try to trick and humiliate his opponent—he is a talented dialectician and knows how to touch the most sensitive areas of a young conscience: truth, honesty, courage, etc. He won't tolerate people who are his equals, and with those stronger than he, maintains a strict silence and tries to cast a shadow of suspicion over them. He is extremely firm in his convictions, but out of self-esteem, to which he is prepared to sacrifice everybody. Thus, the main traits of his character are despotism and self-esteem. All of his declamations are full of passion, but very bilious. He stimulates interest in himself, and the more impressionable and naive simply worship him, the latter a necessary condition of any friendship with him.[65]

It should be remembered that Kapatsinskii gave this deposition in 1869, long before Nechaev had hatched his conspiracy, murdered Ivanov, and acquired his reputation as the archdeceiver and enfant terrible of the revolutionary movement. In addition, Kapatsinskii gave this highly condensed account of Nechaev's ideological position: "He frequently conversed about social questions and put forward a confused communism. In reply to my opinions about the natural inequality of human capacities he said that one could have a juridical system which would force people to be equal."[66]

Another deposition to the police, V. Putsykovich's, also given in May 1869, clarifies our picture of Nechaev.[67] Putsykovich was impressed by Nechaev's perpetual motion, his need to be busy. Nechaev had a mania for books, surrounding himself with them, nervously jumping from one to the other. He tried to acquire any new book in Russian or French that seemed important. Putsykovich claims that his main interests were history and geography, followed by the natural sciences. He also studied various trades—tailoring, boot making, bookbinding, and carpentry. When asked why, he said, "Everything can be useful in life." Once he said he had no intention of becoming a *chinovnik* (a somewhat disparaging term, meaning official or bureaucrat) and that he wanted to go to England to perfect his trade skills and to study toolmaking. As for personal characteristics:

> On the one hand, he was a good comrade: honest, truthful, willing to share all of his material possessions with his friends; but on the other he was unbearable: always asking questions and saying nothing about himself, taking everything the wrong way, extremely callous in his treatment of others. . . . But his most repellent trait was his extreme despotism with respect to one's ideas. He couldn't reconcile himself to the fact that his acquaintances had ideas, convictions unlike his own, and looked at things and acted in a different way than he did. But he didn't scorn these people. No, on the contrary, he tried with incredible persistence to convert them.[68]

Both depositions reinforce what we know about Nechaev as a child but add negative dimensions wholly absent from Fioniia's characterization. As we shall see, even older and more experienced comrades in the revolutionary subculture tended to discount these negative aspects of Nechaev's personality, or to see them as aspects of a useful fanaticism. Unfortunately, neither Kapatsinskii nor Putsykovich helps us to determine the precise moment that Nechaev chose a revolutionary career. It might have occurred in 1867. It certainly occurred by the fall of 1868. There is no story of a conversion experience, or an exemplary figure, although later evidence suggests that either Karakozov might have played that role, or, on another level, the fanatic leader of the Old Believers, the archpriest Avvakum.[69]

Nechaev's teaching position was obviously only a stopgap. The young teacher's attitude toward his subject is revealed in a letter he wrote to Nefedov on October 23, 1864, (that is, two years before he became a teacher of Bible), in which he commented:

> I recently visited Aleksander's father's school; the course of study is not bad, but it's a pity that most of the time is wasted on the teaching and study of the Bible; it appears to be their major subject.[70]

However, the Bible proved useful to Nechaev's followers. Among Kapatsinskii's papers the police found a note from Evlampii Ametistov in which he told Kapatsinskii to read in the Evangels two passages in Luke, and to transmit the "allegory" to Vladimir Orlov. The passages are Luke, chapter three, verses nine and seventeen:

> And now also the axe is laid unto the root of the trees: every tree therefore which bringeth not forth good fruit is hewn down, and cast into the fire.
>
> Whose fan is in his hand, and he will thoroughly purge his floor, and will gather the wheat into his garner; but the chaff he will burn with fire unquenchable.[71]

Chapter II

The Student Rebels

Nechaev had little time for his classroom duties during the autumn of 1868. I. Slivkov, a *storozh* (a helper, evidently entrusted mainly with menial tasks) of the Sergievskii school, filed a complaint with the director of schools in St. Petersburg province in which he claimed that Nechaev often absented himself in order to give private lessons and left the students in the care of an unqualified person.[1] The person in question was Evlampii Ametistov, an eighteen-year-old student of the Medical-Surgical Academy in St. Petersburg, and, next to Vladimir Orlov, Nechaev's closest companion at that time.[2] Nechaev had enrolled as an auditor (*vol'noslushatel'*) in the university, had frequented radical student circles, and, by December 1868, was involved in revolutionary activity. The superintendent of schools investigated Slivkov's complaint, including the assertion that parents had transferred their children to other schools, and his report of gatherings in Nechaev's apartment where, in Slivkov's words, "about fifteen men and also girls create various fires and shots, at which time he commands me to leave the room and go into the kitchen, and even when I hand him the samovar he takes it from me in the hall so that I won't see or hear their conversation."[3] The superintendent found no basis for Slivkov's assertions and wrote a general vindication of Nechaev.[4] Nechaev had explained on January 16, 1869 that the "fires and shots" were chemistry experiments, necessary for his university studies.[5] The unfortunate Slivkov, who had quarreled with Nechaev and had been dismissed by him on January 10, was discharged from his post "for drunkenness" on January 16.[6] Other scattered evidence indicates that Nechaev and others were experimenting with explosives and plotting political assassinations, but Slivkov's report and its implications were ignored.[7]

Nechaev enters Russian revolutionary history by way of the student movement of 1868–1869. He discovered the extent cf his own radicalism through contact with the most radical element in Russian society—the educated youth of the two capitals, St. Petersburg and Moscow. The larger student movement absorbed a number of peripheral elements—nonstudents, part-time students like Nechaev, and others one might call urban mascots. Their character should not be unfamiliar to us, a century later. Major cities, then as now, provided the means—lodging, handouts, and other types of succor—whereby rebellious youths could lead a precarious but independent existence. And within the cities, the universities, technical institutes, and academies were enclaves of a freer life, a more generous corporate spirit, in which mutual aid—both material and spiritual—played no small role in sustaining hundreds of needy students and hangers-on, many of them brothers and sisters of students. In this environment, upwardly aspiring *meshchane* or sons of provincial clergymen mingled with the titled children of noble families, although many of the nobility were financially no better off than their social inferiors. For example, Vera Zasulich, of noble birth, moved to the capital with her sisters and mother and worked at sewing and bookbinding to survive, only to become involved in the student movement of 1868 at the age of sixteen and to remain a revolutionary for the rest of her life.[8] But the revolutionary movement embraced only a small portion of the student movement. The student movement contained both a less radical movement committed to the democratic reform of higher education and student autonomy and a more diffuse rebellion with a distinctive style of life associated with it—the nihilist subculture.

Nechaev partook in some fashion of several of these aspects of the student movement. He affected the curtness of speech, oddness of appearance, occasional studied barbarism (he sometimes carried a cudgel), and ideological extremism of the nihilist subculture. It is difficult to say how the emblematic eccentricities of manner and dress established themselves so widely and firmly in Russia during the 1860s, but having recently experienced something similar, we do not find what happened baffling. Outrageousness in dress and manner, then as now, did not always signify genuine commitment to radical causes, and when it did, did not always lead to revolutionary action. Nechaev proved to be one of the few who committed themselves entirely to revolutionary activity. In fact, he spent all of the period 1868–1872 trying to divert the larger student movement toward his goals.

The atmosphere of rebellion, which had grown in Russian society after the unexpected defeat and national humiliation of the Crimean War (1854–1856), both precipitated the Great Reforms of Alexander II and in turn fed upon their inadequacies. Nihilism was the most extreme response (ignoring, of course, the truly extreme forms of lonely human protest that expend themselves in some quiet corner) to the feelings of frustration that had built up in the educated class during the reign of Nicholas I (1825–1855). All attachments to past forms of culture were called into question by the new critics, save their own passion for the natural sciences, for realism in art—for a "scientific" world view. They proposed to solve all ethical questions by means of rational egoism and all material problems by the conquest of matter. The term "scientism," in the sense of dogmatic naturalism, accurately describes their outlook. The practical implications of both the negative (repudiation of the past) and positive (worship of science and rational social change) aspects of nihilism were as absurd as one would expect any attempt at total, systematic negation and reconstruction according to "scientific" ideas to be. But the doctrine spoke to youth: to its attempt to separate itself from Nicholas I, from Russian backwardness, from serfdom, from oppressive family relationships—in short, from the past. Given its scientistic basis, nihilism tended to increase the mystique of higher education and to attract a multitude of Russian students to medicine, engineering, and agronomy—subjects both scientific and utilitarian. Scientific study did not necessarily imply a love of science, any more than philosophical materialism and determinism implied an amoral outlook or lack of ethical voluntarism in practice. Quite the contrary, they often signified a powerful ethical commitment to human liberation. Hence, nihilism's philosophical aspects, like its stylistic expressions, played an emblematic role. They helped to mark out a group of people who defined themselves as much by what they were not committed to and wished to destroy as by their hopes for the future. In Russia, the conjunction of defeat in war, the death of a Tsar who had become a symbol of repression, the expectation of great changes, the existence of a relatively privileged body of radical students and liberal professors who had access to the latest trends in European thought—all prepared the soil for a nihilist subculture.

Russian nihilism can be seen as one extreme expression of Europe's new age of realism. It began as a renewal of the spirit of the Enlightenment, and its foremost exponents consciously identified themselves with the Encyclopaedists. Ultimately, its philosophical materialism, utilitarianism, and scientism did not give substance and character to the rebellion that occurred in its name. By the 1880s, the term "nihilism" generally stood for Russian revolutionary terrorism in the European lexicon. This, of course, is no more paradoxical than Christianity giving birth to the Crusades, nationalism to imperialism, or Marxism to Stalinism. Doctrines become symbols, and different interpreters can do extraordinarily different things in the name of the same symbols. Nechaev emptied nihilism of its admittedly meager theoretical content and replaced it with his own doctrine of revolutionary action. Nihilism in its scientistic sense was for him only a set of forms, a convenience—not a binding commitment. The third paragraph of "The Catechism of a Revolutionary" sums it up rather well:

> The revolutionary despises any kind of doctrinairism and has rejected peaceful science, leaving it to future generations. He knows only one science—the science of destruction. For this and only for this he now studies mechanics, physics, chemistry, perhaps medicine. For this he studies day and night the living science of people, of their personalities and positions and all the conditions of the present social structure in every possible stratum. The goal is the same—the quickest and surest destruction of this foul structure.[9]

Generally the students interpreted rational egoism according to the ideas of the leading theoreticians of nihilism—N. G. Chernyshevskii, N. A. Dobroliubov, and D. I. Pisarev. The theoreticians of nihilism divided over a number of important issues about the strategies for social progress, but they generally agreed that the rational egoist's self-interest coincided with society's and by this painless device of utilitarianism tried to avoid the moral anarchy that might be deduced from a materialistic and deterministic philosophy. The egoism of the converts to Chernyshevskii's ideas in fact led to communal industrial enterprise (inspired by Fourier) and to rationally examined personal lives, with lovers striving with suffocating attentiveness to ensure each other's happiness. In fact, it seems perfectly clear that the guiding lights of youth culture (this is particularly true of Chernyshevskii and Dobroliubov) had martyrdom in mind, and a cadaverous odor of self-sacrifice pervades their lives and work.[10] Thus, although nihilism may have released youth from Russian society's prevailing norms, it revived the older Russian ideal of sainthood, this time in the service of secular causes.

Chernyshevskii's lugubrious heroes and heroines, unconvincingly rouged with the gaiety and lusty appetites of the healthy, satisfied the moral cravings of more than one generation of self-sacrificing Russian adolescents.[11] The novel's ideally successful sewing *artel'* (a traditional

Russian form of workers' and artisans' cooperative association translated into utopian socialist forms) reinforced the students' own experimentation with communal living and enterprise. As we shall see, the Russian government's interference with student corporate life was an important stimulus to the Nechaev conspiracy. More important for Nechaevism, however, was Chernyshevskii's portrait of a truly unusual person, the "rigorist" Rakhmetov. Chernyshevskii's brief, tangential description of Rakhmetov's personality and broad hints about his significance caught the imagination of youth. He was a hero, a fully developed person who, by the age of twenty, had made himself the physical match of the strongest Volga bargehaulers; who neither drank wine nor touched women throughout his years of training, but ate large quantities of nearly raw beeksteak to sustain his strength; who slept on a felt mat, and once (no doubt in order to test his fortitude under torture) imbedded it with hundreds of nails nearly an inch long and spent an entire night on it; who designed for himself an intellectual regimen of equal rigor; and who busied himself with matters that were secret to everyone, including his closest friends:

> he had a multitude of concerns, but not one of them involved him personally. He had no personal concerns, everyone knew this; but what his concerns were nobody knew. It was only apparent that he had a mass of them. He was rarely at home, always coming and going, mostly on foot. Yet he received a ceaseless stream of visitors, sometimes familiar faces, sometimes new ones. . . . But often he was absent for several days. Then one of his friends received visitors at his place—someone devoted to him body and soul, and silent as the tomb.[12]

Chernyshevskii, a prisoner during the composition of the novel, became the John the Baptist of the Russian revolution, holding before youth a promise: From among your ranks Rakhmetovs will come forth:

> They are few in number, but they enrich all our lives. Without them life would subside, decay. They are few, but they give the rest of us some breathing space—we would be stifled without them. There is a mass of honest and kind people, but few of them. Yet to that mass they are like thyme in tea, like the bouquet of a fine wine. From them it acquires its strength and aroma. They are the flower of the best people, the motive force to engines, the salt of the salt of the earth.[13]

A great many young Russian men and women measured themselves by Chernyshevskii's standards, and he became a cult figure. Although he had no direct hand in the development of revolutionary strategies, his descriptions of Rakhmetov's discipline, secrecy, and extensive travel in Russia and Europe left little doubt about the meaning of the hero's life. Officialdom and the revolutionary underground were rife with false rumors about Chernyshevskii's role in the movement, both before and after his arrest.

Chernyshevskii's promise of a handful of revolutionary paragons contained the assumption that they would not live for the fulfillment of personal motives, mere personal needs. While trying to convince his readers that the chosen few were human and had human failings (Rakhmetov, for example, had an uncontrollable passion for good cigars), Chernyshevskii gave them the capacity to suppress those aspects of their personality not devoted to the larger cause of human progress and welfare. Their program of physical, intellectual, and moral self-development was not an end in itself, but a means to a larger end. Oddly enough, Turgenev shared Chernyshevskii's assumption that the heroes of the revolutionary movement acted out of higher motives. In a letter written in April 1862, shortly after the appearance of the novel, he engaged in some amateur sociology:

> All the great *negators* I have known, without exception (Belinsky, Bakunin, Herzen, Dobroliubov, Speshnev, etc.), came from comparatively good and honest parents. A great idea is contained therein: it removes from the *men of action*, the negators, every suspicion of personal dissatisfaction, personal irritation. They go their way only because they are more sensitive to the demands of national life.[14]

This is surprising indeed from the author of *Rudin* and *Fathers and Sons*, novels that explore with insight the personal lives of rebels. One might even suspect willful misunderstanding, a determined effort on Turgenev's part to believe in the rebels' pure motives, for in *Fathers and Sons* he clearly perceived the controlled violence in his great negator, Bazarov. Nor need anyone acquainted with the biographies of Herzen and Bakunin search further to convince himself of the psychological shallowness of the observation.

Dmitrii Pisarev, the enfant terrible of Russian literary criticism during the 1860s (until his premature death by drowning in 1868), presented a more individualistic interpretation of nihilism and Bazarov. More than Chernyshevskii or Dobroliubov, Pisarev believed in the importance of individual human personality in the actions of heroes. He was opposed to all dogma, all theoretical constructions, all preexisting forms and structures that might be in conflict with the natural actions of a healthy organism. Although ultimately he converted his materialistic individualism into a civic philosophy of useful social labor, he never acknowledged the need for idealism of any sort in ethics. Pisarev often sounded like a nihilist in the Nietzschean sense—a proponent of the idea that everything is permitted to the creative individual.

> You can be as indignant as you please with people like Bazarov, but you absolutely must acknowledge their sincerity. These people can be honorable or dishonorable, civic stalwarts or inveterate swindlers, depending on circumstances and their personal tastes. Nothing but personal taste prevents them from killing or stealing and nothing but personal taste motivates such people to make discoveries in the realism of science and social life. . . . In addition to direct inclination, Bazarov has one other guiding principle in life—calculation. . . . By working tirelessly, Bazarov is following his direct inclination and taste, and furthermore, acts according to the truest calculation. . . . If his imagination sometimes pictures the future, then this future is somehow indefinitely broad; he works without a goal, in order to earn his crust of bread from love of the process of work, but, nevertheless, he vaguely feels through the quantity of his own capacities that his work will not pass without a trace and will lead to something. . . . Neither over himself, nor outside himself, nor within himself does he recognize a moderator, a moral law or principle; ahead—no exalted goal; in his mind—no high design, and yet he has such great capacities. . . . If Bazarovism is a disease, then it is a disease of our time, and must be endured to the end, no matter what palliatives and amputations are employed.[15]

Dostoevsky, of course, agreed that it was a disease, but would have added to Bazarovism a multitude of other isms that had infected the Russian soul. Like Turgenev, he believed that the sources of health and sickness lay in the relationships of fathers and sons, but whereas Turgenev believed that the conflict of generations originated with the sons, he found the source of the contemporary malaise in the intelligentsia generation of the 1840s—the ideological fathers of the nihilists. Dostoevsky found nothing but sick families producing blighted offspring, whereas Turgenev in *Fathers and Sons* (1862) portrayed families that might bind their children by love and join them to the transcendent process of regeneration. The voluminous literature on the rebels of the 1860s does not present a uniform pathology of family life. Tolstoy, who also studied Russian life through the medium of the family, was perhaps closest to the truth in the opening sentence of *Anna Karenina:* "All happy families are like one another; each unhappy family is unhappy in its own way." Russian cultural patterns transmitted through the family tended to limit the psychological strategies available to youths who were trying to cope with cultural change, and the search for individual identity tended to assume the forms described above, but the disruptions in Russian family life caused by cultural change in general and studenthood in particular did not produce any single pattern of rebellion.[16] It is not surprising that writers indulged their own ideological preferences when they portrayed nihilism and its origins and meanings.

One of Nechaev's followers, Prince Varlaam Cherkezov, later a prominent anarchist, found the truest rendering of the younger generation in the work of N. G. Pomialovskii. Pomialovskii, like Chernyshevskii and Dobroliubov a product of the seminary, like Nefedov a participant in the Sunday school movement, rebelled in a traditional Russian way. He found solace in vodka. Pomialovskii's drinking habits prematurely extinguished a brief but brilliant literary career in 1863. His story "Molotov" (1861) belongs to the literature of nihilism through the figure of Cherevanin, though Cherevanin never meant to the younger generation what Bazarov and Rakhmetov meant. Nonetheless, it is the figure of Cherevanin that Cherkezov held up to the court in 1871 as the basic type of young rebel. At the age of twenty-five Cherevanin concluded: "I'm not alive, I'm dying, I'm a riddle to myself. Why should I work when I know that when the younger generation says 'thank you' I won't hear it: my ears will be filled with earth."[17] Unlike Bazarov, Cherevanin renounced a life of toil. He lived only for the moment—a dissolute, unexamined life. According to Cherkezov, the struggle of the "new people" went on in the face of these living dead. Generally, to be a live (*zhivoi*) person meant to commit oneself to larger causes. The student population of St. Petersburg no doubt contained a fair number of nihilists à la Cherevanin. They gambled their money away, drank too much, made use of the city's sizable population of prostitutes, and often suffered the consequences. But when a member of the Russian revolutionary intelligentsia uttered the sacred word "youth" (*molodezh'*) he meant the developed, live segment of the student milieu, and only the detractors of the student subculture exploited the image of the bohemian or debauched nihilist.

One could therefore find under the label "nihilism" every conceivable kind of youthful commitment, state of doubt, or rebellion, but there was a certain solidarity about fundamental issues of human liberation in the student subculture. Nihilists believed that new forms of association had to be developed in order to escape the tyranny of the family, of a backward, patriarchal society, of a meaningless heritage of conventions, forms, and hierarchies embodied in officialdom. The revolutionary segment of the student subculture, with the help of European socialist theory, translated all of this into native social and economic terms and dreamed of a vast upheaval of the oppressed. But at the level of day-to-day activity, the struggle took the form of fighting for student autonomy, organizing mutual aid societies, and arranging a variety of schemes (including fictitious marriages) to help young women escape intolerable family situations. It was at this level that a series of confrontations between students and authorities occurred during the academic year 1868–1869, which gave Nechaev his point of entry into the movement.

The rise in educational standards for those seeking positions in bureaucracies and professions, and the government's failure to provide adequate fiscal support for the growing number of indigent or nearly indigent students, created a chronic problem in Russian institutions of higher education during the second half of the nineteenth century. In 1863, eighteen percent of 4,909 university students received stipends averaging slightly less than 200 rubles per year.[18] Only about one-third to one-fourth of the total number of university students were able to pay their fees when due, even though a sizable number were exempted from the payment of fees. Large numbers filed certificates of poverty. Thus Russian students who had been admitted to universities, usually after an excruciating struggle through a gymnasium, military school, or seminary, found their careers in peril for material reasons above and beyond the lengthy and unremitting process of selection in Russia's system of elite education.[19]

The students responded to the pressures of this system by organizing methods of cooperation and aid that permitted their poor but able comrades to survive. Between 1855 and 1861 student corporate life flourished in the form of *zemliachestva*, groups of students organized on a regional basis (Siberian, Ukrainian, or Caucasian, for example); *skhodki*, student assemblies formed on an ad hoc basis, which had first appeared in 1857 after police had beaten up a group of Moscow University students; student-run newspapers; libraries and reading rooms; organizations that helped distribute stipends; *kassy*, student banks for needy students; *arteli*, small enterprises organized and run by students on a profit-sharing basis; and *stolovye*, cheap dining arrangements. In addition, the students formed *kruzhki*, circles of different types that usually ministered to some of the material needs of the participants, whether in a formal commune or in a loose arrangement in which students lived together in apartments, exchanged books and tutoring, engaged in literary, scientific, or political discourse, and in general made life easier and more stimulating for each other.[20]

In some ways, the *kruzhok* was a surrogate family. In fact, one often found brothers, sisters, or other close relatives in the same *kruzhok*. In other ways, it was an extension of the cultural life of the university or technical institute. But a number of circles obviously were self-education groups organized according to socialist ideals and devoted to discussion of Russia's "accursed questions." To the most radical students *kruzhkovanie* (the formation of circles) and mutual aid arrangements of the types described provided opportunities for recruitment and in some cases for the diversion of funds in *kassy* to radical purposes. In sum then, the *kruzhki* served material, cultural, and political purposes, although the most radical students found that they had to separate themselves from the usual types of circles and organize their own on conspiratorial principles. The growing importance of ideology in *kruzhkovanie* is evident in the use of the term "party" during the late 1860s and early 1870s to describe different types of circles. But these circles were not usually exclusive, and active individuals might circulate in several *kruzhki*.

By 1861, the government had grown increasingly alarmed about the flourishing student corporatism and the style of life it supported. They had every reason to be alarmed; they had lost control over youth. It was not merely a matter of dress or deportment since Nicholas I's regulations about student garb and facial hair had been abolished. The students also wanted a kind of extraterritoriality—complete freedom from police control. The authorities not only refused them this, but added insult to injury by making cooperative arrangements with the police in order to curb student disorders. In addition, the university authorities tried to squelch the students' increasing tendency to demonstrate against unpopular or incompetent professors. In 1861, the government launched a counterattack against the students, and new regulations in effect abolished privileges that the students had enjoyed for several years. Although the regulations forbidding student *skhodki*, committees, and deputations were severe enough, the new policy on tuition and fees, which discriminated against poor students, caused the greatest resentment. The government's attack was two-pronged: it made matriculation more difficult for undesirable elements and threatened the activities that had made life easier for the students.[21] In addition, it made it harder for radicals to exploit or control student libraries, newspapers, banks, and assemblies. Officialdom practiced its own rough sociology. For many officials "revolutionary," "poor student," "nihilist," and "former seminarian" were nearly equivalent terms. One contemporary official historian of the revolutionary movement speculated that these "proletarians of thought" projected their own misery onto the masses—the peasants and factory workers—imagining that they too were revolutionary.[22] Thus, the authorities assumed that measures designed to deny the poor access to the system might also decrease the amount of frustration in the institutions of higher education, remove an important factor in student rebelliousness, and simultaneously reduce youthful revolutionary zeal.

Instead, the new measures only caused rebelliousness to boil over. During the autumn and winter of 1861–1862, student demonstrations in St. Petersburg led to the use of mounted troops wielding sabers and rifle butts, hundreds of arrests, and numerous expulsions. A student walkout in St. Petersburg was followed by the closing of the university in December 1861. In Moscow, local *meshchane* joined the police in assaults upon the student demonstrators. During the course of 1862–1863 a number of events—but mainly the mysterious fires in St. Petersburg in May 1862 (attributed to student revolutionaries), the almost simultaneous appearance of a bloodthirsty revolutionary proclamation, "Young Russia," the most radical appeal to youth of the period, and finally the Polish rebellion of 1863—exhausted whatever support had existed in liberal, educated society for the student rebellion. The students' own efforts to organize a free university were unsuccessful; their experiment lasted for only a few weeks between January and March 1862. But the resistance by both students and faculty to the new regulations forced the government to yield some concessions to the universities. The university statute of 1863 strengthened faculty governance and thus gave the university more autonomy as an institution, but it did not remove the regulations against student autonomy.[23]

Ultimately, the partial victory of 1863 reinforced the spirit of elitism in higher education because it confirmed the privileged status of institutions of higher education. The word "student" still evoked the idea of privilege, of relative freedom, and of a better future. A great variety of sources attest to the mystique of studenthood in Russian society and to the students' sense of self-importance. The life of the student still had greater appeal than the call of the revolutionary émigrés—Alexander

Herzen, Michael Bakunin, and Nicholas Ogarev—to leave the lecture halls and go to the people. The students did not leave. Instead, they found ways to carry on the corporate, comradely existence that had been officially denied them. The universities and other institutions of higher education still attracted the live members of the younger generation, and they in turn sustained a subculture that attracted hangers-on, like Nechaev. On the other hand, the defeats of 1861–1863 encouraged a conspiratorial outlook among radical students, who had witnessed the failure of a revolutionary front to coalesce around the student movement and who had experienced instead the devastating reaction of 1862–1863.

Radical students had tried to divert discontent toward revolutionary goals but had overestimated the likelihood of revolution. The complex character of the serf reform of 1861 and the confusion surrounding it led radicals to assume that a vast peasant uprising was imminent. Although the assumption proved to be wrong, it was a reasonable one, given the increase in peasant disturbances during the years before the serf reform and the first chaotic months after its promulgation. But the government's short-term strategy succeeded. A lengthy, phased disengagement of peasants and landlords, the complex land settlement, continuing promise of a "real" reform, and the ruthless use of military force when necessary checked the tendency toward large-scale disturbances. To the radicals, however, the precisely demarcated phases of the land settlement appeared to be major opportunities for revolutionary action, first in 1863, after the landlords' land inventories were due, and then in 1870, when the temporarily obligated peasants had to accept either drastically reduced allotments or long-term indebtedness under the forty-nine-year redemption scheme. In effect the land settlement and other provisions of the serf reform paid off the gentry for their loss of peasant laborers and renters. The revolutionaries assumed that the peasants would see that the Tsar was simply an agent of the landlords, but they were wrong. The peasants still clung to the idea that the Tsar would grant them the "land and freedom" that the Great Reforms of the 1860s never really gave them. The militant wing of the student movement and the revolutionary émigrés (with Ogarev in the lead) named their organization Land and Freedom with the peasant slogan of the great seventeenth- and eighteenth-century jacqueries in mind but failed to ignite a peasant uprising. Worse still, the connections of Russian students, military officers, and revolutionary émigrés with the Polish uprising of 1863 played into the government's hands during the chauvinistic reaction that followed.

An essential element was lacking in the revolutionary situation of 1861–1863—mass participation. The attempt to coordinate the Polish uprising with a Russian uprising failed, although Lithuania, White Russia, and to some extent the Ukraine were affected. How to draw the masses of former serfs—the vast majority were still tied to communes in order to fulfill the collective responsibilities laid upon the commune by the Russian government; some, though, were drifting into the cities and proletarianization—into a full-scale uprising remained the major question facing the Russian revolutionaries during the 1860s and 1870s. But the peasants lived according to their own commitments and symbols and by a different sense of space and time, and the revolutionaries found themselves rediscovering and repeating the limited number of strategies that isolated groups of young men and women—aided by middle-aged theoreticians and historical examples—deduce by the logic of commitment. Radical students often started their active careers as teachers, sometimes hoping to destroy ancient peasant loyalties to the Tsar by propaganda, but more often hoping to clarify to the peasants the system of exploitation that victimized them and to awaken and amplify the socialist instincts they believed already existed in the peasants. The more impatient among them moved swiftly from programs of enlightenment to conspiratorial schemes or carried on both simultaneously. The conspirators always acquired their greatest cogency in the revolutionary movement at moments of clear defeat, when propaganda and agitation had failed to yield revolutionary cadres and popular movements of anticipated scope and effectiveness, and at moments when a relatively less organized phase of the movement had been brutally repressed and hundreds of comrades arrested. At these moments revenge seemed to be as powerful a motive as constructive revolutionary goals.

Peter Zaichnevskii, inspirer and coauthor of "Young Russia," played a role in the early 1860s similar to that played by Nechaev in the late 1860s and early 1870s.[24] Zaichnevskii tried to divert the revolutionary movement to Jacobinism but failed. That is, he carried the idea of revolutionary organization and methods to an unacceptable extreme. His Jacobin means appeared inappropriate to his democratic ends, and however inspiring he may have been as an activist, his proclamation failed to animate a large following. In it one finds both the passionate vindictiveness and spirit of self-sacrifice that distinguished Nechaev. The bloodthirsty rhetoric of "Young Russia" in its day affected readers in much the same way that Nechaev's *Narodnaia rasprava* did in 1869 and 1870. Zaichnevskii seemed to welcome the blind violence of revolutionary struggle:

There is only one way out of this horrible, oppressive situation . . . a revolution which must radically change everything, all of the bases of contemporary society without exception, and destroy the allies of the existing order.

We do not fear it although we know that rivers of blood will flow and that innocent victims will perish; we foresee all of this and nonetheless welcome its coming. We are ready to sacrifice our own heads, if only what we have long desired were to come sooner![25]

There is as well in Zaichnevskii's rhetoric well-focused hatred of the Tsar and the court:

From below is heard the remote and suppressed murmur of the masses, a people oppressed and humiliated by everyone who possesses the slightest bit of authority—a people plundered by officials and landlords, who sell to them their very own property—the land, plundered by the Tsar, who doubles direct and indirect taxes and uses the money, not for the benefit of the state, but for an increase of profligacy at court, for wardrobes to fraulein-mistresses, for rewards to his slaves, for troops, who protect him from the people.[26]

But the most singular feature uniting different generations of extremists in the revolutionary movement was a sense of immediacy, a belief that the revolution lay just around the corner—a feeling of tense expectation and alertness.

Soon, soon the day will come, when we will unfurl the great banner of the future, that red banner, and with a great shout: Long live the socialist and democratic Russian republic! we will march on the Winter Palace to destroy those who live there. Perhaps the whole business will end with only the destruction of the royal family, that is, of some hundred or so people, but perhaps—and the latter is more likely—the entire imperial party, to a man, will stand behind the sovereign, because it will be a question of their own survival.

In the latter case, with complete faith in ourselves, in our strength, in the people's sympathy with us, in the glorious future of Russia, which has come forth as the first to realize the great moment of socialism, we shall give forth one shout: "to the axes," and—then . . . then smash the imperial party . . . smash them in the squares, if those dirty swine dare to enter, smash them in their houses, in the narrow alleys of the city, on the broad streets of the capital, in the countryside and villages.

Remember, that at that time, he who is not with us is against us;

> he who is against us—is our enemy; and enemies must be destroyed by any means.
>
> But don't forget to repeat with every new victory, during every battle: long live the Russian social democratic republic!
>
> And if the rebellion does not succeed, if we have to pay with our lives for an audacious attempt to give to man human rights, we will go to the scaffold without a quiver, fearlessly, and placing our head on the block or in the noose, will repeat that very same great cry: long live the Russian social democratic republic![27]

Words like "fanatic" and "millenarian" fit revolutionaries like Zaichnevskii and Nechaev well, although this does not imply that one should expect uniform behavior from extremists. Strikingly different personalities responded to their appeal, but very few could carry out the demands of the leaders. For some, attachment to a conspiratorial organization signified a natural expression of commitment. They had little sense of the concrete tasks before them. Furthermore, many of those who entered conspiracies were quite young and experienced several changes of mind and affiliation during their revolutionary careers. But there were others who had a sense of personal responsibility for the revolution, who believed that it had some special claim on their lives which in turn gave them the license to act as avengers. They carried to a logical extreme the belief of leaders like Zaichnevskii that by destroying the pillars that supported the Imperial structure, one could bring down the entire system. These were the Tsaricides. The strategy of Tsaricide should not be confused with Jacobinism, although the two sometimes appeared together. The Tsaricides believed that under the right circumstances assassination of the Tsar could touch off a vast uprising. Some revolutionaries, who realized that the vast majority of peasants still believed in a benevolent Tsar, planned to accuse the propertied classes of the murder and lead the masses in a social revolution. Others believed that the crushed, disunited peasants would take heart if they saw they had allies who could strike a blow at the very top and accept the leadership of revolutionary youth. But in spite of all the talk of Tsaricide in revolutionary circles, there were only two attempts on the life of the Tsar during the 1860s—Dmitrii Karakozov's attempt of April 4, 1866, and the Pole Anthony Berezowski's of May 1867.

Karakozov's attempt had far greater significance. He touched off the second wave of reaction in postreform Russia but also became the hero of the revolutionary underground. He himself was a product of the underground. Despite the breakdown of the frail network of opposition groups during the reaction of 1863, former associates of Land and Freedom and new recruits tried to revive the revolutionary optimism of 1861.[28] However, the almost total subsidence of peasant disorders in 1863 gradually forced the new leaders of revolutionary circles to shift from propaganda to terror. Nikolai Ishutin was the central figure in this transitional phase of the movement of the 1860s, although his followers were later called *Karakozovtsy*. The complex story of the development of Ishutin's conspiratorial groups in Moscow between 1864 and 1866 and their liaison with Ivan Khudiakov's St. Petersburg circle will not be told here.[29] Suffice it to say that the two groups entertained a variety of strategies for achieving a Russian and international socialist revolution that reflected the experiences of the preceding years and anticipated those of the subsequent period of revolutionary populism. Ishutin distinguished himself from his predecessors (including Zaichnevskii) by his ruthless approach to conspiracy and by introducing into the revolutionary movement of the 1860s the principle that violence within the party was justified against members who endangered its goals. Any means might be used against anyone. Although it is difficult to establish precisely when the group began functioning (and indeed, if it ever really functioned), Ishutin created within his revolutionary organization an elite terrorist group called "Hell." Its members evidently earned their status by virtue of extreme discipline and self-sacrifice:

> A member of "Hell" must live under a false name and break all family ties: he must not marry; he must give up his friends; and in general he must live with one single, exclusive aim: an infinite love and devotion for his country and for its good. For his country he must give up all personal satisfaction and in exchange he must feel hatred for hatred, ill-will for ill-will, concentrating these emotions within himself.[30]

"Hell" watched over the activities of the broader organization and had the right to assassinate refractory members. But the most notable revolutionary duty assigned to "Hell" was the assassination of Alexander II.

The extremes of violence, deception, and self-sacrifice characteristic of the new trend in the revolutionary underground merged in the contemplated act of Tsaricide. The assassin was to bite a capsule of mercury fulminate after completing his assignment, thereby disfiguring his face. He was to carry in his pocket a proclamation telling of the existence of a vast revolutionary organization and to threaten Alexander II's successor with his predecessor's fate if he failed to yield to the demands of the revolutionaries.[31] However, the terrorist plans were vague, and the place of Tsaricide in revolutionary strategy was never fully clarified. The idea of Tsaricide no doubt served personal fantasy as much as, if not more than, revolutionary purpose. The role of hero-martyr appealed to Ishutin and his followers, and one can hardly imagine a better way of achieving it than by a suicidal act of Tsaricide which would unleash the (imagined) revolutionary fervor of the masses and simultaneously remove a singularly important obstacle to the quick realization of a socialist republic. Karakozov chose to play the role.

How much planning and how many people were involved in the assassination attempt has never been definitely determined, even by the assiduous scholarship of Soviet historians. However, it is quite clear that many of the defendants in the trial that followed Karakozov's arrest and the discovery of Ishutin's and Khudiakov's organizations lied about their relationship to Karakozov, just as the members of Nechaev's did five years later; and it is certain that Karakozov did not act on his own. He belonged to Ishutin's "Hell" (indeed, he and Ishutin had grown up together) and received support from it, but evidently the decision to make the attempt was his own. The dramatic events of the last few weeks before the attempt suggest he was an unbalanced and suicidal person. It has been established that Karakozov spent the two months between November 11 and January 13, 1865, in the clinic of Moscow University. Three weeks later he disappeared for several days, having left a suicide note behind a commode.[32] When he returned, he expressed a desire to assassinate the Tsar. In addition to his revolutionary purpose, Karakozov evidently wanted to use the assassination to destroy himself. One source claims he had been treated for syphilis. In any event, he appeared in St. Petersburg toward the end of February and shortly thereafter contacted an intern in one of the hospitals. A. A. Kobylin later testified that he had found nothing seriously wrong with Karakozov but had given him some sort of electric treatment. Evidently, Kobylin lied, for he was connected with the St. Petersburg underground. He supplied Karakozov with poison after learning about his plans.[33] An atmosphere of sickness and irrationality surrounds the entire affair. Three weeks before the assassination attempt Karakozov distributed a proclamation, "To My Worker-Friends," in which he explained and justified his contemplated act. The police received a copy through the mail but did nothing to prevent the attempt. It was, of course, a failure. Karakozov's pistol shot missed. Legends surrounding the affair gave Karakozov the hero-martyr role he sought, despite the fact that some of those who knew about the attempt blamed him for botching it. But Karakozov presented another image of himself to the prosecutor at his trial:

Prosecutor: [referring to the formation of the secret society, "Hell"] Did you have any influence on the formation of the society?
Karakozov: No. I didn't have any influence.
Prosecutor: But didn't you propagate the . . . idea of the necessity of Tsaricide? . . .
Karakozov: I was at first a student and then became a sick person—nothing more.[34]

In the student underground a cult soon formed around Karakozov. Stories of Karakozov's heroic behavior after his arrest circulated widely. Alexander Herzen published several of them in the revolutionary émigré journal *Kolokol* (*The Bell*) during 1866–1867, and his savage attack on the authorities enhanced the spirit of violence in the student underground. In reply to a Russian official's reference to the "unheard of crime of Tsaricide in Russia," Herzen wrote:

What is unheard of about it? Only that the attempt did not succeed. Is it possible that Murav'ev's mouthpieces haven't heard of the murder of the tsarevitch Dmitrii? Or of the murder of the only decent man ever to be a Russian Tsar, Dmitrii the Pretender? Or of the murder of Boris Godunov and his son? Or of the murder of Peter III by his wife's lovers? Or of the murder of Ivan Antonovich by the self-same fine lady? Or of the murder of Paul I by the leading generals with the participation of his inconsolable son—and of the murder of the tsarevitch Aleksei, at the command of his most tender parent? Haven't Murav'ev's mouthpieces heard the French saying about an "autocracy limited by assassination?" That was our Magna Carta. Poison, the knife, and the garrote (*sharf*)—to this we must add two more limitations upon power—bribes and filth.[35]

Herzen claimed to have received from reliable sources stories about Karakozov's ordeal. First, Karakozov tried to commit suicide by biting through an artery in his wrist. His captors tied him up crosswise, his right arm to his left leg and the reverse, and belted him around with an iron band.[36] Then he defied General Mikhail Murav'ev, known as the "hangman of Vilno" for his bloody suppression of the insurrection in Lithuania in 1863, now commissioned to investigate and crush the new conspiracy. When Karakozov refused to answer questions Murav'ev reputedly said: "You my little dove will confess to me. I'm a Russian bear, and when I strike, bones splinter," upon which Karakozov rattled his chains, strode toward his tormentor, and said in a deep, tense voice: "You may be a simple Russian bear, but I'm a polar bear, and we'll see who handles whom." The frightened Murav'ev jumped toward the door and called the guard.[37]

Karakozov's captors allegedly interrogated him in a special padded room in the Third Section for four days without cease.[38] When this method failed, they whipped him every day for more than a week, but he still refused to answer questions and went on a hunger strike. They had to force feed him bouillon through a tube. Doctors trained in new scientific techniques of torture were called in, and they finally resorted to electric shocks.[39] Herzen explained Karakozov's fortitude with considerable insight (although some of the stories sound like fantasies about the diabolical ingenuity of the authorities):

> Karakozov did not fear and could not fear death. He had long ago settled all of his accounts with life and had signed his own death sentence not only before Prince Gagarin and September 3 [1866], but much earlier than April 4.[40]

Stories of Karakozov's heroism and martyrdom reached Nechaev. According to Zemfiri Ralli, who knew Nechaev during 1868–1869, Nechaev read avidly the back issues of *Kolokol* devoted to the Karakozov affair, and they evidently excited his imagination, although like other members of the underground he found fault with his predecessor. In a conversation (later reported to the police) he reputedly said:

> Karakozov acted stupidly and rashly. He shot without figuring out the best way to carry it out and paid with his life, and in memory of this [the Tsar's escape] they built a chapel in Petersburg for 50,000 rubles, which is enough money to support 1000 [?] students for a year.[41]

Nechaev added to this: "There are many people to take Karakozov's place."

There were indeed people to take Karakozov's place, some of them former members of the Ishutin conspiracy who had been acquitted and formed a group called the Smorgon Academy. They and other student revolutionaries evidently planned to blow up Alexander II's train at Elizavetgrad in the Ukraine in late August or early September 1869. Felice Orsini, who had attempted to assassinate Napoleon III with a bomb in 1858, had inspired Ishutin to pursue more advanced technology. Though the members of "Hell" never got beyond the planning stage,

Feofan Borisov, Mikhail Troitskii, and Vasilii Kuntushev evidently did.[42] Nechaev, as we shall see, tried to join this assassination plot but nothing came of it. Local police were alerted, and the three were arrested. In any case, there is clear continuity in philosophy, technique, and even personnel between the Ishutin-Karakozov type of conspiracy and Nechaev's. The White Terror did not destroy the student underground. Indeed, the inability of the vaunted Russian system of repression to stamp out revolutionary circles is striking. Student revolutionary leaders continued to find receptive audiences everywhere, and the repression in higher education that followed Karakozov's attempt actually increased the number of recruits.

Nechaev inherited all of the expectations, hopes, schemes, and techniques of the revolutionaries of 1861–1863 and 1864–1866: the assumption of a peasant uprising, now expected in 1870 (the final phase of the land settlement); hopes for cooperative ventures with the radical émigré community, with the newly established International and other European revolutionary centers, and with non-Russian Slavs who combined nationalistic and socialistic aspirations; and the idea of political assassination. More important, Nechaev exploited the expectations and hopes aroused in others by earlier revolutionaries. Chernyshevskii, Zaichnevskii, Ishutin, and Karakozov had created the heroic models and the rhetoric, and the revolutionary underground had created the organizational schemes, which he would develop according to his own lights. The autocracy and the educational system provided him with his recruits.

The student movement of 1868–1869 followed hard upon the new regime in higher education established by Dmitrii Tolstoi. To quote one historian of the Russian student movement:

> The Nikolaeven parade-ground principle [referring to Nicholas I's mania for military discipline]: "Flog ten people to death if you can get one to drill properly," was applied by Tolstoi to the gymnasiums and, insofar as possible, to the university.[43]

The regulations of May 1867 created a system of surveillance designed to prevent a recurrence of the student conspiracies of the early and mid-1860s. University authorities and police were to inform one another about student delinquencies and "in general, about all activities raising doubt about the moral and political reliability of the students."[44] Other regulations made it more difficult for students to raise funds for indigent comrades. They forbade student-sponsored concerts, plays, literary evenings, and similar public events.[45] As in earlier reactions against student manners, morals, and politics, the reaction of 1867 failed to change the student subculture or erode the student underground. Radical students applied pressure from the other side but failed to change the basic orientation of the largest body of students, who wanted academic and personal freedom and a rich, autonomous corporate life but did not want to sacrifice these to political causes. Few of them wanted to use institutions of higher education merely as a base for radical activity. In the 1860s when the question: Science or Labor? (meaning labor for the cause of revolution) arose repeatedly, the vast majority of students chose science.

Students of the Medical-Surgical Academy in St. Petersburg set off the disturbances of 1868–1869. Perhaps the most organized body of students in Russian higher education, they reacted with singular energy against any infringement of their individual or collective rights. Since medicine had become the ideal discipline of "new people," Russian medical faculties tended to attract a high proportion of students with radical inclinations, and since the Medical-Surgical Academy was the best as well as the most liberal medical school, it naturally became a center of revolutionary ferment and the nihilist subculture.[46] Thus, in autumn 1868, the medical students began to mobilize and by December 1868, had organized *skhodki* in student apartments and university halls. The *skhodki* spread to other institutions in St. Petersburg, and during the second half of December 1868, and all of January 1869, they were held almost daily.[47]

In the course of the *skhodki* Nechaev revealed the full extent of his radicalism. He become an active member of the more radical student party and attracted the attention of the police in late January 1869, but fled abroad on March 3, 1869, before the student movement reached its peak. By that time, he had acquired a wide circle of acquaintances, partly through his connection with Vladimir Orlov. Nechaev befriended Orlov in Ivanovo, where he spent the summer vacation in 1868.[48] Orlov, a twenty-five-year-old teacher, son of a village priest, had studied in the Vladimir Religious Seminary in the mid-1860s. He recruited several students and former students of the seminary, all of them sons of priests like himself: Ivan Florinskii, Fedor and Vasilii Mavritskii, and Ivan and Evlampii Ametistov. All of them except Evlampii Ametistov—an eighteen year old—were in their early twenties.[49] Furthermore, all except Vasilii Mavritskii abandoned their religious calling for secular education in St. Petersburg and Moscow. Orlov recruited also Nikolai Nikolaev, Aleksei Zubkov, and Vasilii Kukushkin.[50] Nikolaev was the only member of the Ivanovo circle to participate in the fully developed conspiracy. His early career bore some resemblance to Nechaev's. The illegitimate son of a Moscow *meshchanin,* he grew up in a foundling home in Ivanovo, worked in a factory office there, and after a brief career as a clerk in a legal office, found employment in 1868 in a house of detention in Moscow. He was only seventeen or eighteen at the time of his initial involvement with Nechaev's and Orlov's revolutionary circle.[51] Zubkov, a merchant and factory owner in Voznesensk reputedly worth 5,000,000 rubles, was only peripherally involved. Kukushkin, of petty merchant background, employed as a photographer in Ivanovo, acted as intermediary between Zubkov and Orlov. Zubkov gave the circle several hundred rubles.[52]

According to Florinskii, who studied with him at the seminary, Orlov was an ambitious, intelligent, and gifted person. Although he abandoned the priesthood, he retained a religious streak, expressed in his penchant for quoting Biblical texts. He had a special talent for poetry and had written a poem to Alexander II during the Tsar's visit to Vladimir province. Florinskii described him as a liberal and an optimist during those years. Orlov's main ambition was to be a *narodnyi uchitel',* a teacher to the peasants, but he also aspired to higher education.[53] Nechaev evidently prodded him to come to St. Petersburg in 1868. In Ivanovo Orlov was a popular teacher. Zubkov, presumably an admirer of Orlov, testified at the trial of the Nechaevists that Orlov taught not only reading and arithmetic, but carpentry and bookbinding, and took his young charges on trips into the woods surrounding Ivanovo to gather wood.[54] Orlov quite clearly had injected nihilist ideas into his pedagogy. Elizaveta Tomilova, one of Nechaev's collaborators who knew Orlov in St. Petersburg during March and April 1869, described him as a vaporous socialist theoretician attempting to ground his new society in cosmic, physiological, and historical laws. Both she and Anna Nechaeva (with whom Orlov was smitten) were completely bewildered by Orlov's abstract, repetitious monologues, rendered all the more difficult to understand by his stammering. Nechaev called Orlov a "fantasizer" and poked fun at him while he rambled on, but Orlov never noticed. According to Tomilova, his behavior was quite odd. He crept about like a shadow and would suddenly appear before her with a wild look in his eyes.[55]

Feliks Volkhovskii played some role in the early phase of Nechaev's career—that is, before his first flight abroad in March 1869. At the age of twenty-two, the young *dvorianin* (nobleman) was already a veteran of the revolutionary underground. He had been involved with Ishutin through a Ukrainian commune in Moscow University and suffered his first arrest in 1866 after Karakozov's assassination attempt. Shortly afterward, he helped organize the Ruble Society, an early *narodnik* circle devoted to testing the revolutionary temper of the countryside and to educating the peasants. Like so many of these circles, it had an ambiguous character, designed on the one hand to further popular enlightenment and bridge the abyss separating the intelligentsia from the peasants, and on the other to merge with the revolutionary movement.[56] It was discovered by the police in the spring of 1868 and dissolved by arrests. The coorganizer of the society, German Lopatin, like Volkhovskii, devoted his life to the movement, although he was never part of the Nechaev conspiracy. In fact, it was he who unmasked Nechaev in 1870, at a time when Nechaev held in thrall the leaders of the Russian revolutionary émigré community in Switzerland. His brother Vsevolod, however, did work with Volkhovskii and Nechaev. Twenty years old at the time of his involvement with Nechaev, Vsevolod Lopatin later joined one of the most important socialist circles of the early 1870s and conducted revolutionary propaganda in the Ukraine in 1873.[57] Unlike the recruits from Ivanovo (with the exception of Orlov perhaps) the former members of the Ruble Society who mingled with Nechaev in the revolutionary underground were his equal in commitment, and they were more experienced. There is no evidence that he controlled them. It is not even possible to reconstruct from the obviously false information given to investigators before the trial and later to the court who was in control or how deeply individuals were involved. But Volkhovskii and Vsevolod Lopatin played at least minor roles in the development of Nechaev's conspiracy.

Grigorii Enisherlov's role is also difficult to establish, not so much because of false testimony, but because in his memoirs, written long after he had dropped out of the revolutionary movement, he may have exaggerated his influence on Nechaev.[58] Like Volkhovskii and the Lopatins a member of the gentry, he was only eighteen or nineteen when he chose a revolutionary career. He ran away from home in June 1868 with the intention of enrolling as an auditor in the Technological Institute in St. Petersburg,[59] one of the three centers of the student movement there. His father soon learned from one of Enisherlov's confidants that Grigorii had enrolled him in a gang in Khar'kov; that the gang was one of several planned for the purpose of robbing the rich to collect money for the "general cause"; that Grigorii planned to rob a local monastery (in Khar'kov) and use the funds to buy a house near the Winter Palace; and that he would then tunnel under the palace and blow it up with nitroglycerine.[60] The elder Enisherlov informed the governor of

Khar'kov, whose investigation yielded nothing but the fact that Enisherlov was in St. Petersburg without a passport. Briefly detained by the police in St. Petersburg, Enisherlov convinced them and his father that his friend's story was a complete fabrication. His father permitted him to enroll in the Technological Institute, where he became an active member of the student movement and one of the most fanatic (in an adolescent way) members of the revolutionary underground.

Zemfiri Ralli, another who began a long revolutionary career as a leader in the student movement, recalled a meeting in Nechaev's apartment with Nechaev, Orlov, Evlampii Ametistov, and Enisherlov. After the meeting Enisherlov urgently pressed Ralli to accompany him home. Once there, Enisherlov wrote on a scrap of paper and handed it to Ralli. Ralli read: "When Ralli needs a person ready to shoot the ruler he can ask me, and I will carry it out." Enisherlov announced that his apartment was surrounded by spies and that he probably would be arrested the next day. It immediately occurred to Ralli that Enisherlov himself was an agent provocateur, but he decided that he was merely naive. He destroyed the note and related the incident to Nechaev the next day. Nechaev, at first displeased that Ralli had destroyed the note, later agreed it was the correct thing to do.[61] One detects the instincts of the manipulator and blackmailer in Nechaev's initial reaction. The episode suggests that Enisherlov might have been a bit unbalanced at the time. A prison story related by Lev Nikiforov, like Ralli one of the student emissaries from the Medical-Surgical Academy to Moscow in February 1869, reinforces this impression. Nikiforov was Enisherlov's cell neighbor in the spring of 1869, after both had been arrested for their roles in the student movement. A number of Nechaev's other associates were in prison as well, among them Feliks Volkhovskii and Vera Zasulich, and Enisherlov blamed himself for Volkhovskii's arrest. When he learned that he and Zasulich were going to be freed, he began to beat his fists against the window panes and appeared before the prison commandant, hands dripping with blood.[62]

In March 1870, after a second arrest, this time in connection with the Nechaev conspiracy, Enisherlov claimed that Nechaev had to be punished. He considered it a matter of personal honor and begged the authorities to release him so that he could kill Nechaev. In a statement to the police of March 6, 1870, Enisherlov denied that he had taken seriously Nechaev's talk about the use of terror in political organizations. Nechaev had proposed killing spies and agents by first strangling and then shooting them in the head—the method actually used in Ivanov's murder—as a distinctive warning to others.[63] Yet in his memoirs, written in the 1890s and entitled "My Confession," Enisherlov boasted that he had formed a "Jesuitical" theory of revolution and had influenced Nechaev.[64] During a programmatic session of a revolutionary *kruzhok*, presumably in the autumn or winter of 1868–1869, Enisherlov had championed military coups and political assassination. Nechaev and Orlov were present. Only Nechaev supported him fully:

> Only one, lean with a vindictive face and a convulsively compressed mouth, a beardless youth, warmly shook my hand and said: "I'm with you—forever. You can't do anything by taking a direct path; it ties your hands . . . Jesuitism is exactly what we have lacked up to the present moment. Thanks, you hit upon it and spoke out. I'm with you."[65]

The *kruzhok* then voted on a number of questions. No one besides Enisherlov and Nechaev unconditionally accepted the Jesuitical approach to revolution. To the question: What kinds of restrictions will be placed upon members who leave the society?, Nechaev alone responded with the answer: "death." The others contented themselves with a demand of strict silence about the revolutionary organization. The circle, however, voted unanimously for the death sentence in reply to the question: What will be the punishment of traitors, that is, informers?[66] Enisherlov therefore lied to the police about his own position, although he may have accurately described the reaction of others to Nechaev.

Tomilova, if we are to believe Enisherlov, tried to dissuade Nechaev from his terrorist position. She jokingly told Enisherlov:

> You . . . gave him the idea—now I can't do a thing with him! . . . He used to go where one led him—dug his heels in, but went on—but now you've discovered his America for him, and it will cost a lot of effort to calm down this bandit-Pizarro.[67]

Elizaveta Tomilova, wife of a retired colonel, at the age of thirty was one of Nechaev's oldest collaborators. She boarded Anna Nechaeva in her home shortly after Anna arrived in St. Petersburg in December 1868.[68] Tomilova influenced Enisherlov, according to Enisherlov's account, in a liberal-gradualist direction, but Nechaev savagely fended off her and any attempts to get him to moderate his position. He viewed Tomilova and all liberals with profound contempt.

> You've . . . frightened our fine lady . . . and now for appearance' sake we've got to "calm down," so we can suck them dry . . . and then throw them into the garbage, to the Third Section . . . Here's where your theory will be confirmed splendidly.[69]

Tomilova may have talked like a liberal, but she acted otherwise: All the evidence suggests that she collaborated closely with Nechaev from before his first flight abroad until her arrest in April 1869. She was the recipient of the clumsily devised conspiratorial letters he sent from Geneva at the time of his first exile. During the police raid on her apartment she tried to tear up Orlov's notes, which clearly implicated her:

> All friends of the cause, those of you who are acquainted with the names Nechaev, Ralli, Ametistov, etc., place your trust in Tomilova in all matters. She is privy to the entire plan associated with our cause and through her you will find both the means and the best friends for the continuation of our cause . . .
>
> V. Orlov[70]

Furthermore, in the 1870s she became involved in another terrorist conspiracy, that of The People's Will.[71] It is easier to assume that Nechaev and Tomilova had been deceiving Enisherlov, or that Nechaev had been deceiving both of them, than it is to reconcile with Enisherlov's memoirs the evidence of Tomilova's radicalism and closeness to Nechaev. Although the facts do not completely vitiate Enisherlov's claim about his influence over Nechaev, they do cast some doubt on it.

Ralli is the most reliable source for information about the influences on Nechaev during the winter of 1868–1869. His memoirs, like Enisherlov's, contradict the information he gave the authorities. In addition to being Nechaev's inside informant on the Karakozov affair, Ralli participated with Nechaev, Orlov, the Ametistov brothers, and several other students in a political circle, which met in Nechaev's apartment during December 1868. They read old issues of *Otechestvennye zapiski* (*Notes of the Fatherland*) containing articles by Robert Owen, *La Lanterne*, Philippe Buonarroti's *Conspiration pour l'égalité dite de Babeuf*, and Thomas Carlyle's history of the French revolution (like Owen's essays, translated into Russian) and discussed Russian revolutionary history—the Decembrists, the Petrashevskii Circle, and Khudiakov's group. The knowledge Nechaev gained in this study group is reflected in some of his later pamphleteering. He must have been fascinated by the Terror in the French revolution. At some of the *skhodki*, portraits of Robespierre and Saint-Just graced the tables, while photographs of the martyred poet

Mikhail Mikhailov, Herzen, and Chernyshevskii adorned the walls.[72] Nechaev's penchant for centralized control and conspiracy found support in the left wing of the French revolutionary tradition, as did his crude, material egalitarianism. Michael Bakunin's anarchist program, published in the first issue of the journal *Narodnoe delo* (*The People's Cause*), also circulated in radical circles with electrifying effect. Although the Jacobin spirit of central control and anarchism are not congenial partners, Bakunin's uncompromising radicalism set forth simply and directly in "Our Program" appealed generally. One can easily see how a young Jacobin-communist might respond enthusiastically to and interpret the following:

> We want full intellectual, socioeconomic, and political liberation of the masses.
>
> I. *Intellectual liberation*, because without it political and social freedom can be neither complete nor secure. Belief in god, belief in immortality of the soul and any species of idealism in general, serves, on the one hand, as the necessary support and justification of despotism, of all species of privilege and of the exploitation of the masses, and on the other hand, demoralizes the masses themselves . . .
>
> From this it clearly follows that we are exponents of atheism and materialism.
>
> II. *Socioeconomic liberation* of the masses, without which any kind of liberation must be a repugnant and hollow-sounding lie. The economic existence of the masses was always the cornerstone, and contained within itself the real explanation of their political existence. All the . . . existing political and civic organizations in the commune rest mainly on the following foundations: on the fact of conquest, on the right to hereditary property, on the familial rights of the father and husband, and on the sanctification of all of these by religion—all of these together constitute the essence of the state. An inevitable consequence of the entire state structure was and must be a slavish subordination of the simple laborer and the uneducated majority to the so-called educated, oppressive minority. A state without political and juridical privileges, based upon economic privileges—is inconceivable.
>
> Desiring the genuine and decisive liberation of the masses we seek:
>
> 1. Abolition of the right to hereditary property.
> 2. Equalization of the rights of women, both political and socioeconomic, with the rights of men; consequently we seek destruction of familial law and marriage, both religious and civil, since they are indissolubly connected with inheritance rights.
> 3. With the destruction of marriage arises the question of the up-

bringing of children . . . From the time of the established pregnancy of the mother to their [the children's] majority, the upbringing and education, equally for everyone—from the lowest level to specialized higher scientific development—at one and the same time industrial and intellectual, preparing a person for both muscular and intellectual work, must be largely the responsibility of a free society.

As a basic economic truth we set forth two fundamental positions: The land belongs only to those who work it with their hands—to citizens' communes. Capital and all of the tools of labor belong—to the workers—to workers' associations.

III. The entire future political organization must be nothing more than a free federation of free workers, both agricultural and factory-industrial *arteli* [associations].

Therefore, in the name of political freedom we seek above all the decisive destruction of the state, the uprooting of all aspects of the state principle with all of its clerical, political, military- and civil-bureaucratic, juridical, scholarly, and financial-economic institutions.

We seek full freedom for all peoples, presently oppressed by the empire, and full rights of self-determination on the basis of their own instincts, needs, and wills . . . federalizing from the bottom up, those who *want* to be members of the Russian nation, could create a genuinely free and happy society in friendly and federative ties with the same kinds of societies in Europe and in the entire world.[73]

Whatever the relative impact of "Our Program," on the various circles that Nechaev frequented, or on people like Enisherlov and Ralli, the evidence suggests that Nechaev reacted immediately and enthusiastically to revolutionary strategies employing terror, deception, and dictatorial organization. Furthermore, despite the absence of any mention of political plots associated with the study group meeting in Nechaev's apartment, Slivkov's report of "fires and shots," as noted earlier, suggests preparation for direct action. Documents belonging to Feliks Volkhovskii and annotated by him tend to reinforce the hypothesis that Nechaev and others were hatching a political plot under the cover of the student movement during the winter of 1868–1869. In fact, it seems likely that Nechaev was involved in more than one plot, although no statements to the police, trial testimony, or memoirs permit us to reconstruct precisely their immediate objectives or the extent of various individuals' collaboration.

The most important document of this period of Nechaev's activity is "A Program of Revolutionary Actions." It was found among Volkhovskii's papers during a police raid in January 1870.[74] Volkhovskii's annotations to the "Program" tend to support his denial of authorship. The manuscript was in Nadezhda Uspenskaia's handwriting. She belonged to a circle of revolutionaries based in Cherkesov's Moscow bookstore which included Volkhovskii, the central figure in the group, Mariia Antonova, who married Volkhovskii in 1871, Pavel Prokopenko, a former member of The Ruble Society, Vsevolod Lopatin, Nikolai Nikolaev, Viktor Skipskii, and others. Uspenskaia, the fifteen-year-old sister of Petr Uspenskii, Nechaev's steadfast supporter in Moscow, copied the manuscript from the original, which Volkhovskii claimed to have received from Orlov during the Lenten season, 1869.[75] The original mysteriously disappeared, and the investigation and trial failed to establish who wrote the "Program."[76] Scholarly speculation has attributed the "Program" to Nechaev alone, or to Nechaev in collaboration with Petr Tkachev. Tkachev's role in the revolutionary underground during 1868–1869 before his arrest on March 26, 1869, is as difficult to establish as those of less significant figures.[77] He lied systematically and had others do the same for him during the investigation and trial. Tkachev, along with Volkhovskii, Ralli, V. Lopatin, and Varlaam Cherkezov (the last, like Ralli, linked to the Karakozov affair), a veteran of revolutionary activity, was the outstanding theoretician among Nechaev's revolutionary colleagues of that period. He had a long record of radical activity beginning in October 1861, when he was a seventeen-year-old law student in St. Petersburg University. During his incarceration after his first arrest for participating in the student movement of 1861, he befriended one of Zaichnevskii's future disciples, Leonid Ol'shevskii. In 1862 he began a journalistic career as a writer on legal questions, but in his numerous articles he dealt with the "accursed questions." Furthermore, Tkachev never severed his ties with the revolutionary underground. His writing career was punctuated with an arrest in 1862 and a police search in 1866. He remained a consistent extremist of the Jacobin-communist variety both before and after the Nechaev affair, and ended his career in Paris, where he collaborated with French Blanquists. Tkachev died in 1886, after four years of progressive paralysis and symptoms of insanity.[78]

The first Soviet scholar to examine the question of who wrote "A Program of Revolutionary Actions" at first simply attributed it to the circle that had formed around Nechaev.[79] Later, he gave Tkachev a role in its composition and spoke of a circle forming around Nechaev and Tkachev.[80] Unquestionably, Tkachev knew Nechaev and Orlov and had conspired with them about the formation of a central committee to guide the student movement in a revolutionary direction. There had been meetings in Tkachev's quarters as well as Nechaev's. Ivan Likhutin, one of Nechaev's followers, in a letter to his mother of February 8, 1869, (intercepted by the police) wrote that Tkachev had formed a *kruzhok*.[81] The same Likhutin, in a protocol given on January 18, 1870, to the Senate committee investigating Nechaev's political plot, testified that Nechaev dominated (*orudoval tam*) Tkachev's circle and developed there his idea of organizing the revolutionary network into *kruzhki* of five members.[82] Nechaev's actions after his first flight abroad fulfilled the prescriptions of the "Program," insofar as it was possible, and there is no reason to doubt that he played a role in its formulation. Tkachev preferred to remain a shadowy figure in the underground, to lend his pen and knowledge to the movement, often for purposes of giving it a respectable cover, and to publicize positions with which the liberal reading public might sympathize. He only unfolded his program fully in 1874, several years after his third arrest and imprisonment—this time for his connection with the student movement and the Nechaevists—and his emigration. The extent of Tkachev's contribution to the "Program," if any, will never be known. Given the modus operandi in revolutionary circles described by Enisherlov in his memoirs, it is probable that the various points of the "Program" were voted upon and then written at a single sitting of the *kruzhok*. The language of the "Program" indicates that it was designed to proselytize as well as to guide.

A Program of Revolutionary Actions

We cannot fail to recognize that the chief reason for the misery of our society issues from its bad economic structure, permitting and legitimating the dominance of the strong over the weak, the parasitism of the capitalist on the exhausted worker. Some work from early morning until late at night and receive for it a miserly wage, insufficient to support them and to restore their wasted energy. Instead of clothes they have filthy, pitiful rags, instead of a dwelling—some kind of repulsive kennel, a damp, stinking cellar, and even this only in the happy event that they have work. And what are the others doing all the while—those upon whom they depend for work, and consequently for their existence? They gather up from them the entire product of their labor, leaving them only the bare essentials to sustain their hungry and cold existence. In order to avoid this irksome task of collecting, they hire managers, foremen, etc., etc., and for this *dolce far niente* they are afforded every possible comfort and consideration. The more developed among them use the money taken from peasants and craftsmen to encourage the fine arts and literature, or they deplore the sad fate of the paupers and engage in petty charity. If you reflect about what's around you, it must seem like a kingdom of the insane—

so strange and unnatural are the mutual relations of people, so strange and incomprehensible their placid attitude in the face of a mass of filth, meanness, and injustice which issues from our social structure. You steal and consider yourself honest, you give the person you've robbed of hundreds some kind of pittance and sincerely consider yourself his benefactor. This goes beyond naiveté—it's insanity. But how are we to understand that such things are considered normal by those who have been robbed themselves? Such an arrangement can't continue forever. The *narod* will realize that right and might are on its side, and then they will be victorious. This outcome is inevitable. Everything we do must hasten it, by explaining to the *narod* its strength, the necessity of unification and revolt.

The full freedom of the rejuvenated personality lies in social revolution. Only a radical reconstruction of absurd and unjust social relations can give people enduring and genuine happiness. But it is impossible to achieve this under the present political structure because it is in the interest of the existing power to prevent it by all possible measures, and as is known, the authorities possess all possible means for this purpose. Therefore, as long as the present political struture of society exists, economic reforms are impossible, and the only way out—is political revolution, the annihilation of the nesting places of the existing power, a reform of the state. Thus, *social revolution—is our final goal and political revolution—is the only means for achieving this goal.* In order to make use of this means, to apply it to the cause, we already have methods worked out in the history of previous revolutions. It is up to us to apprehend them consciously, that is to grasp that since they are phenomena repeating in history, one must recognize the historical law and, not waiting for this law to appear in all of its fullness by virtue of time and circumstance, which is inevitable—since all things occur in due course—to hasten this development, prepare it, try to affect minds in such a way that this development would not be unexpected for them and they would act consciously, as calmly as possible, and not under the influence of passion, their eyes bloodshot. Of course, many years have intervened between earlier revolutions and our era, many changes have occurred, and consequently the methods must necessarily be modified and adjusted to the present time, but all the same a law is a law, and we may modify methods, introduce new principles into them, but we cannot ignore them.

We must try to create the greatest possible number of revolutionary types, to develop in society consciousness of the necessity and possibility of revolution, as the only means for achieving the best order of things, and carefully construct a revolutionary organization.

In order to achieve this we must distribute certain types of proclamations in a certain spirit, arrange *skhodki* and personal protests as preliminary probes, as a practical method for developing revolutionary types and for separating from the masses the types which are already developed, finally, as a method for bringing together both individuals and numerous but uncoordinated circles; recruit people and form everywhere private *kruzhki* with the same direction and the very same, single goal—revolution; set up *kassy* toward the formation of a revolutionary fund; try to enter into relations with European revolutionary organizations and maintain constant ties with them. We must infuse into our organization those *social-economic* principles, which will be at the bases of the future state and political order. The organization must be established according to the spirit of decentralization and on the law of mobility, that is, its members must move from place to place, that is, after a certain time move from one place to another, which is necessary because the activity in various places calls for it, and the organization at first will not be in any condition to send separate agents to every locality, and because this kind of activity maintained constantly by the same person in one place will undoubtedly attract too much public notice and place the agent in a dangerous position, from which follows inevitably, that the authorities will make it impossible for him to act. It is decentralization in the sense of a weakening of the main center and the allocation of a great deal of initiative to the activities of provincial centers. Then, those entering the organization must renounce property, studies, family ties, insofar as the latter (family and studies) might impede the activities of the members—to demand total renunciation of them the organization cannot, since this would restrict without need or cause individual freedom, which is incompatible with an organization based upon rational principles. Until May the activity of the best people must be concentrated in Petersburg and Moscow, and also in part in other university cities. At this time a protest of university students and those of other institutions of higher education for the right to have official *skhodki* must be prepared and completed; and simultaneously the principle of propaganda must be applied to the poor by the very same poor—it follows that an organization must be formed from the poor. Beginning in May activity must be transferred to provincial and district towns and concentrated mainly among the *raznochintsy* [roughly, educated commoners], seminarists and provincial poor, etc. Beginning in October all of the forces of provincial activity and activity concentrated in the capitals by propagandists must be introduced into the milieu of the *narod* itself (which is difficult in the summer because of the heavy working season). Therefore, in October at least three-fourths of the active workers must move from the capitals to the provinces, toward the western border, to Dinaburg—an important route for emigration, and thus the preparation of the area around this route has special significance. From May until September no more

> than one-fourth of the members will remain in the capital. Specialists from among the best writers on the social and natural sciences must be among them. Before September, they must define in detail the structure and rules of the Russian revolutionary organization, create a catechism, the rules of which must be observed by everyone entering into direct relations with the organization; define the activity of the center and the provinces, the methods and everything relevant to the creation of particular protests (of course, theoretically) in the mass of people in 1870, as well as the rules for agricultural and artisans' associations; provide instruction in other methods of recruitment; create the form of the future state structure and define the time of revolution. In October members from all of the provinces must assemble, and all of the problems that have been theoretically solved must be discussed and accepted by a majority. From this moment the organization must begin systematic revolutionary activity embracing all of Russia.
>
> NB. The composition of the form in which the future state structure will be organized must occur with the agreement of revolutionaries abroad and consequently a system of foreign correspondence will be created. The best time for the uprising is—the spring of 1870, because in this year many serious and immediate problems will be confronting the *narod*, and because in the event that the uprising fails in the central areas, the summer period will be favorable for a separate war along the Volga and Dnepr and for the concealment of large masses of the *narod* in the forests. The major condition which the members of the organization must observe is to avoid diffusing themselves through multifaceted activities, and once having taken up the cause, to push aside everything not relevant to it, to expend all of their means and all of their time, insofar as their material resources permit, since at this time the organization is not able to provide material security for its members, and consequently, they must expend a certain amount of time on the acquisition of the means to live, if they aren't able to get private stipends or haven't their own resources.[83]

This programmatic statement—sentimental but sardonic, visionary, yet oddly concrete—is a pale preface to Nechaev's more personal statements in *Narodnaia rasprava* (*The People's Revenge*), "The Catechism of a Revolutionary," *Obshchina* (*The Commune*), *Kolokol*, and several proclamations. It is not clearly a product of his pen. For example, Nechaev would never have assigned to theory and theoreticians the role given them by the author(s) of the "Program." One might even suspect Orlov as the major author, since nihilist scientism dominates the theoretical outlook of the document, and a vague Jacobinism its strategic perspective.[84] But it contains as well typically *narodnik* ideas about the nature of a peasant uprising—for example the assumption that chronically disaffected areas in the Ukraine would behave in a traditionally explosive manner, once the proper leadership appeared. This odd mixture of Jacobinism and *narodism* is typical not only of Nechaev, but of an entire wing of the revolutionary movement during the 1870s and after, as is the lightly posed and crudely resolved theoretical problem of historical law and revolutionary action. The revolutionaries of the 1860s and 1870s were impatient. They wanted to give history a push. The most impatient and willful tried to create the perfect instrument: the disciplined revolutionary organization that might accomplish in months what would otherwise take years or even decades. And they promised to manage all of this and simultaneously control the violent passions of revolution.

Despite its specific timetable and its discussion of broad strategies of recruitment, organization, and coordination, the "Program" does not fully clarify what the new methods appropriate to the new revolutionary era were. It did not attempt to reveal either the structure and rules of the Russian revolutionary organization, or the "catechism" that would provide a code of conduct for its members. The author(s) of the "Program" may have solicited suggestions about methods, organizational rules, and rules of conduct. Volkhovskii's annotations, for example, are obviously an attempt to specify appropriate methods:

> An axiom having the same significance in both physics and sociology, especially forcefully put by Buckle is—"No effect can be greater than the cause producing it." It follows that in a struggle with an authority, which rests upon force, every party of action must also be based upon an even greater force, that is, from the army or the *narod*. From history I know whenever the party of action tried to create a revolution by means of a conspiracy, it suffered a series of defeats so long as revolutionary ideas did not penetrate little by little into the masses. . . . Arrange it so that these forces will be approximately equal, so that one fine day the party of action will find arrayed against it, not the "court" supported by the army, but only the "court," in itself weak. It seems not at all impossible that a swift and daring action by a well-organized party might seize this trifle. . . . We have only "regiments," politically indifferent and inert, unaccustomed to any political role, well disciplined and therefore knowing nothing besides the commands of the nearest authority. . . . If these leaders disappear on one fine day . . . then it will be easy. . . . Everywhere we see evidence of one and the same law: the smaller the mass participating in political life, the easier it is to have a political revolution (*pravitel'stvennyi povorot*). Insofar as humanity passes through all of

> the stages of development, from absolute monarchy to democratic republics they become more and more difficult. . . . In chemistry and physics a small, vital force liberates huge reserves of potential force (a spark, gunpowder). . . . If a provisional government during the earliest period of its existence clearly and strongly shows the *narod* its misery, the reasons for it, and the means for curing it, then important consequences must follow. It is remarkable that all radical measures are extremely simple, their significance and value can be explicated to the dullest person from the simple people, that is from among those persons whom these measures will not harm. Thus, I presume that if a provisional government decrees a series of measures, whose positive consequences will be tangible to the peasants and the mass, it will thereby summon the masses to participate in its cause, in the completion of the revolution, and will create in its own support the desired force, which will help it defend its friends and suppress its and the people's enemies, which, of course, will get up a terrible struggle in view of the radical measures.[85]

Volkhovskii's commentary continues the scientistic perspective of the "Program"; it also includes the idea of a two-stage revolution: first, a coup d'état engineered by a "small, vital force" and then a series of measures designed to bring the masses into the revolution. The importance of this idea in the Nechaev conspiracy has been obscured, probably for the simple reason that it remained primarily an idea. But it was almost certainly a preferred method for setting off the popular revolution. The assassination of the Tsar figured prominently in the conspiracy contemplated by Nechaev, although it is not mentioned by Volkhovskii.

Rumors (recorded by police agents), statements by Nechaev's followers, and occasional statements by Nechaev himself, suggest that between 1869 and 1872, when he was still at large, he was plotting an attack on the Winter Palace. One police report specifically names Nechaev and Vsevolod Lopatin:

> On the night of February 19 [1870] Nechaev, Lopatin and others . . . dressed as peasants, intend to stay in one of the houses surrounding Haymarket Square, with the aim of fulfilling their criminal intentions in relation to the Sacred Person of the Lord Emperor.[86]

A police agent planted in the Agricultural Institute in St. Petersburg heard that Nechaev controlled 200 people and had a cash reserve of 100,000 rubles and a printing press. With these resources, he planned to kill the Tsar and call the masses to revolution.[87] More important, on at least two occasions Nechaev expressed to his close followers views that resembled both the rumors and Volkhovskii's notes to the "Program." Nikolai Nikolaev in his deposition claimed that Nechaev had said:

> On February 19, 1870 it's necessary only to gather together thirty persons, disperse them on various squares in Moscow and begin to yell these words: "The Tsar has been killed and they want to make everyone serfs."[88]

Although nothing is said here about a plan to kill the Tsar—only to announce his murder—shortly after he had killed Ivanov, Nechaev said to Kuznetsov:

> "The realization of this plan [killing the Tsar] does not present any great difficulty. One only needs an organization of forty to fifty loyal persons, which having broken into the palace and disarmed the guard could finish off the Tsar and his family." The palace guard in this period was extremely undisciplined, some of the Tsar's lackeys and servants neglected their duties, and under such conditions, according to Nechaev's assurances, it would be possible to carry out a coup.[89]

Nikolaev's deposition reveals that Nechaev planned to add an element of deception to the preferred method, but as we shall see, it gives only the faintest flavor of the fully developed methods of deception Nechaev was to suggest to The People's Will ten years later.

Nechaev abandoned the theoretical outlook of the "Program," or perhaps he openly broke with it, almost as soon as he began to write his own appeals. He also summarily dispensed with the relative moral delicacy of the "Program," especially its recognition of the personal rights of members of the revolutionary organization. In fact, Nechaev deviated so far from the morality of the revolutionary subculture that he became an embarrassment to it.

While Nechaev conspired in the underground, he maintained a reasonably respectable front in the student movement. He worked for the radical party, which wanted large-scale *skhodki* (as opposed to the smaller *kruzhki* preferred by the moderates), a single *kassa*, ostensibly for needy students, a central committee, and unification of the movement in a network of institutions of higher education.[90] In general, the radicals wanted confrontations with authority and politicization of the movement, but they distinguished themselves from the moderates more by their methods and hidden motives than by their overt demands. The radicals too demanded student rights, emphasized the plight of the poorer students, and showed how their demands for autonomous student institutions were connected with their concern for poor students. Both Enisherlov and Tkachev contributed proclamations to the student movement, while Ralli, Nikiforov, Volkhovskii, V. Lopatin, and others tried to stir up the students in Moscow. Nechaev began to take a leading role at *skhodki* in early January 1869. Stepan Ezerskii, a leader of the moderates, attended a *skhodka* where Nechaev was the main orator. He later testified to the police that Nechaev's "sincere passion" attracted the students, but that Nechaev did not exceed the limits of the usual student demands.[91] Nikiforov, however, related one incident in which Nechaev had evoked a strong protest because he strayed to other concerns.[92]

The most interesting of Nechaev's overt activities was his attempt to get students to sign a petition. The petition was apparently a device for testing the degree of commitment of the students at the *skhodki*. At the very least it committed the signers to support the demand for the right to have official student *skhodki;* at the most it committed them to some form of protest at a later time. Nechaev gathered ninety-seven signatures. Somehow the petition (perhaps it is better to call it a commitment to protest) fell into the hands of the Third Section. They treated it with special care, although why they did remains a mystery.[93]

Ivan Likhutin told the Senate investigating committee that he had asked Nechaev what he intended to do with the list of names. Nechaev had replied that since the signers belonged to a variety of institutions under different jurisdictions, their request could not be submitted to any given minister, and hence would be submitted to the Tsar himself. For this purpose everyone would go to the square (though not specified in Likhutin's protocol, probably the square before the Winter Palace). Likhutin suggested that only Nechaev should go, but Nechaev had replied: "Either they go to the square and take their chances, or else answer for certain to the authorities."[94] Independent testimony establishes that Nechaev threatened to give to the authorities the names of those who refused to attend the protest on the square.[95] Evidently, the impatient Nechaev thought he could recruit and radicalize people for the movement by implicating them, exposing them to arrest and police brutality, and cutting their ties to the existing order. Vera Zasulich claims in her memoirs that Nechaev had a fully developed rationale for this technique of "recruitment." Once expelled and radicalized, the students would settle in provincial areas and serve as agitators. They would convert the local seminarists, who would presumably be more receptive to propaganda, and they in turn would propagandize the local peasants.[96] One can easily connect Nechaev's tactic with the strategy of the "Program."

Whatever the case, Nechaev's prominence at the *skhodki* and, no doubt, his circulation of the petition, attracted the attention of the police. On January 29, 1869, he received an order to appear before the authorities (*Upravlenie Sanktpeterburgskogo Gradonachal'nika*) and evidently did so on January 30.[97] He left instructions with Evlampii Ametistov to contact Nikiforov if he should be arrested. In the belief that Nechaev had been arrested, Ametistov went to Nikiforov's apartment, but Nechaev appeared shortly after, out of breath, and hurriedly told them that he had been at the Third Section, that they knew almost everything about the *skhodki*, and had asked him a lot of trivial questions. He had to go back in an hour. Later that evening, he appeared at Tomilova's looking completely distraught and said that he had been placed under the sponsorship of the director of the Sergievskii School.[98] The next day, Nechaev disappeared. There is no evidence that the Third Section had either arrested him or planned to arrest him. Perhaps they had asked him for the list of names—they undoubtedly knew it existed—and Nechaev served his own purposes by giving it to them. Furthermore, the interview with the police and, presumably, his double dealing marked the end of the first phase of Nechaev's activity. During the first phase, like almost all members of the revolutionary underground, he had played the role of teacher or student while serving his primary goal of revolution. Henceforth he became a full-time underground revolutionary. Evidently, he had rehearsed a theatrical departure with a few close comrades in St. Petersburg and Moscow. To others who knew him well, he had signaled his departure. He had been studying French assiduously, and shortly before his disappearance on January 31 had sold his books.[99]

Nechaev chose Vera Zasulich as the instrument for his disappearing act. The Zasulich family in a sense had become wards of the revolutionary movement. The widowed mother and four daughters (one of whom died at the age of fifteen) eked out a living in the capitals, where they entered into the nihilist subculture. Aleksandra Zasulich married Petr Uspenskii, and Ekaterina, Lev Nikiforov. Ekaterina, the eldest sister, had been a member of a sewing *artel'* organized by Ishutin, and for a while mother and daughters worked together as seamstresses. Vera, youngest of the three surviving sisters, also tried her hand at bookbinding. But the young imitators of Vera Pavlovna, heroine of Chernyshevskii's novel, found that in real life the *arteli* quickly broke down because of incompetence and lack of commitment.[100] (The *nigilistki* sometimes found themselves before courts of arbitration when the experienced seamstresses whom they hired to teach them lost patience with the apprentices and appropriated the sewing machines.) Zasulich drifted into the student milieu, where she met Nechaev. He struck her, as he had others, as an extremely energetic, self-made person. Nechaev was quite adept at picking out those whom he'd impressed, and he soon invited her to the gatherings at his apartment. He assumed that the seventeen-year-old was smitten with him, and he declared his love to her. She was shocked and as gracefully as she could indicated that she had in mind only comradely relations.[101] Zasulich became a regular participant in Nechaev's circle and a committed revolutionary. She evidently already supported the strategy of political assassination. At student gatherings she spoke of the need to "deliver Russia from the Tsar." Almost ten years later she tried to assassinate the military governor of St. Petersburg, General F. F. Trepov.

On the eve of his disappearance, Nechaev stayed with his sister Anna and Zasulich in Tomilova's apartment. Shortly before dawn, he appeared in the room where Zasulich slept and handed her a parcel for safekeeping. The parcel probably contained notebooks or sheets of paper with the names of hundreds of radicals.[102] That very morning Nechaev left the apartment, and Zasulich never saw him again. On the first or second of February, she received in the mail an envelope containing a letter and a scrap of gray paper. The anonymous author of the letter wrote:

> While walking today along Vasilevskii Island, I encountered a carriage carrying a person under arrest. A hand was thrust out and threw a note, and I heard a voice say: "If you are a student, take this to the designated address." I am a student and consider it my duty to fulfill the request. Destroy my note.[103]

On the slip of gray paper, Zasulich found a penciled note in Nechaev's hand: "They are taking me to a fortress, which one I don't know. Tell this to the comrades. I hope to see them. Let our cause continue."[104] Anna Nechaeva, like Zasulich seventeen years old, but barely literate—a simple girl who adored her older brother—desperately made the rounds of the authorities, trying to find him.[105] The director of the Sergievskii

School, who had supported Nechaev against Slivkov's complaint two weeks earlier, made his own inquiries, but was told the same thing. Nechaev had not been arrested.[106] Everyone assumed the authorities were lying and feverishly speculated about the reasons for Nechaev's secret arrest. Already a prominent figure during the January *skhodki*, Nechaev now became a celebrity in the radical underground. That is precisely what he had intended.

In reality, Nechaev went to Moscow, found Orlov, and arranged to stay in Nikolai Nikolaev's apartment. Orlov was Nechaev's stage manager and factotum during the next few weeks. They traveled from Moscow to Ivanovo, where they got 200 rubles from Zubkov, and back to Moscow, from which Nechaev departed alone with Orlov's passport for Odessa. Nechaev returned to Moscow at the end of Lent. Orlov spread the rumor that Nechaev had escaped from the Peter and Paul Fortress, and then had been recaptured in Odessa, but had eluded his captors, run and walked about thirty miles, and hitched rides in ox carts on his way to Moscow. Nechaev later published his own account, which included additional details about his struggles with his captors. Actually Nechaev's and Orlov's journey were mainly occupied with preparations for Nechaev's first flight abroad. They needed cash and an external passport. Nikolaev gave Nechaev his external passport and Nechaev left Moscow on March 3, crossing over the border the next day.[107]

Nechaev's and Orlov's feverish machinations seem strangely out of place in the context of the student movement then. Although the movement did shift to the left because of the hard line taken by the university authorities, it never acquired the momentum of the rebellion of 1861. The students of the Medical-Surgical Academy, the vanguard of the movement, on March 11, 1869 forcibly occupied an auditorium that had been denied them for their *skhodki*. On March 13, they beseiged an officer of the Academy in a campus building for the better part of a day. Arrests of student leaders followed that night, and the next day the "soft" president of the Academy was replaced by a more "energetic" one. On March 15, the St. Petersburg police closed the grounds of the Academy to students. Students of the Academy carried their demonstrations into the streets. The disturbances spread to the Technological Institute, where mounted police were called in (though violence was averted), to the Agricultural Institute, to the University, and to the Petrov Agricultural Academy and the University in Moscow. All of these institutions were shut down for several days, and student leaders were arrested and expelled.[108]

However, the anticipated mass radicalization of the student bodies of the capitals and other university cities did not occur. Many students used the closing of the schools as an excuse to bend their elbows at local taverns, sometimes to the annoyance of the regular patrons.[109] In Khar'kov, students contented themselves by venting their hostility on students who didn't support the "cause," men in uniform, and well-dressed citizens.[110] Reports of student rowdiness and debauchery began to pour into the offices of the police, and in St. Petersburg an odd rumor circulated that students of the Medical-Surgical Academy were going to poison the city's meat supply.[111]

The student movement in Moscow proved to be more important for the history of the Nechaev conspiracy. Volkhovskii, V. Lopatin, and Nikiforov were singled out as instigators of the disturbances at Moscow University who were more interested in political, social, and economic issues than in the students' narrower causes.[112] Their arrests in April 1869, along with the March and April arrests of most of Nechaev's developed comrades in St. Petersburg, left the position of leadership open to him when he returned. He was one of the few proponents of the "political" approach to revolution still at large after the spring of 1869. A handful of veterans, notable among them Varlaam Cherkezov and Petr Uspenskii, became important figures in Nechaev's conspiracy when he returned six months later. The Ishutin tradition barely survived. However, disturbances in the Petrov Agricultural Academy and Moscow University helped Nechaev's cause. Founded in 1865, the Petrov Agricultural Academy had a reputation for liberalism. A great many students lived in state-funded rooms, while the rest lived in the student quarter of the city, making it easier to arrange corporate dining rooms, libraries, and a secret *kassa* with numerous subscribers. The students ran their affairs with no interference from Academy authorities. In addition, they had the use of a spacious park belonging to the Academy.[113] But in March 1869, the students of the Academy protested to the Academy Council against recently issued rules forbidding women to visit state-owned rooms at night. The minister of state property retaliated by converting the dormitory space into classrooms.[114] In Moscow University, the central incident occurred several months after the March demands, in October 1869, when eighteen students of the Medical School were expelled for leading a student boycott of the lectures of Professor A. I. Polunin, whom they judged incompetent.[115] Most of the expelled students joined Nechaev's conspiracy.[116]

More generally, the failure of the March protests in the University and Petrov Academy, followed by the Polunin incident, convinced a small number of students that the only proper protest was revolution, and the only way to fight was to go underground. But the strategy of the "Program" could not be served well by such modest numbers. The radicals had anticipated mass expulsions and the closing of institutions of higher education for a long period as had occurred in 1861–1863. Nothing of the sort happened in 1869. Most students pursued the moderate strategy of forming clandestine self-education circles for their mutual support, and the authorities avoided mass expulsions. In addition, Russian educated society failed to rally behind the students as it had in the earlier period of student rebellion, when the opposition front had been broader. The events of the 1860s had clearly separated the radicals from the liberals. They regarded one another with (respectively) hatred and contempt and suspicion and fear. It seemed that the radicals, their ranks depleted by the arrests of key figures (among them, Tkachev, Ralli, Orlov—who remained at large until the end of June 1869—Enisherlov, Tomilova, Zasulich, the Ametistov brothers, and several members of Volkhovskii's Moscow circle) would have to abandon the strategy of the "Program." Instead they increasingly relied upon Nechaev, whose stubborn fidelity to the timetable of the "Program," refusal to admit defeat, and Jesuitism kept alive the illusion that the revolution was near at hand.

Chapter III

Nechaev and the Émigrés

The First Proclamations Campaign

When Nechaev arrived in Geneva in March 1869, he brought with him the promise of a revived revolutionary movement. Rumors about peasant rebellions and the story of the student disorders arrived almost simultaneously with him. Aging émigré veterans of the socialist cause, like Herzen, Ogarev, and Bakunin had already experienced a similar moment in 1861–1863. The consequences had been disastrous for them. Their prestige and influence among Russian liberals had virtually disappeared after the Polish uprising of 1863, and the new generation of radicals tended to see them as creatures from another world, often treating them condescendingly. Ogarev in particular had suffered during the post-1863 decline. He had played a major role in lining up *Kolokol* with the student underground. After the failure of the Polish rebellion, the dissolution of the first Land and Freedom, and the decline of *Kolokol*'s popularity, he drifted further into alcoholism.[1] Unlike Herzen, who was able to distance himself from the movement and its basic assumptions, he could not engross himself in a literary career and a richly complicated personal life. He needed the stimulus of a movement; in this respect he resembled Bakunin, although he lacked Bakunin's quixotic energy and capacity for contriving the semblance of a movement out of thin air. One would think that Ogarev and Bakunin would have learned something from the disasters of 1862–1863, yet instead of raising their threshold of resistance to exaggerated tales of revolutionary preparedness, the events of that period seem to have lowered it. Bakunin and Ogarev were captives of their commitment to an immediate revolution. Young emissaries from Russia simultaneously revived their hopes and exploited their resources and reputations.

Ogarev evidently was Nechaev's first contact among the émigré triumvirs.[2] Long before the demise of *Kolokol*, Ogarev had tried to embody in his personal affairs the antiphilistine ideals of his romantic youth. The fascination with fallen women that haunted his generation (and the next one as well) inspired him to marry an English prostitute and raise her son as his own. Ogarev's young ward, Henry Sutherland, became one of Nechaev's followers in Switzerland. Ogarev himself welcomed Nechaev with the enthusiasm of a patriarch reunited with a prodigal son. The émigrés had anticipated a new breed of revolutionary more sympathetic to them, better organized, and capable of carrying on the unfinished business of 1861–1863. To Ogarev, Nechaev signaled the end of the doldrums.

With Ogarev's help Nechaev launched the first proclamation in the campaign of 1869. Copies of "To Students of the University, Academy, and Technological Institute in St. Petersburg" began to arrive in St. Petersburg on March 30. From one to five or six were in each envelope, with instructions to the addressees to spread the word to other universities and other students.[3] Nechaev's first published piece is fairly moderate in tone compared to his later efforts, yet Ogarev wrote to Herzen on March 20/April 1:

> Yesterday a letter arrived in your name with a request to print a message to the students from one student, who has just escaped from the Peter and Paul Fortress. The message is perhaps a bit overdone, but one must print it. I am deeply convinced that it will, in any event, turn things around and resurrect the émigré press.[4]

Two days later he wrote: "This student message is very immature, very immature, yet reminds me of my own youth and offers hope of new forces."[5]

Nechaev informed his student audience that good fortune had permitted him to escape the "frozen walls" of the Peter and Paul Fortress and the "evil, dark force" that had imprisoned him there. In a further attempt at self-promotion, he pursued a theme familiar to his personal acquaintances—his own bitter experiences as a child of the people:

> Thousands of emaciated, ragged, humiliated, plundered persons live in our memory. We recognize in them our fathers and near ones. They are all exhausted in the struggle with something vague, and they vainly call out for help. They continue to struggle blindly, but waste their strength fruitlessly on an enemy which they cannot see, but

> which crushes them. But to us this dark force is clearly visible, luring us to serve it by showing us luxury and glory.[6]

Playing as usual on the sense of guilt in his relatively privileged and idealistic readers, Nechaev described a series of paths that led to debauchery, parasitism, worldly comforts, and privileges; to selling out to the bourgeoisie, the liberals, and the educational establishment that served despotism. The dead weight of the past threatened to crush all health and life out of the younger generation. What could the students do? Nechaev called on them to confront the bayonets of the government, not isolated as in the past, but united in a movement that was purified of its unreliable elements and strengthened by the addition of allies from all discontented groups. Friends and enemies had to be judged by what they did and who they were, not by what they said. Revolutionary types (though he did not once use the word "revolution" in the proclamation) could not develop in the passive world of books but only in persistent struggle. The more frequent and greater the clashes with the dark force, the greater the number of tempered fighters. Some would be sacrificed, to be sure, but that was a small price to pay for the rapid process of conversion and commitment that would occur during the struggle. Finally, Nechaev appealed to a desire for revenge. The survivors would exact a hundredfold vengeance upon the enemy. The themes that appear here recur with added pathos and savagery in Nechaev's later writings.

Meanwhile, Ogarev began to slip into a role similar to that he played during the era of Land and Freedom. He was the first to oblige Nechaev (who arrived in person shortly after the letter to Herzen mentioned by Ogarev) with a proclamation. Ogarev failed to convince Herzen that it should be issued over the signatures of the triumvirate and thus had to change his initial title, "From Old to Young Friends," to "Russian Students."[7] A brief exhortation to the students, it is not one of Ogarev's better efforts and is notable mainly as a preface to his and Bakunin's efforts on Nechaev's behalf. Once again (as in 1862–1863) Bakunin became the major collaborator and intriguer, although Ogarev produced a number of short pieces, both poetry and prose,[8] and did editorial work for Nechaev during the course of 1869 and 1870.[9] Nechaev quickly saw that Ogarev was an easily manipulated, pathetic ruin. But Bakunin at first impressed him.[10]

We know little about Nechaev's movements in Europe immediately after his arrival there. He sent two telegrams from Brussels to Tomilova, who received the first on March 8 and the second a week later. Tomilova sent Nechaev 100 rubles at his request. Then she received another telegram, this time from Geneva and dated March 17/29,[11] asking her to get money from Zubkov. Presumably this was the date of Nechaev's arrival in Geneva. He sent his first letter from Geneva on March 25/April 6, after his first meeting with Bakunin—at least so it would appear from his crude attempt to hide Bakunin under the name "Bakurskii," a ploy that failed to deceive the agent of the Third Section who analyzed the letter. Nechaev displayed unusual laziness in devising code names. Vera Zasulich became "Grandmother Vera"; Vladimir Orlov, "Grandfather Vladislav Fedos'evich"; Zubkov, "Zubatov."[12] Nechaev tried to pass himself off as a wine merchant. Evidently, when he referred to "merchandise" he meant the revolutionary "types" called for in the "Program of Revolutionary Actions." He wanted Zasulich to come to Geneva with lists of names—presumably those he had left in her possession—and a picture of the state of the revolutionary underground. Nechaev mentioned a trip to France that depended upon his receipt of the information, but this may have been simply a fiction. Herzen is referred to as "that businessman who had a porter factory in London for such a long time."[13] Presumably, with Herzen's backing Nechaev could arrange for a major contribution from Zubkov, and to convince Zubkov, Nechaev was willing to send documents verifying his ties with Bakunin, since he had not met Herzen. Tomilova was to tell Orlov that "one could get genuine, unadulterated wine only from Bakurskii," which apparently meant that only Bakunin could be relied upon to follow the revolutionary line of the student underground. However, Nechaev continued, Orlov had to close the deal with Zubkov in order to ensure Bakunin's delivery of "the barrels" he was preparing. Nechaev obviously was using his new relationship with Bakunin to strengthen his credit in Russia while simultaneously trying to impress Bakunin with the extent of the movement and its backing. He told Bakunin and Ogarev that he was an agent of a powerful, widespread network of revolutionary organizations and showed them phony letters from all over Russia as evidence.[14] The lists and notebooks left with Zasulich would back up his story and the letters, and he therefore asked Tomilova to convince Zasulich to go to Geneva.

Nechaev's second letter, the last Tomilova received before her arrest, followed on April 7/19. He hardly troubled to keep up his front as a wine merchant. The urgent tone of the letter and most of its substance suggest something other than anticipation of the purchase of some barrels of wine:

> I just received your second letter from which, just as with the first one, I could gather nothing! . . . Surely you should be able to find time to give a thorough account of everything that is going on and write more often! . . . I'm surprised!? . . . You must think I'm made of stone, to leave me ignorant about the cause which is as dear to me as my life. Reading the newspapers and not receiving a single line from you, I was tormented the whole while, and if I didn't lose my mind, it was probably because matters here keep me busy full time!? When I went away I didn't sever ties with the cause the way others have, just as soon as they can make connections here. . . . You . . . must know that while I'm alive I'll never retreat from that which I pursue, and if you know this, then you have to inform me about the slightest changes, about all the details, if the cause is dear to you as well! . . . Why have all of you over there dropped everything!? Things are hot, like iron, and have to be beaten while hot! . . . The matter which has to be discussed does not touch upon our trade alone, but Europe in general! . . . For God's sake, don't be so slow![15]

By the time he wrote the letter, Nechaev had established connections with Italian revolutionaries in Geneva and told his friends to contact him through one of them—Zamperini.[16] The police could hardly fail to see through the second letter, although one agent picked up the rumor that Nechaev was involved in a counterfeiting ring.[17] The Third Section managed to decipher the clumsy code names devised by Nechaev. In a raid on Tomilova's apartment on April 13, they found Nechaev's telegrams and letters and the two notes by Orlov that established Tomilova's credentials in the conspiracy. The raid not only implicated Tomilova, it also permitted the police to connect the St. Petersburg group with Volkhovskii's Moscow circle through Mariia Antonova, who appeared at Tomilova's house during the raid.[18] Andrei Kolachevskii, who had been associated with the Ishutin circle, had accompanied Antonova and was also arrested. By the beginning of May, fourteen people, including most of Nechaev's closest collaborators, had been implicated. The arrests that followed the raid foiled the group's plan to print revolutionary proclamations on a secret printing press. Those arrested included Tomilova, Anna Nechaeva, Antonova, Andrei Kolachevskii, the Zasulich sisters, Nadezhda Uspenskaia, the Ametistov brothers, Liudmila Kolachevskaia (Andrei's sister), Volkhovskii, and Ralli. Orlov fled to the Ukraine and hid first in Khar'hov and then in Kuban province but was apprehended on June 28, 1869.[19]

Other central figures, most notably Tkachev and Vsevolod Lopatin, were also arrested—the former on March 26, 1869, for composing a proclamation "To Society," outlining the student demands and printed on a press owned by his common-law wife, Aleksandra Dement'eva, and the latter on April 16 for his role in the student movement in Moscow. The March and April arrests all but destroyed the groups that had formulated the "Program of Revolutionary Actions." Nechaev and Orlov had demonstrated an unusual capacity for conspiratorial incompetence. Although the evidence cited earlier establishes that Nechaev wanted large numbers of students arrested, it is difficult to believe that he also wanted those involved in the formulation of revolutionary strategy and tactics—the fully developed revolutionary types—to fall as well. There is something odd about the paper trail Nechaev left behind him. By scattering as much material about as possible he may have hoped to create an atmosphere of furious activity and revolutionary preparedness that would encourage recruitment. On the other hand, exhibitionism and an irrational desire for detection may have been involved. These last two may even be connected as symptoms of the hero-martyr fantasy suggested in his descriptions of his alleged escape from the fortress and in the image of himself as a heroically struggling victim in the proclamation to the students. As we shall see, these early fantasies were only stage sets for the real drama. What is certain is that Nechaev's methods and those of his coconspirators assured the collapse of the still rudimentary organization forming in St. Petersburg and Moscow.

While all the arrests were taking place, Nechaev was busy taking Ogarev and Bukunin in tow. As already noted, Bakunin's uncompromising extremism in the first issue of *Narodnoe delo* had at first impressed Nechaev. Now, face-to-face meetings with the physically gigantic and verbally expansive old revolutionary confirmed his initial reaction. The enthusiasm in Nechaev's second letter to Tomilova was undoubtedly genuine. To be sure, like the other émigrés, Bakunin later suffered Nechaev's contempt and had to fend off brazen attempts at extortion. But for a moment, something like mutual admiration and respect existed between the cosmopolitan veteran of failed revolutionary causes and the raw youth from the provinces. Bakunin lived in anticipation of the reappearance of youthful leaders like Andrei Potebnia. Of all the revolutionaries of 1861–1863, Potebnia seems to have impressed the triumvirs the most. A person of enormous personal integrity, Potebnia had none of the long-windedness of the intelligentsia. He was a military officer, a man of action, with the conscience and commitment of an *intelligent*. Potebnia led the futile revolt of 1863 among the Russian officers who were sympathetic to the Polish cause and died in battle at twenty-four. Although it is possible that Bakunin projected some of Nechaev's features onto Potebnia, it is more likely that his acquaintance with Potebnia had prepared the way for Nechaev. The following passages from Bakunin's pamphlet, "To the Officers of the Russian Army"[20] (written in January 1870, during Nechaev's second exile), might just as well have been about Nechaev as Bakunin perceived him in 1869:

> Potebnia was a simple man; humble in station, in rank, and by education. . . . Everything that he knew he got mainly from Russian journals. Reading *Kolokol* had greatly influenced him as it had all of his contemporaries. He had a simple but healthy mind, distinguished only by sober, practical thought. But he had a chivalrous soul and was an unstudied, unrhetorical hero. He believed in the cause, was convinced of its necessity. He dared to act, and once having undertaken action, he followed through, unswervingly forward, turning off neither to the right nor to the left and not stopping before any obstacle. He lay down his life for the cause. . . . Potebnia gave himself entirely to the sacred cause of destruction, to the cause of popular liberation.[21]

There is an even more striking passage in the same vein:

> A daily witness to the boundless suffering of the *narod*, he [Potebnia] gave to them his soul, and gave himself over to the great cause of their liberation, and also their revenge. Potebnia hated the existing order with the very same ardent and deep passion with which he loved the people. Both passions, love and hate, fused into a single one, became the exclusive stimulus for all of his actions and for his entire existence. . . . He had a warm heart but a cold exterior. . . . He was stingy with words, sober in the discussion of any matter.[22]

Bakunin then went on to describe the kind of conspiratorial organization Potebnia had tried to create in 1862–1863. In the autumn of 1862 he had first come to the émigré leaders for help in arranging contacts between the Russian and Polish military organizations. They had sent him to the committee of Land and Freedom.

> A month later he returned to London, and this is what he said about the Committee:

> "There's nothing serious there, not even the embryo of something serious. Most of its members are conspiratorial and revolutionary braggarts, children showing off for each other and consoling themselves with loud but empty phrases; children not only by age . . . but in mind, in abilities and in their complete absence of will power, strength and real knowledge. . . . Nevertheless," added Potebnia, "we must act, though independently in the name of the Committee, because there is no other organization and no other committee in Russia. . . . Finally, in time, serious people can join this fake Committee and convert it into a real one."[23]

Unwittingly (though by January 1870 he was perhaps on the verge of conscious recognition) Bakunin had described Nechaev's position in 1869–1870. Bakunin evidently at first believed that Nechaev was a Potebnia representing a new Committee with a large organization of disciplined, self-sacrificing revolutionaries behind it. More than a year later Bakunin wrote to Nechaev, "The first serious Russian revolutionary was Potebnia; the second was you."[24] He revealed admiration and enthusiasm for the new generation in general and Nechaev in particular in other correspondence and in his first proclamation for Nechaev, written in May 1869, "A Few Words to the Young Brothers in Russia":

> Where did you get your faith and strength? Faith without God, strength without personal hopes and aspirations. Where did you get this capacity to give yourself up to death without vanity and fine phrases? Where is the source of that wildly destructive and coldly passionate inspiration, which paralyzes the minds of our opponents and freezes the blood in their veins?[25]

Nechaev obviously had considerable psychological leverage over Bakunin and Ogarev. Herzen remained relatively aloof. He quickly recognized the symptoms of 1862–1863 in both the situation and the rhetoric. After reading Ogarev's proclamation he sadly noted that Ogarev had acquired the strident tone of the new revolutionary generation.[26] When Ogarev somewhat repentantly sent Herzen a new, less strident manifesto entitled "Our Story" (published in May 1869), Herzen agreed to issue it over the signature, "The Publishers of *Kolokol*," but convinced Ogarev that it had to be modulated even more. Bakunin found it too moderate and refused to add his signature.[27] Eventually, Ogarev yielded to Bakunin's influence, and his later efforts brought down more of Herzen's rebukes. In a letter written to his daughter Natalie on June 10/22, 1869,

Herzen described the split with Ogarev and Bakunin, which he feared would lead to open warfare in the press. Herzen had arrived in Geneva on April 28/May 10. He met Nechaev soon thereafter, developed an instantaneous dislike for him, and later referred to him as a reptile.[28] Herzen had little stomach for the "bloodthirsty" rhetoric inspired in Ogarev by Nechaev and Bakunin and even less for Bakunin's "doomsday" preaching.[29] He tried to restrain his comrades from writing on Nechaev's behalf, but they proved impervious to his efforts to stop them from "le déchaînement des mauvaises passions."[30]

There was small likelihood that Herzen could divert Bakunin from collaboration with Nechaev, much less from his pursuit of *buntarstvo*—of an explosive release of the destructive powers of a vast rebellion led by ruthless men of action. Bakunin had an almost mystical faith that the Russian masses would repeat in 1870 the one-hundred-year cycle of insurrection suggested by Stenka Razin's rebellion of 1670 and the Pugachev revolt of 1773.[31] Furthermore, Bakunin discounted the unattractive personal qualities of the young fanatics who approached the émigrés—something Herzen found impossible to do—achieving at the personal level the same kind of synthesis that guided him in his philosophy of history: Processes of creation and destruction interpenetrated; the new society could not be built with clean hands. In June 1867, he had written to Herzen:

> In the younger generation, taken separately—in separate cases there is a multitude of unpleasant, dishonorable, even filthy features. It is, however, a quite natural phenomenon: The old morality based upon religious, patriarchal, and estate [*soslovnye*] traditions has collapsed, never to rise again. The new one is far from realization, but one has presentiments of it. Only a radical social revolution can realize it fully. The isolated strength of a single person, no matter how clever and powerful he might be, is not enough for this. Therefore the new morality does not yet exist. The younger generation searches for it, but still has not found it—hence the waverings, contradictions, ugliness and not infrequent filthy scandals. So it was in '93—only then the guillotine purified morals, and didn't give the immature sprouts a chance to decay. All of this is very unpleasant, painful, and sad, but natural and inescapable. All of this in the midst of our poor, inexperienced Russian émigré world is aggravated further by that émigré disease, which you so accurately studied and described in your writings. But all of this does not have to prevent us from seeing the important, indeed mighty qualities of our younger generation—in it

> there are not hothouse, artificial or intellectual [*reflektivnye*] passions only, but a genuine passion for equality, labor, justice, freedom, and reason. Because of this passion, tens of them have already gone to their deaths, and hundreds to Siberia. Among them, as always and everywhere, there are many empty braggarts and phrasemongers, but there are heroes—heroes without phrases. . . . No, if you please, Herzen—these unwashed, awkward pioneers of the new truth and the new life are a million times better than your proper corpses.[32]

Bakunin, still trying to live down the artificial passions of his own youth, was neither emotionally nor intellectually prepared to fend off a young man who roughly embodied his conception of heroism. Thus, both in Russia in the student underground and in the émigré milieu, Nechaev was well served by the eager anticipation of a man of action—abrasive, somewhat inarticulate, but wholly dedicated to the cause. Nechaev had left Russia with the preconception that the émigrés were parasites but indispensable for his purposes.[33] After a while he began to treat Bakunin as a subordinate, and the older man became a willing accomplice in his own humiliation.[34]

Bakunin quickly followed his first proclamation for Nechaev with another, "The Posing of the Revolutionary Question," in May 1869. In an ambiguous statement, Nechaev later seemed to claim authorship of the proclamation, although it was undoubtedly written by Bakunin. Nechaev with greater accuracy claimed as his own "Principles of Revolution," written during June or early July 1869. There is no mistaking Bakunin's *narodnik* anarchism in "The Posing of the Revolutionary Question." He called for a general *bunt*, not a series of disunited and easily crushed uprisings, such as had occurred time and again in isolated villages or districts in the Russian countryside over the course of two centuries. The general *bunt* would be led by the hardy, refractory young men who had escaped into the forests and become brigands.

> Brigandage is one of the worthiest forms of Russian folk life. . . . The brigand is a hero, a protector, a popular avenger; an irreconcilable enemy of the State and the entire social and civic order erected by the State; a life-and-death fighter against the entire bureaucratic-noble and official-priestly civilization.[35]

Bakunin justified the savage cruelty of the brigand by calling him a product of the cruelty of the ruling powers. He urged university youth to abandon the false, doctrinaire, perverted "science" of the Academy and to help the *narod* unite into a general *bunt*. Bakunin did not encourage the formation of secret conspiratorial circles. Quite the contrary, he derided the pretensions of "doctrinaire-educated, conspirator-socialists" separated by a vast gulf from the only true source of revolutionary strength—the *narod*.

There is a substantial difference between the historical-theoretical justification of merciless revenge rendered in Bakunin's pungent, but nonetheless restrained prose and Nechaev's harsh vindictiveness. Whereas the State and *Narod* appear throughout Bakunin's proclamation as Evil and Good, they figure very little in Nechaev's. Furthermore, it is not difficult to detect an undertone of mutual criticism or mistrust in the two proclamations. Bakunin's "The Posing of the Revolutionary Question" had made light of the pretensions of "conspirator-socialists." Presumably, Nechaev had shown him a copy of the "Program of Revolutionary Actions," and it had evoked a contemptuous response. By contrast, Nechaev's "Principles of Revolution" posed a direct challenge to the émigrés:

> We are severing ties with all political émigrés who do not want to return to the homeland to stand in our ranks; and while these ranks are still not visible—with all of those who will not further their open appearance on the stage of Russian life. (Exceptions for those émigrés who have already declared themselves workers for a European revolution.)[36]

The awkwardness of the passage and its dictatorial tone—not to speak of its content—leave little doubt about who wrote it. Nonetheless, the influence of Bakunin on Nechaev is unmistakable. Nechaev found in Bakunin an anarchist's hatred for coercive political, social, economic, and cultural forms. Nechaev added a surcharge of vengefulness, which the aging anarchist admired and encouraged but did not feel. On the other hand, Nechaev exploited Bakunin's love of intrigue which involved Bakunin in conspiracies no less vaporous than those dreamed up in the student underground. One therefore cannot draw a solid line between Bakunin and Nechaev. In their first collaboration during the spring and summer of 1869, Bakunin's influence is apparent. A passing reference to Schiller's hero-brigand, Karl Moor, in "The Principles of Revolution" no doubt owes something to Bakunin's tutelage, as does the glorification of total destruction.[37]

Nechaev's individual contribution begins where methods of revolutionary struggle and the selection of revolutionary targets (or victims) intersect. One stylistic clue to Nechaev's authorship of the following passage in "Principles of Revolution" is the repeated use of the word *fakticheskii* ("real" or "actual").

> For the present revolution we do not need individuals standing at the head of the crowd and commanding it, but hidden inconspicuously in the crowd itself, and inconspicuously using themselves to tie one crowd to another, in addition inconspicuously giving one and the same direction, one and the same character to the movement. . . . Actors in the present popular revolution, once they have worked out their life plan, declare themselves in real actions (*zaiavliaiut o sebe fakticheski*), unifying and organizing during the very action. Long underground work, separated from real activity, often filled the ranks with weak people, who caved in at the first pressure. The closer one approaches the time for a genuine popular movement, the less one finds a split between thought and action. More deeply infused with revolutionary ideas, the generations preceding the revolution contain individuals who cannot restrain their passion for destruction until the outset of the general struggle, who quickly seek out enemies and do not hesitate to destroy them. At first appearing as exceptional events, called acts of fanaticism or frenzy by contemporaries, they must recur more and more frequently in various forms, and then become transformed into something like a general passion in the youth, and finally, into a general insurrection.[38]

Nechaev was describing himself and some of his comrades in the student underground. Unlike Bakunin, who repeated the émigré call of 1861 to leave the university lecture halls and go to the people, Nechaev called the students underground. One should note that Nechaev did not condemn but welcomed unrestrained avengers. Nechaev's sequence of revolutionary actions moves from individual youths in the revolutionary underground, to the youth movement as a whole, and only then to the masses. He was a *Pugachev d'université*, a fulfillment of Joseph De Maistre's prophesy. Bakunin had not really diverted Nechaev from his main base of action nor affected Nechaev's inclination toward political terrorism, as is revealed in the following passage:

> The annihilation of highly placed persons, in whom are embodied governmental forms or forms of economic corruption, must begin with isolated acts. Later this work will become easier, in proportion to the increase in panic in that social stratum which is doomed to perish. The cause begun by Karakozov, Berezowski and others must pass over, constantly increasing in frequency and magnitude, into the actions of collective masses, like the actions of Karl Moor's comrades in Schiller, except for the idealism which prevented the actions which were called

> for which must be replaced by stern, cold, merciless consistency. . . .
> . . . . Our first business is struggle, cold, fierce; our goal—the total destruction of restraining bridles.[39]

Nechaev's contempt for the Academy and for any attempt by philosophers or scientists to impose their order upon the "amorphousness" that would emerge after the universal destruction wrought by revolution matched Bakunin's, at least in "Principles of Revolution." Later, Nechaev's Jacobinism gained the upper hand, and he violated his own anarchist prescription against utopian formulations:

> And since the given generation itself was subjected to the influence of those repulsive conditions of life, against which it rebels, it cannot participate in the business of creation, the business of those pure forces, which will work themselves out in the days of renewal. We say: The abominations of the contemporary civilization in which we grew up deprived us of the ability to erect the building of Paradise of the future life, of which we can have only a vague conception according to our understanding of something opposite to the filth of the present! . . . For persons beginning the practical action of revolution we consider any discussion of this vague future criminal because it interferes with pure destruction, holds back the movement to begin the revolution, and consequently delays its finish. During practical action it is a fruitless dissipation of the mind, mental onanism.[40]

The plea for destruction, total destruction, continues, but in addition one finds a recurring, unusually strongly expressed hatred for words, thoughts, or a passive attitude that leads to relaxation or withdrawal from ceaseless activity:

> The struggle will grow, our forces will grow! . . . From this issues our hate of surcease, in anyone or in anything! . . . We must disturb this pernicious social slumber, this monotonousness, this apathy by any means! . . . We believe only those who really declare their devotion to the cause of revolution, fearing neither torture, nor imprisonment, because we repudiate all of those words which are not quickly followed by action. Aimless propaganda not setting forth a definite time and place for the realization of the goals of the revolution are no longer needed! . . . We want to hear talk only about action now, so that the mind doesn't get confused by idle words; so that the tone of polemics, of journalistic enthusiasm doesn't corrupt character, doesn't give birth to new chatterers, and doesn't divert attention to trifles. . . . We will use force to silence all chatterers who refuse to understand this![41]

Further, Nechaev threatens to "smash to pieces" the timid souls who hold back and fail to join the revolution. He no longer searches for euphemisms for the method of struggle he has chosen. It is terrorism, and all means are legitimate:

> Not recognizing any kind of activity other than the act of annihilation, we agree that the forms in which this activity can appear are extremely varied. Poison, the knife, the noose, etc.! . . . Revolution consecrates everything equally in this struggle. Thus, there is an open field! . . . Let the last days of the social bloodsuckers be darkened! Wails of terror and repentance will resound in society, rag-picker writers will emit lyrical groans. Should we pay any attention to this!? . . . No! . . . We must remain profoundly indifferent to all of this howling and not enter into any kinds of compromise with those who are doomed to perish. They call this terrorism! . . . They have a loud epithet for it! Let them, we don't care. . . . Let all healthy young persons take up without hesitation this sacred cause of annihilation of evil, of purification and enlightenment of the Russian Land by fire and sword, fraternally uniting with those who will do the same in the whole of Europe.[42]

One need not comment on the Manichaean spirit of "Principles of Revolution." Its truly notable feature is its frenzied commitment to action. Nechaev had defined anything other than direct revolutionary action as a form of masturbation. The following passage from the first issue of *Narodnaia rasprava* intimates a similar message:

> We have lost all faith in words. Words have significance for us only when . . . actions follow immediately after them. For example, a modest and extremely cautious organization of secret societies without any open, practical manifestations is in our eyes no more than a little boy's game, silly and disgusting.[43]

His terminology must have had an interesting effect upon Bakunin, whose youthful elevation above the coarse and immediate had been described by Vissarion Belinsky as that of a "eunuch and onanist."[44] But Belinsky himself had complained of the same affliction, of a reasoned idealism that "made life a gloomy dream and turned joys into specters."[45] He called this striving for a "higher" plane of life "spiritual onanism."[46] Belinsky, the father of social, didactic literary criticism in Russia and Herzen's and Bakunin's colleague during the 1830s and 1840s (he died in 1848), like them had fled philosophical idealism. Bakunin, however, like the character modeled after him in Turgenev's novel *Rudin*, abandoned his Hamlet-like flight from action for quixotic activity. Bakunin had been known as a coward in love and in combat. Mikhail Katkov, later Russia's leading conservative-chauvinist journalist, but in the 1830s and 1840s a friend and associate of Belinsky and Bakunin, in a dispute had called Bakunin a eunuch, spat in his face, and accepted with alacrity an invitation to a duel, from which Bakunin withdrew. Belinsky was Bakunin's courier, and he described with contempt the avalanche of words used by Bakunin to hide his cowardice.[47] Bakunin had a great deal to live down. Nechaev's psychological leverage over him worked at a level deeper than the homage of the older generation to the young, than the émigré afflictions of remoteness from the battlefield and dependence on young emissaries like Nechaev, even perhaps than the anxiety that age might cheat them of participation in the revolution.

"Principles of Revolution" also reveals a great deal about Nechaev's personality. Expressions of anxiety about passive repose, about a deathlike existence, about seductive substitutes for life rather than the "real" thing occur repeatedly in his writings and recorded conversations. There is no mistaking the deep anxiety that lay behind his biting his fingernails down to the quick, his perpetual motion, his sleeplessness, and his need to have someone with him at all times. All the descriptions we have of Nechaev suggest that he was in flight not merely from the external "dark, brute (*grubyi*) force" threatening the life of the young, but from something inside himself as well. The struggle taking place in the political and social world paralleled an inner conflict. Compulsively, he provided clues to that inner conflict and glimpses of his real revolutionary intentions in his writings and personal contacts, while simultaneously wrapping his conflicts and intentions in layers of deception. Conflicting desires to sink imperceptibly into the underground—to become depersonalized—and to be a hero no doubt issued from the same inner ambivalence. He failed to control in himself the very ambivalence he manipulated in others.

The proclamations written by Nechaev, Bakunin, and Ogarev began to pour into Russia during the spring and summer of 1869. They came not only from Geneva but from Naples, Genoa, Leipzig, Nuremberg, Hamburg, Koblenz, Cologne, Nyon, Freiburg, Bonn, Tübingen, Berlin, Mainz, Stuttgart, and Frankfurt-am-Main.[48] The German cities predominate because Nechaev asked sympathizers traveling through Germany to mail his proclamations from railroad stations. In late July they began sending Ogarev's "*Vol'nyi pesennik*" ("The Freedom Songbook")[49] and in August, the first publications bearing the imprimatur of *Obshchestvo Narodnoi Raspravy*—The Society of the People's Revenge.[50] Eight titles had appeared by August, but only one of them—the first—was signed by Nechaev.[51] He had definitely written three of them ("To the Students of the University, Academy, and Technological Institute," "Principles of Revolution," and the first number of the serial *Narodnaia rasprava*), Bakunin two, and Ogarev the remainder. Although he usually expressed contempt for the written word, Nechaev seemed to be trying to have a revolution by means of it. In one St. Petersburg post office alone the authorities detained 560 proclamations addressed to 387 people.[52] At first it was not difficult to intercept the packets. The proclamations were large; anywhere from three to twelve were placed in large, easily identifiable, envelopes. Furthermore, Nechaev had at first addressed all the packets in his own handwriting, with which the postal inspectors were familiar. He later switched to a smaller format, ordinary envelopes, and varied handwriting, and the proclamations once again got through.[53] He sent them to students, bookstore owners, heads of schools, shopkeepers, apothecaries, doctors, clerks, police officials, military officers—to people of every calling. Occasionally, Nechaev asked his addressees to write to several different people (including Zamperini) in Geneva if they had fulfilled the requests hastily scrawled in pencil ("Distribute in St. Petersburg, Khar'kov, and Kazan' "; "Distribute to the student body"; "Read at the *skhodki* of the students of the Technological Institute," for example) and enclosed with the proclamations.[54] In addition, Nechaev sent letters to friends, like Kapatsinskii, without hiding his identity or intentions—thus incriminating them.

Most of the proclamations belong to the ephemera of the history of the revolutionary underground. The distinguishing features of the proclamations campaign of the spring and summer of 1869 were its millenerianism—its promise that the revolutionary moment was near at hand—and its savage spirit of vengefulness. There can be no doubt that Nechaev inspired the campaign and, with his usual zeal, almost singlehandedly dispatched the paper flood. In addition to the proclamations written for the campaign, Nechaev sent copies of the first issue of *Narodnoe delo* and the *Communist Manifesto*, which he probably commissioned one of the young émigrés to translate into Russian.[55] It is almost impossible to assess the impact of the campaign, since virtually no one, either at the trial of the Nechaevists or in memoirs, admitted to being influenced by the proclamations. Quite the contrary, they seemed to want to save the reputation of the postal inspector, who had tried to make the best of a bad situation by announcing that: "Full publicity of the views of the émigrés will quickly convince the public that they are fools and scoundrels."[56]

Of all the writings noted above, the *Narodnaia rasprava* acquired the most notoriety. The first issue of *Narodnaia rasprava* elaborated the themes presented in "The Principles of Revolution." It should be noted that Nechaevism is not the most ruthless form of terrorism. Nechaev spoke of the panic that acts of violence against highly placed persons would unleash, but unlike some modern terrorists, he never suggested that innocent victims be selected as targets. He continued the tradition of the Terror against enemies of the people and the revolution, and anyone he considered an enemy or traitor to the cause might become a target of The People's Revenge. Thus, he practiced terror more in the eighteenth-century sense of the word than in its modern sense. *Narodnaia rasprava* makes this quite clear. Real (*fakticheskii*) revolutionary actions had to destroy a specific target: a person, a thing, or a relationship hindering the liberation of the people. Nechaev specified primary targets: first, high-ranking military men with major commands who had reputations for zealous loyalty; next, magnates who used their wealth exclusively for themselves, their estate, and state purposes; finally, the pens-for-hire who had sold out to the government. People in the first category had to be exterminated without further ado. The wealth of the people in the second category would be expropriated when possible or else destroyed. The writers would be silenced by any means, "even if their tongues had to be removed."[57] An especially vindictive note enters his writing when he meditates the fate of the hirelings of the Third Section and the police in general. It is worthwhile to examine another example of his rhetoric for its typically sadistic imagery of victimizer and victim:

> But now we must pursue without delay the extermination of his Arakcheevs, that is, of those monsters in splendid court uniforms who, spattered with the people's blood, are considered to be the pillars of the state; those who organized and still organize the slaughter of the rebelling peasant folk; those administrative bloodsuckers ceaselessly sucking away at the yearning breast of the people who have shown and will show special zeal in devising measures and means for squeezing the last vital juices out of the people in order to dull their incipient understanding.[58]

The sexual aspect of Nechaev's rhetoric appears most clearly in *Narodnaia rasprava* in his list of the "pillars of the state" and their crimes. He exhibited a special delight in exposing real or imagined court scandals—palace orgies, the debauchery of the Tsar, high officials achieving their status by acting as procurers for the Tsar. For example, General N. V. Mezentsev, director of the Third Section, is accused of having "palmed off his pretty little sister" on the drunken Tsar.[59] The Tsar is typically described as weak minded, lecherous, and dissipated.

Nechaev's unusually concrete and specific strategy and his attempt to expose the entire sordid spectacle of court life are aspects of his apparent compulsion to seem to declare everything, even while concealing something. Thus, in a footnote in the first issue of *Narodnaia rasprava* he wrote that there was an urgent need for a detailed, alphabetical list of the people's enemies, including their ranks, occupations, and locations.[60] Nechaev compiled such a list in an alphabetized pocket notebook, which has been preserved.[61] It contains hundreds of entries—not only the names of the malefactors, but sometimes those of their wives as well. Given his compulsion to reveal what his real intentions were, Nechaev could not refrain from mentioning the fate of the Tsar. But given his equally strong compulsion to deceive, one may assume that he did not reveal his true plans for dealing with the Tsar, his family, and his entourage. Nechaev promised in *Narodnaia rasprava* that the Tsar would not be touched during the assassinations campaign. He would be preserved until the day of the people's revenge, when, surrounded by the ruins of the state, the people themselves would "smash in his skull together with the hated crown." In the same article Nechaev wrote: "We must view Karakozov's deed as a prologue! Yes, it was the prologue! Let us make every effort, friends, to hasten the onset of the drama itself!"[62]

Finally, *Narodnaia rasprava* was Nechaev's guarded declaration of independence from émigré tutelage. Although both issues were printed in Geneva, they listed Moscow and St. Petersburg respectively as place of publication, as if signifying the autonomy of the new organ of the Russian Revolutionary Committee.[63] The anonymous author(s) of the first issue of *Narodnaia rasprava* recommended the first issue of *Narodnoe delo* as a programmatic statement coinciding in essential points with *Narodnaia rasprava*, but criticized its literary form, moderate tone, and abstract and theoretical way of posing issues. Bakunin had not signed his work in *Narodnoe delo*, but it is unlikely that Nechaev did not know about Bakunin's authorship, even though he referred to the "unknown" author of the first issue. Bakunin is also praised for his proclamation to the students but criticized for not providing any answer to the questions: What will the students do when they leave the Academy? How will they go to the people and what will they do? The Russian Revolutionary Committee recommended three proclamations that broached these problems openly and solved them directly: "The Posing of the Revolutionary Question," "Principles of Revolution," and Nechaev's proclamation to the students. It is not completely clear whether or not The Russian Revolutionary Committee claimed that Nechaev wrote all three proclamations. (Placing his name in the genetive case at the end rather than the beginning of the sentence rendered the meaning ambiguous.[64] He might have been the author of only the last proclamation or of all three.)[65] In all probability Nechaev in the name of the fictitious committee was building his own reputation as a superior strategist, and doing it at Bakunin's expense, or else he felt he could claim for his own those of Bakunin's productions he had inspired but not written.[66]

The only document of this period to have had other than historical interest—"The Catechism of a Revolutionary"—did not belong to the proclamations campaign as such. It was written in code and smuggled into Russia by Nechaev when he returned in August 1869. Once again, the authorship is uncertain, although the inspiration is definitely Nechaev's. Of all the works attributed to Nechaev, Bakunin, or their joint effort, "The Catechism of a Revolutionary" is the most extreme. In the words of a prominent student of anarchism

> it expresses ideas and sentiments that had already been propounded by Zaichnevsky and Ishutin in Russia and by the Carbonari and Young Italy in the West. Yet by carrying to an ultimate extreme the ruthlessness and immorality of its predecessors, it constitutes the fullest statement of a revolutionary creed that has occupied a prominent place in revolutionary history for more than a century.[67]

Although all of the proclamations issued by Ogarev, Bakunin, and Nechaev have been republished by scholars either fully or in part, only "The Catechism of a Revolutionary" has been reissued recently (as late as 1971) by contemporary extremists. At the risk of exaggerating its importance, one might say that "The Catechism" is to modern extremism what the *Communist Manifesto* is to communism. There is no way to measure its popularity in the revolutionary underground in

Russia. However, it is impossible to think of a document that better sums up the commitment or modus operandi of the revolutionary extremist. Few revolutionaries, to be sure, can live according to the rules in "The Catechism."[68] Not even Nechaev did. These rules propound an extreme inversion of conventional morality that is no less impracticable for ordinary human beings than the scrupulous performance of a monastic regimen.

The booklet containing "The Catechism" in coded form was found during a police search in the apartment of Petr Uspenskii on November 26, 1869. Police investigators found the key to the code among the papers of Aleksei Kuznetsov. With the key and Uspenskii's help (one had to know as well that the words had to be read from right to left), the document was deciphered on February 20, 1870, and read at a session of the trial of the Nechaevists in July 1871.[69] "The Catechism" appeared in the stenographic account of the trial published in the official organ, *Pravitel'stvennyi vestnik* (*The Government Herald*). It is not clear how widely it circulated in Nechaev's organization before Ivanov's murder and the discovery of the Moscow circles put an end to the conspiracy, but "The Catechism" is almost certainly Nechaev's fulfillment of the catechism called for in the "Program of Revolutionary Actions."[70] Indeed, Nechaev evidently still adhered to the timetable of the "Program," which stated that the structure and rules of the organization and its catechism had to be established by September 1869.

The prominence of "The Catechism" has made the question of who wrote it far more interesting to scholars than the equally difficult problems of finding out who wrote the proclamations. Bakunin's reputation as a historical figure is affected by the outcome of the research and anti- and pro-Bakunin biases have affected analysis of the document and of the evidence about its authorship.[71] Like "Principles of Revolution" and other proclamations, it appears to be a collaborative effort. Although there is evidence that Bakunin wrote down a complete copy, that copy has not been preserved.[72] Even if it had been, it would prove very little except Bakunin's collaboration, which can hardly be doubted. There is also external evidence that Nechaev wrote it in a letter from Bakunin to Nechaev dated June 2, 1870, which contains this sentence:

> Remember how you got angry at me when I called you an Abrek [a Caucasian mountaineer-outlaw bound by oath to perform the equivalent of a vendetta] and your catechism a catechism of the Abreks, how you said that all people have to be that way, that the

> most complete renunciation of oneself, of all personal needs, satisfactions, feelings, affections and ties must be the normal, natural everyday condition of all people without exception.[73]

Bakunin referred to "your catechism," and some scholars have taken that as final proof that Nechaev was the author, in spite of the evidence for Bakunin's contribution.

It is not difficult to understand why Bakunin might try to disassociate himself from "The Catechism." It was such a shocking document, even for the revolutionary underground, that Nechaev himself more than a decade later denied to The People's Will that he had written it.[74] Anyone who has read "The Catechism" realizes that, by definition, anyone associated with it would lie without a second's hesitation about who wrote it or what its standing was as a guide to conduct in the revolutionary organization. But the problems of analysis are not insuperable if several assumptions are made: Some of Bakunin's turns of phrase had become the common property of the younger generation, including Nechaev. Conversely, Nechaev had inspired Ogarev and Bakunin to produce their most bloodthirsty rhetoric, as Herzen had remarked, and thus, in a letter Bakunin might refer to the "Catechism" as "your catechism" because it was, in a sense, Nechaev's. "Your catechism" surely implied that Bakunin repudiated Nechaev's most savage positions and the Jesuitism he perceived and condemned in Nechaev. Nechaev and his "Committee" had initiated the project, and Bakunin, whatever his misgivings, had committed himself to them. He could hardly object to a division of labor and joint authorship, but, no less than Ogarev, he must have tried to exercise editorial control over Nechaev. In the process Bakunin rendered some of Nechaev's more shocking ideas in a prose style that gives some passages in the "Catechism" singular power.

On his side, Nechaev felt no compunction about joint authorship. His relative respect for Bakunin at this stage in their relationship and, indeed, his dependence on him imply collaboration. In addition, we know from Nechaev's modus operandi in Russia that he believed in dividing up the labor and liked to assign his followers tasks according to their backgrounds and expertise. Surely, he must have granted Bakunin a role in the formulation and writing of the "Catechism" befitting the older man's contribution to the revolutionary movement. Finally, there is a great deal of other evidence, both internal and external, that the document is a product of both Bakunin's and Nechaev's ideas and prose styles.[75]

Both Nechaev and Bakunin wanted to use the "Catechism" to revise aspects of "The Program of Revolutionary Actions." As noted earlier, the "Program" was a mixture of ideas and was neither consistently anarchist-populist nor Jacobin-conspiratorial in outlook. Bakunin apparently wanted to stress the anarchist-populist side and play down the other, while the opposite was true of Nechaev. It is therefore not surprising that the "Catechism" perpetuates rather than resolves the polarities in the "Program." On the other hand, since Bakunin and Nechaev shared an antitheoretical outlook, they rid the "Catechism" of the scientistic perspective that had informed the "Program." Nechaev in addition excised the "soft" aspects of the "Program" and replaced them with his singularly "hard" ideas about revolutionary organization, commitment, and morality. Here he differed significantly from Bakunin.

The "Catechism" is therefore rather uneven in both ideology and style. Textual analysis suggests that Bakunin was responsible for the style and some of the substance of the first seven paragraphs, but that Nechaev injected into them his extreme asceticism and fascination with martyrdom. The second section, comprised of four paragraphs, contains some Bakuninist phraseology but is substantively mainly Nechaev's work. The third and lengthiest section is almost certainly Nechaev's, both stylistically and substantively, whereas the last section appears to be wholly Bakunin's. But it is best at this point to let the "Catechism" speak for itself.[76]

The Attitude of the Revolutionary toward Himself

1. The revolutionary—is a doomed man. He has neither his own interests, nor affairs, nor feelings, nor attachments, nor property, nor even name. Everything in him is absorbed by a single, exclusive interest, by a total concept, a total passion—revolution.

2. In the depths of his being not only in words but in action he has sundered any connection with the civil order and with the entire educated world and with all the laws, proprieties, conventions, and morality of this world. He is—its merciless enemy, and if he continues to live in it, then it is only in order the more certainly to destroy it.

3. The revolutionary despises any kind of doctrinairism and has rejected peaceful science, leaving it to future generations. He knows only one science—the science of destruction. For this and only for this he now studies mechanics, physics, chemistry, perhaps medicine. For this he studies day and night the living science of people, of their personalities and positions, and all the conditions of the present social structure in every possible stratum. The goal is the same—the quickest and surest destruction of this foul structure.

4. He despises public opinion. He despises and hates the existing

public morality in all its motives and manifestations. Everything that facilitates the victory of the revolution is moral to him. Everything that hinders it is immoral and criminal.

5. The revolutionary—is a doomed man. Merciless toward the state and generally toward the entire society divided into estates and by education, he does not expect from them the least mercy toward himself. Between them and him there exists a concealed or manifest, but constant and implacable life-and-death struggle. Every day he must be ready to die. He has to train himself to withstand torture.

6. Stern with himself, he must be stern with others as well. All tender, effeminizing feelings of kinship, friendship, love, gratitude, and even of honor itself must be suppressed in him by a total cold passion for the revolutionary cause. For him there exists only one comfort, one consolation, reward, and satisfaction—the success of the revolution. Day and night he must have one thought, one goal—merciless destruction. Striving coldbloodedly and tirelessly toward this goal, he must always be ready to perish himself and to destroy with his own hands everything that hinders its realization.

7. The nature of a true revolutionary precludes any kind of romanticism, any kind of sensitivity, enthusiasm, and excitement. It precludes even personal hate and vindictiveness. Revolutionary passion, having become in him normal and constant, must be united with cold calculation. Always and everywhere he must be, not a person guided by personal inclinations, but the kind of person prescribed by the general interest of the revolution.

The Attitude of the Revolutionary toward His Revolutionary Comrades

8. The only person who can be a friend and cherished by the revolutionary is a person who has declared himself by actually engaging in the very same revolutionary activity that he has. The measure of friendship, devotion, and other duties with respect to such a comrade is defined solely by the degree of his usefulness in the cause of an all-destroying practical revolution.

9. There is no need to say anything about the solidarity of the revolutionaries. In it resides all of the strength of the revolutionary cause. Comrade-revolutionaries standing at the same level of revolutionary understanding and passion must, insofar as possible, discuss all major matters together and decide them as one man. In fulfilling the plan determined in this manner, each must count on himself, insofar as possible. In the fulfillment of a series of destructive actions each must act himself and seek the counsel and help of comrades only when it is essential for success.

10. Every comrade must have at his disposal several revolutionaries

of the second and third rank; that is, not fully initiated ones. He has to look upon them as part of the general revolutionary capital placed at his disposal. He must expend his portion of the capital economically, striving always to extract from it the maximum utility. He looks upon himself as capital foredoomed to be expended for the victory of the revolutionary cause, but as a type of capital which he himself cannot dispose of without the agreement of the entire association of completely initiated persons.

11. When a comrade gets into trouble, in resolving the question, shall he be saved or not, the revolutionary must not let personal feelings enter into his deliberations, but only the benefit of the revolutionary cause. Therefore he must weigh on the one hand the usefulness of the comrade, and on the other—the expenditure of revolutionary forces needed to save him and must decide the issue by where the balance lies.

The Attitude of the Revolutionary toward Society

12. The acceptance of a new member into the association who has declared himself not only in words but in actions cannot be decided in any other way than by unanimity.

13. The revolutionary enters into the official world, the world of estate rankings, and the so-called educated world and lives in it only with the aim of destroying it more completely and sooner. He is not a revolutionary if he pities anything in this world, if he can hold back before the annihilation of a position, a relationship, or some person belonging to this world, in which everyone and everything must be equally despicable to him. All the worse for him if he has in it family, friendly, or love relationships; he is not a revolutionary if they can stay his hand.

14. With the goal of merciless destruction the revolutionary can and frequently even must live in society, pretending to be something other than what he is. The revolutionary must penetrate everywhere, into all strata[77]—upper and middle, into the merchant's shop, into the church, into the manor house, into the bureaucratic, military, and literary worlds, into the Third Section, and even into the Winter Palace.

15. This entire rotten society must be split into a few categories. The first category—is sentenced to death without delay. The association will make up a list of condemned people of this sort and rank them according to their relative harmfulness for the success of the revolutionary cause, so that the higher numbers will be cleared out before the lower.

16. During the composition of such a list and the establishment of the order designated above one must be in no way guided either by the personal villainy of the man, or even the hate aroused by him in

the association or the people. This villainy and this hate can even be partly and temporarily useful, facilitating the incitement of a *bunt* in the *narod*. One must be guided by the amount of benefit which must accrue to the revolutionary cause from his death. Thus, above all, those people especially harmful for the revolutionary organization must be destroyed whose sudden and violent death can inspire the greatest fear in the government and, having deprived it of clever and energetic figures, paralyze its power.

17. The second category must consist of those people who will be permitted to live only provisionally, so that by a series of bestial acts they will drive the people into an inevitable *bunt*.

18. To the third category belong the multitude of highly placed brutes or individuals, neither especially distinguished by intellect nor energy, but enjoying because of their position wealth, connections, influence, and power. We must exploit them in all possible ways and by all possible means, entangle them, confuse them, and having found out everything we can about their filthy secrets, make them our slaves. Their power, influence, connections, wealth, and strength can in this way be made into an inexhaustible treasure and powerful aid for various revolutionary undertakings.

19. The fourth category consists of ambitious statesmen and liberals of various stripes. We can conspire with them according to their programs, making it appear that we are following them blindly, but all the while taking them in hand, learning all their secrets, hopelessly compromising them, so that they have no way out, and we can use them to stir up trouble in the state.

20. The fifth category—is the doctrinaires, the conspirators and revolutionaries idly prating in *kruzhki* and on paper. One must ceaselessly push and drag them forward, into real skull-cracking commitments, as a consequence of which the majority will perish without a trace and a few will yield some genuine revolutionary results.

21. The sixth, important category—is women, who must be divided into three major groups: some—empty-headed, mindless, and spiritless, who must be used like the third and fourth categories of men; others—zealous, devoted, able, but not ours, because they still haven't achieved a genuine straightforward and practical revolutionary understanding—they must be used like men of the fifth category; finally, women who are fully ours—that is, who are completely dedicated and have accepted our program in its entirety. They—are comrades to us. We must regard them as our most valuable treasure, without whose help we cannot possibly manage.

The Attitude of the Association toward the *Narod*

22. The association has no other goal besides the complete liberation and happiness of the *narod*, that is the laboring people. But being

convinced that this liberation and the achievement of this happiness are possible only by way of an all-shattering revolution of the *narod,* the association with all of its power and means will facilitate the development and dissemination of those troubles and evils, which must at last drive the *narod* beyond the limits of its patience and incite it to a massive rebellion.

23. By a revolutionary *narodnoe* association we mean not a regulated movement in the classical Western form—a movement of the sort which, always stopping short before respect for property and the traditions of the social orders of so-called civilization and morality, until now everywhere limited itself to the overthrow of political forms alone in order to substitute another for them and tried to create a so-called revolutionary state. The only revolution which can save the people is that revolution which will destroy at its roots any kind of statehood and annihilate all state traditions, structures, and classes in Russia.

24. The association therefore does not intend to thrust upon the *narod* any organization from above, no matter what kind. A future organization, without doubt, will be produced from the *narod*'s movement and its way of life, but this—is the concern of future generations. Our concern—is passionate, complete, general, and merciless destruction.

25. Therefore, when drawing near to the *narod,* we must before all else unite ourselves with those elements of the *narod*'s life, which since the time of the founding of the Muscovite state power have not ceased to protest—not with words—but with deeds against everything, which directly or indirectly is connected with the state—against the gentry, against officialdom, against the priests, against the world of the guilds, and against the *kulak*-devourer. We will unite ourselves with the dashing world of the brigand, with this true and unique revolutionary in Russia.

26. To unify this world into one invincible, all-shattering force—that is the whole of our organization, conspiracy, task.

The only surviving copy of "The Catechism" is called neither "The Catechism of a Revolutionary" nor "The Rules Which Must Guide the Revolutionaries," but both titles passed into usage since at the trial of Nechaev's followers it became clear that the document contained the rules of organization and conduct called for in the "Program of Revolutionary Actions," which did mention a catechism. In addition to the twenty-six paragraphs specifying rules of conduct, the booklet contained "The General Rules of the Organization" and "The General Rules of the Network for the Sections."[78] The organizational rules call for centralization, strict subordination, division of labor, and secrecy. The organization depended upon the efforts of a prime mover, who would found the initial cell of five or six members. Each member in turn would found a second-degree cell of the same size, and so on. Each new cell would be subordinate to the cell of its organizer. Theoretically, each cell (aside from the organizing cell) would have immediate ties with one cell above it and five or six below it. All information would flow upward to the organizing cell. The organizer of each cell would collect information from below but was not bound to pass any down. In the rules for the sections—groups formed from the cells for specific tasks and security purposes—the first mention of a Committee appears. This, no doubt, is a reference to the Russian Revolutionary Committee of *Narodnaia rasprava*. One of the main functions of the sections would be to raise money, one-third of which would go to the Committee. In Russia, Nechaev manipulated these rules for his own purposes; he became the Committee. When he organized the founding cell, he made the fictitious Committee the authority of last resort, thereby making himself the dictator of the entire organization. The odd vagueness about the Committee in the rules is therefore quite understandable.

With astonishing rapidity, Nechaev transformed his revolutionary fantasy into the semblance of reality. Having won over the émigrés, he used them to enhance his reputation and authority and to acquire funds. Bakunin and Ogarev obliged him in all respects. Bakunin had given Nechaev a document signed by him and bearing the seal of The European Revolutionary Alliance attesting to Nechaev's status as a secret representative of the Russian section of The World Revolutionary Alliance. To add verisimilitude to his fiction Bakunin affixed "No. 2771" to the document. It was dated May 12, 1869.[79] With Bakunin's help, Nechaev now bore the credentials of two spectral organizations. To be fair to Nechaev, a Russian Revolutionary Committee probably existed briefly during the winter of 1868–1869, but even then it was more an idea than a genuine organization.[80] The suppression of the student rebellion and the arrest of Nechaev's closest collaborators, some of whom were implicated by receipt of letters from Nechaev, certainly destroyed whatever "Committee" had existed. Bakunin designed his deception mainly as an organizational expedient. He did not want to enroll Nechaev directly in his already existing anarchist Alliance but decided rather to create a Russian wing which would report to Bakunin himself.[81] Both Nechaev and Bakunin can be judged guilty, not so much of mutual deception, as of self-deception. In the last analysis, Bakunin's somewhat silly methods could not harm Nechaev. The credentials he concocted for Nechaev gave Nechaev greater cogency. As an active organizer in the International and a revolutionary veteran with considerable influence in European revolutionary politics, Bakunin had a great deal to lose in the event of Nechaev's duplicity, while Nechaev had little or nothing to lose. In this respect too, it was an unequal relationship.

Ogarev strengthened Nechaev's mystique by dedicating a poem (which he had originally written for Sergei Astrakov, a friend who had died in Moscow in 1867) entitled "A Student" to his "young friend Nechaev." He did this at Bakunin's prodding—another bit of evidence attesting to Ogarev's weakness and the fact that Bakunin was ready to abandon ordinary rules of decency for Nechaev's sake. They printed the poem as a separate proclamation, and it circulated widely in Russia. The poem described the hard life and martyrdom of a young fighter for the *narod* who had died "in the snowy labor camps of Siberia," prompting Herzen to remark in a letter to Ogarev: "How is it that you've buried Nechaev alive?"[82] While Nechaev prepared for his departure from Switzerland, Ogarev and Bakunin busied themselves with several new proclamations. Only Herzen refused to join the campaign to build up Nechaev's image and presumably his movement. But even Herzen, in the end, was forced to play a role in Nechaev's intrigues.

Herzen and Ogarev had come into possession of £800 (20,000 francs) in 1858 as a result of the revolutionary philanthropy of a young Russian nobleman, Pavel Bakhmetev. They were to use the money for revolutionary propaganda. Instead, they invested the capital and spent only the interest earned over the years, so that in 1869 the original sum was still intact. Although as noted before, Herzen had taken an immediate dislike to Nechaev, he was in no position to deny Ogarev half the sum for Nechaev's use and reluctantly settled with him in late July 1869. Ogarev received something less than 8,000 francs, since he had already spent part of the fund on the proclamations campaign in the spring.[83] It is not clear how much of the total sum ended up in Nechaev's hands or how much Ogarev and Bakunin used to defray the costs of the proclamations campaign, which continued after Nechaev's departure. In any case, the transfers of money during the spring and summer of 1869 marked only the beginning of Nechaev's efforts to control the entire fund.

The time for Nechaev's departure arrived in August, since he had to return with his rules of organization and conduct by September. Once again, he used Bakunin's connections, this time with a group of Bulgarian revolutionaries. They accompanied him to Bucharest where a member of the Bulgarian underground, D. Panichkov, supplied him with a fake Serbian passport.[84] Henceforth, he traveled as a Serb. In August 1869, he slipped across the Romanian border into Bessarabia and from there into Kherson province. Toward the end of August Nechaev reached Odessa. He presented himself as a Serbian mechanic named Katarzhianets, seeking work on the railroad.[85] During the first days of September, he stayed with Nikolai Sobeshchanskii, a young parochial school teacher, whom he had met on the way to Odessa. They had taken a room together in a hotel in Odessa for a day. According to Sobeshchanskii, his new acquaintance claimed that both the *narod* and the *dvorianstvo* were unhappy with the Russian government; that he had connections with 300 people in various cities who were ready to begin a liberation movement; that the assassin of Serbian Prince Michael Obrenovich had done the right thing; that Russia needed a government like that of the United States of America; and that he was being hunted by the Russian government. When Sobeshchanskii defended the government, Katarzhianets leaped from his chair, drew a revolver from his pocket, and threatened to kill him or to commission one of his agents to do the job if Sobeshchanskii should inform on him.[86] The next day Sobeshchanskii left for his family estate in the village of Popushai near Odessa. Five or six days later Nechaev turned up in Popushai, which he used as a base for several trips. On the fifth day of his stay there, he took a cab into Odessa and returned dressed up in a frock-coat with copper buttons and an official's hat with a cockade. Finally, according to Sobeshchanskii, Nechaev left Popushai at 2:00 A.M. no earlier than September 10 or 11, presumably for Elizavetgrad on the way to Moscow.[87]

What had Nechaev been doing during this time? There is some evidence that he had been conspiring with members of the revolutionary underground who were planning to blow up Alexander II's train when it passed through Elizavetgrad. A pseudonymous letter of October 26, 1869, informed the police in Elizavetgrad that "two young persons recently settled in your city" in order to place a mine under the railway there. Actually, three were involved. One of them, Feofan Borisov, had been a member of Ishutin's Organization and later the Smorgon Academy. Vasilii Kuntushev had also belonged to the Smorgon Academy and had participated in an abortive attempt to liberate Chernyshevskii in 1868. The third conspirator, Mikhail Troitskii, who later married Tomilova and became a member of The People's Will, had belonged to a circle of revolutionaries in Saratov, where he had met

Kuntushev and Borisov. Nechaev contacted the group at the beginning of September in Odessa. In an oral memoir recorded sixty years later, Borisov claimed that they had planned only to organize the smuggling of émigré literature from Geneva, the same story he had told the authorities.[88] Kuntushev, however, had a sledgehammer in his possession when searched by the police. He had claimed at first that he and Troitskii planned to rob a rich estate owner (a woman named Sokolovskaia) in the area and had purchased the sledgehammer as a weapon to use against her, should she resist! Only later did all three admit to a plot to smuggle contraband literature. None admitted to the assassination plot against the Tsar. Borisov stated in his oral memoir that his group and Nechaev had at first planned to act together but had been repelled by Nechaev's "extreme unscrupulousness."[89]

Although it is impossible to establish definitely what was going on in Elizavetgrad, the pseudonymous letter, the sledgehammer, Nechaev's disguise as a machinist seeking work on the railroad, Borisov's and Kuntushev's connections to Ishutin's Organization and the Smorgon Academy, the fact that the method for assassinating the Tsar described in the pseudonymous letter had been discussed in Ishutin's "Hell," and Troitskii's later connection with The People's Will, which carried on the same tradition, taken together suggest something other than a plot to smuggle contraband literature. And given what we know about Nechaev, if Borisov, Kuntushev, and Troitskii had failed to accept his methods, then it is not inconceivable that he was behind the pseudonymous letter. One can only imagine what they might have deemed "extremely unscrupulous."

Nechaev's brief adventure in the environs of Odessa ended with his departure from Sobeshchanskii's estate. The young man who returned from Switzerland carrying a coded copy of the rules of organization and conduct for a new breed of revolutionary had already begun to live according to "The Catechism." He had made himself a mediator between the older émigrés and the youthful underground in Russia. To Bakunin and Ogarev, he was one of the heroic young *praktiki*, an enthusiastic organizer who might help them fulfill their hopes of 1861–1863. Now he would present himself to his peers as a human whirlwind, a comrade to international revolutionaries who dashed back and forth between Europe and Russia and from city to city in Russia on trains—that era's symbol of dynamism. Nechaev was undoubtedly as much a captive of the symbolism of the revolutionary subculture as a manipulator of it. He entrained for Moscow to arrange the next act in the strange drama of his career.

Chapter IV

The People's Revenge

Nechaev arrived in Moscow early in September 1869, almost precisely on schedule. Petr Uspenskii, one of the few figures in the underground associated with Volkhovskii's circle who still remained at large, quickly joined forces with him. Uspenskii had maintained contact with Nechaev while Nechaev was in Geneva and had sent money for his return. As the manager of Aleksandr Cherkesov's bookstore in Moscow, Uspenskii not only was able to satisfy his love of books, but was in a peculiarly good position to coordinate communications in the Moscow underground. The twenty-two year old *dvorianin,* a dropout from Moscow University, was Nechaev's first contact in Moscow. Uspenskii's claim that Nechaev arrived in Moscow on September 3[1] is difficult to reconcile with Sobeshchanskii's account of Nechaev's activities in and around Odessa at that time; but it may be that Sobeshchanskii had lied. Perhaps Nechaev had actually left Popushai earlier than September 10 or 11; or perhaps for some reason Sobeshchanskii used the Gregorian calendar, which would account for the discrepancy; or else Uspenskii lied to cover up Nechaev's connection with the Elizavetgrad affair. Uspenskii's loyalty to Nechaev—and his wife's as well—never diminished. Unlike most of the other members of Nechaev's organization, he refused to denounce Nechaev and portray himself as the innocent victim of malicious cunning. Nechaev entrusted Uspenskii with the society's most precious secrets, including the coded booklet containing the rules of the organization and "The Catechism." Generally, Uspenskii performed the same functions that Orlov had performed before his arrest.

He became Nechaev's closest confidant but was not an organizer or stage manager in quite the sense Orlov had been.

In Moscow Nechaev was a relatively unknown figure. At first, only Uspenskii and Cherkezov knew his real identity. To most of those recruited into the conspiracy he was "Ivan Petrovich Pavlov," an engineer, but he had several other aliases: Panin, Petrov, Kiniavskii, Nachalov, Dmitrii Fedorovich, Ivan Korol'. He tried to build up his image with Uspenskii and Cherkezov by stories of his escapes. Nechaev also claimed that he had organized a factory strike, in Belgium, in gratitude for which the workers had sent him as their deputy to the International; that he had quickly distinguished himself there; and that he had met Bakunin as an equal, not as an unknown student.[2] Finally, he told Cherkezov that he had brought sixteen émigrés with him.[3] Although Cherkezov later testified that he neither believed all of Nechaev's stories nor was impressed by his qualities of leadership or level of development, he nonetheless joined forces with him. A veteran of Ishutin's conspiracy and the Smorgon Academy, he saw Nechaev as an energetic fanatic who could further the unfinished business of the underground. To him Nechaev was just another hired gun:

> a person neither particularly clear minded, broadly developed, nor equipped to direct the movement, nor even to be a serious and consistent political agitator. But he possesses one quality—decisiveness to the point of fanaticism, a passion for work in the popular cause and an equally fanatic devotion to it. In this last quality one must seek whatever influence he has over any particular group of people. He didn't give them anything. Didn't help their development—they're more developed than he is—didn't clarify the program or the state of the popular cause—they knew it anyway and better than he did. Without having given them anything he got them involved in the movement because he is an energetic and active person; though he was tainted he appeared as a person standing for the cause . . . As far as his personal qualities are concerned, I can say only one thing: His personality . . . is not particularly attractive. . . . His personality had only this significance for me—as an intermediary between separate dissatisfied personalities; but his mediation becomes superfluous just as soon as they get together.[4]

Cherkezov had underestimated Nechaev's capacity for controlling the individuals brought together by his devious methods; indeed, there is no evidence that he ever resisted Nechaev's leadership. All of Nechaev's other close comrades in The Society of the People's Revenge attested to the power of his personality, his rhetoric, and his example. He kept in constant motion to convince them that a large organization existed and that he was overworked by the Committee. For example, he would come to a meeting dressed as a military officer and claim that he had just attended a meeting of a revolutionary military circle.[5] Or he would feign a disconsolate mood and announce that five circles in St. Petersburg had been uncovered and the members arrested.[6] He would act out the full range of emotions appropriate to each imaginary situation. Despite his unattractiveness, his physical appearance and nervous manner reinforced the impression of fanatic commitment.

He was of average height but quite strongly built. The only decent photograph of Nechaev's face shows that he had a high forehead with straight, chestnut hair brushed straight back; an unhealthy complexion, with small moles or blemishes on his cheeks and around his mouth; patchy, silky whiskers, lighter colored than the hair on his head; straight, medium-sized eyebrows; a sullen, penetrating squint; brows furrowed at the peak of a pointed, medium-length nose; and tightly compressed lips. Nechaev sometimes wore blue spectacles, and it may be that he was near-sighted, for later in prison he kept his spectacles with him. He had a number of disguises: various officers' uniforms, a priest's cassock, a peasant costume, the accouterments of a bureaucrat. Finally, he had his stories, proclamations, credentials, and cash with which to impress his comrades. If all of his stage effects and revolutionary rhetoric failed to convert a candidate, Nechaev resorted to threats—the threat of popular vengeance against those who had not joined the movement, the more immediate threat of denunciation to the Third Section, or even the threat of violence. It was well known that he carried a revolver.

Although they cannot always be taken at their word, Nechaev's co-conspirators rarely admitted that they were influenced by his writings. *Narodnaia rasprava* in particular evoked negative responses. Uspenskii claimed that most members of the organization found it "repulsive." Pimen Enkuvatov, a twenty-one-year-old student at the Petrov Academy and one of the recruits in the autumn of 1869, admitted that he had shown the proclamation to his comrades but "with the same purpose with which he once showed them a tarantula he had caught."[7] Nechaev's personal impact was far more important. He impressed some with his passionate love of the people and made them feel they were parasites unless they joined the cause. At first, he might demand only a small act of commitment—a seemingly trivial errand, a copying task. He would then interpret its acceptance as a sign of total subordination to him. Some were impressed by his command of a large number of facts about social and economic conditions and his self-confidence, but most were impressed by the sheer energy and strength of character with which he exhibited his commitment. Cherkezov was quite correct in his analysis of Nechaev's development. To be sure, to a semieducated adolescent like Nikolaev Nechaev seemed more developed; and Ivan Pryzhov, the oldest member of Nechaev's organization, himself the son of a liberated serf and largely self-educated, was taken in by Nechaev's half-lies about his autodidactic feats. Nechaev had told Pryzhov that he was barely literate at the age of sixteen but had gone abroad at the age of nineteen, so that when Pryzhov met him he could read philosophical essays in French and knew by heart entire passages from Kant's *Critique of Pure Reason*.[8] The forty-year-old Pryzhov, an odd, compulsive man, had pursued a career as a *narodnik* historian of the folkways of the poor and outcast. He had written a *History of Pot-Houses* in 1868. The research had taken him into the taverns and dens of the Moscow underworld, and he had become an alcoholic during the course of his studies, to the point of delirium tremens.[9] Nechaev impressed him as a person from the *narod*, like him but better—someone who had come through intact and able to apply himself fully to the cause of popular liberation. Nechaev's energy astonished him. Pryzhov had met a great many people, but according to his testimony he had never before encountered nor even conceived of that much energy in one person.[10]

The central point—one made by Uspenskii repeatedly—is that Nechaev did not have to convince people with words and arguments. He merely had to push them into motion by providing an example, setting them some task, and then initiating them into the organization by showing them its rules, some of the proclamations, and documents stamped with the oval seal of the Committee—an axe around which was written "The Committee of the People's Revenge of February 19, 1870." Many of his followers claimed to be confused or ignorant about the goals of the society. Most admitted to *narodnik* ideals or to support of the goals of the student movement. They appeared to be guilty only of a desire to improve the welfare of the *narod* and their less fortunate fellow students through cooperative associations, enlightenment, and mutual aid—and of gullibility and pliancy. All of this, while true, fails to capture the atmosphere of the conspiracy. Uspenskii, who was far more inventive in justifying Nechaev and providing a rational explanation for his appeal than any other defendant at the trial of the Nechaevists, ended on this note during one session: "I must add to what I have said one powerful cause, an undefined force dragging us forward. I refer to that psychological state in which we found ourselves at that time, to that nervous agitation which possessed us."[11]

Uspenskii introduced Nechaev to Nikolai Dolgov, a twenty-five-year-old student in the Petrov Academy who had been expelled from St. Petersburg University during the disorders there. Dolgov was well known at the Academy for his *narodnik* spirit of self-sacrifice. He spent most of his free time teaching peasant children how to read, and he and several other students of the Academy who were to graduate that year planned to work in the agricultural association movement and as village teachers. They even had dreams of converting a plot of land near the Academy into a model commune. With this in mind they all attempted to work themselves into good physical condition.[12] Presumably, Nechaev convinced Dolgov that his group's efforts would yield greater results if placed in the service of the Committee. He moved in with Dolgov and began to recruit from the group, which consisted of Ivan Ivanov, Aleksei Kuznetsov, and Fedor Ripman. With Nechaev and Dolgov they formed the founding circle of The Society of the People's Revenge.[13]

Kuznetsov, one year Nechaev's senior, came from a merchant family of high standing, received his secondary education at the Moscow Commercial School, and had been at the Petrov Academy for three years when Nechaev met him. He was especially impressed by Nechaev's capacity to remain alert on a schedule that permitted only two or three hours of sleep a night. In a charade of rational organization Nechaev assigned Kuznetsov the task of stirring up opposition to the government in the merchant community.[14] Nechaev took his recruits as they came and assigned them what was for the most part meaningless busywork, except when it came to collecting funds. Kuznetsov, who was able to get money from his wealthy family, was with Zubkov and Cherkezov, one of the organization's most successful fund raisers.[15] He became one of Nechaev's most assiduous coorganizers and faithful servants. According to Cherkezov, he was "like wax, upon which Nechaev could impress any shape he pleased."[16]

Ripman, also slightly older than Nechaev and of gentry origin, did not distinguish himself as a member of the conspiracy. In addition to the usual recruiting, he was encouraged to familiarize himself with the true mood of the *narod*, for which purpose Nechaev apprenticed him to Pryzhov. Pryzhov acquainted his charges with the underworld dens of

Moscow where they might meet the "lower layers of society"—swindlers, pickpockets, prostitutes, and gypsies. Ripman described his experiences to the court:

> Pryzhov showed me a place where I could go, namely Khitrov Market. . . . When I went in I almost fainted at the sight of the filth, physical and moral, which prevailed in that den. But for the vodka which I drank I would have collapsed. The first time I didn't stay long. Afterwards I went several times, but each time this place produced a more painful impression. Things reached the point where my health began to fail. . . . Consequently, I soon stopped going altogether.[17]

Ripman learned from a prostitute that some of the tavern's patrons were considering mugging him, and so he terminated his brief exposure to the lower layers of Moscow. He contented himself with using the Bible to spread literacy and subversive ideas among a few peasants he knew in the Moscow suburb where he lived.

Ivanov was the outstanding figure in the first circle recruited by Nechaev. Data on his background have not been preserved, but he had been involved in the student disorders in March 1869, and was one of the most vigorous and dedicated student activists. A number of the Nechaevists commented on his physical strength. Uspenskii, Kuznetsov, and Enkuvatov described him as an irritable, limited, and stubborn person, who acted out of egoism rather than convictions about the cause. Ivanov's duties in the Petrov Academy made him a central figure, since it was the conspiracy's most immediate and rewarding recruiting ground. In addition to recruiting, he had to arrange lodgings for conspirators, influence "public opinion," arrange literary gatherings for propaganda purposes, and establish ties with lower bureaucrats (*volost' pisari*) in the region of the Academy. (The last duty may be a clue to Ivanov's family background.) Like the others he had to collect funds; unlike them he gave no evidence of being impressed by Nechaev and refused to subordinate himself unconditionally to the Committee. By all accounts, he was the only person who argued heatedly with Nechaev or, indeed, showed any spine at all.[18]

After September 20, when Nechaev revealed to the nuclear group the rules of the organization and told them about the Committee, they began to create circles of the second degree. Each member of the founding circle received a number: Dolgov became "1"; Ivanov "2"; Kuznetsov "3"; Ripman "4." The first person recruited by Dolgov became "11," the second "12," and so on. The numbers of members of all degrees were formed by adding a number signifying order of recruitment to the right of the recruiter's (*organizator*) number. All of this elaborate play with numbers and with aliases as well (some members used both aliases and numbers) permitted Nechaev to perpetuate the game begun by Bakunin with the numbered blank from the General Committee of his international organization. Not all members played the game well. Dolgov recruited three new members: Porfirii Korob'in, Nikolai Abramov (only peripherally involved), and Elizaveta Beliaeva, who fell in love with Nechaev. Ivanov recruited Eduard Lau, Valentin Lange, Pimen Enkuvatov, and Vladimir Popov. Kuznetsov formed a circle consisting of Innokentii Klimin, Georgii Gavrishev, his (Kuznetsov's) brother Semen, and the brothers Vladimir and Ivan Riazantsev. Ripman's circle was formed later and was recruited by him, Nechaev, and Cherkezov from a group of students expelled from the Medical School of Moscow University. It included Dzhavad Ishkhanov, Lazarev Mutafov, and Nikolai Piramidov. Ultimately, ten expelled medical students were associated with the conspiracy. Three members of circles of the second degree formed circles of the third degree with eleven members. All of the basic organizing in Moscow was done in September and early– to mid-October, but the Polunin incident at the end of October filled out the ranks, so that by early November the fundamental structure had been created.[19]

Nechaev masterminded the activities of the entire organization. He almost immediately began to intimidate the circles by threatening them in the name of the stern, Argus-eyed Committee. There is no evidence that any of the central figures saw through his manipulations until Ivanov's rebellion. They held meetings, collected funds, and turned in reports to the appropriate figures in the organization, although some of them, Kuznetsov for example, failed to fulfill the numerous commissions forwarded through "Pavlov" and falsified their reports.[20] Nechaev sometimes sent observers to meetings to impress the members. Nikolaev played this role under the alias Aleksandr Vasil'evich. Toward the end of September, Nechaev traveled to St. Petersburg to contact those of his friends who had not been arrested in the spring. Ivan Likhutin, his closest collaborator in St. Petersburg, returned to Moscow with him and posed as an agent of the Geneva Committee.[21] Nechaev evidently did this to authenticate his story that sixteen émigrés had returned with him, to intimidate the first circle—Likhutin questioned Uspenskii and Pryzhov and attended a meeting of the founding circle[22]—and to bring news of the existence of the organization to St. Petersburg. It is likely that St.

Petersburg ultimately would have been Nechaev's main base and that he intended the organizational work in Moscow merely as the dress rehearsal for the formation of a more powerful St. Petersburg organization which would carry out the assassination of the Tsar and other political assassinations preliminary to a coup, but the murder of Ivanov and the discovery of the Moscow organization aborted Nechaev's scheme.

The impression of well-intentioned naiveté, or helpless entanglement in Nechaev's web, projected by most members of The Society of the People's Revenge does not accord well with their later careers as revolutionaries, with postrevolutionary memoirs, or indeed, with communications intercepted by the police. The correspondence between Valeriian Smirnov and Aleksandr Buturlin of January 1870, dramatically illustrates the mood of some of Nechaev's recruits. Both Smirnov and Buturlin had been expelled from Moscow University because of the Polunin affair. Smirnov was one of the most respected students in the Medical School and acted as treasurer of an aid fund gathered for the eighteen expelled students. He was therefore a natural target for Nechaev. Buturlin belonged to a wealthy gentry family and in the mid-1870s contributed thousands of rubles to the revolutionary movement. The circle to which they belonged is notable among the Nechaevists for its revolutionary activism. Smirnov, Aleksandr von El'snits, and Vladimir Gol'shtein all emigrated illegally in 1871 and actively participated in émigré revolutionary circles—though the last two (who had also been expelled for their part in the Polunin affair) dropped out of the movement after a few years. Smirnov's letters confirm Uspenskii's statement, quoted above, about the "undefined force . . . that nervous agitation which possessed us." In a letter of January 9, 1870, he wrote to Buturlin:

> The moment of truth draws near. For me, just as for many others, it has fatal significance. Perhaps my days are numbered, perhaps they will be summed up on the gallows, or on the square [where political criminals were subjected to a ceremony of public disgrace].[23]

And on January 25:

> Bitterness, titanic bitterness that begs to express itself and can be restrained in only one way—by the hope that our time will come, when we will mete out wholehearted *bloody* retaliation, if I didn't have this hope there would be no reason to write you this letter. But now I highly value my death; I know that I am not alone, that our entire brotherly circle lives for the sake of one and the same ideal, is nourished by one and the same merciless bitterness.[24]

Nechaev was not alone in his bloody millenarianism or in his appreciation of the hero-martyr role. News of arrests and expulsions and stories about Siberian exiles did not act as a deterrent, but instead encouraged some of those who joined the conspiracy. The description of Nechaev's imaginary martyrdom in Ogarev's poem—a sickly, melodramatic fraud to the detached observer—evidently produced the anticipated effect. Buturlin, like Smirnov one of the more developed members of the conspiracy, wrote that his "spirit caught fire, reading the news about all of those persons, suffering courageously for their convictions."[25] However, the fraternal bitterness and anger expressed by Buturlin and Smirnov found its outlet in hate of external authority. Nechaev's perpetually burning rage, on the other hand, might devour his brothers in the cause as well as the "dark force" oppressing them.

Dostoevsky's insight into Nechaev as a type should be noted here, lest a one-sided picture of him and the conspiracy emerge. When he was first working on *The Devils*—before the stenographic account of the trial of the Nechaevists appeared—Dostoevsky wrote to Mikhail Katkov that to his amazement, the type of character pictured by his imagination was half-comic. Dostoevsky sustained this image, and in the finished novel Peter Verkhovenskii is a comic-sinister figure. To be sure, there may be a comic element in the most serious business. Lenin, for example, in his furious effort to get back to Russia after the outbreak of revolution in 1917 entertained the idea of wearing a blond wig and carrying the passport of a deaf-mute Swede. (In fact, later in 1917 while in hiding Lenin *did* wear a blond wig as part of his disguise as a Finnish laborer.) Dostoevsky pictured Nechaev as a naive Jesuit, a conspirator who badly conceals what he is doing. Nechaev was rendered equally well by Bakunin who likened Nechaev to an "ostrich hiding its head behind a tree but unable to conceal its huge body."[26]

Nechaev and his followers botched everything. Ivan Likhutin, for example, at Nechaev's request asked Pryzhov for some forms bearing the Committee's seal. Pryzhov tried to make them up but failed, and Uspenskii and his wife were no more successful. Eventually, Likhutin himself managed to get a clear imprint. In his deposition Likhutin noted that the seal was like a new toy, and that the entire business seemed like play. This was extreme candor indeed for a man who played a central role in the most comic episode of the conspiracy—the extortion of 6,000 rubles from one member of the conspiracy by three others—in the course of which Likhutin got his brother Vladimir to dress up in an officer's uniform. Vladimir and a third accomplice both wore false whiskers and "arrested" Andrei Kolachevskii, to whom Ivan Likhutin had just entrusted "Nechaev's very secret notebook."[27] The two "agents" took Kolachevskii to a hotel and told him either to hand over his check for 6,000 rubles or else be taken to the Third Section. This took place in St. Petersburg in October 1869, and Nechaev picked up the check on November 24, although Likhutin's quick exposure by Mikhail Negreskul prevented Nechaev from using it. Anna Uspenskaia provides still another example of the clumsiness of the young conspirators. In October, Nechaev asked her to dig up some type for a secret printing press which Liudmila Kolachevskaia, the unfortunate Andrei's sister, had buried in a suburban park in April 1869. She and Pryzhov went to retrieve it, but first ran afoul of the park keeper and then simply couldn't find where it had been buried.[28]

Occasionally, Nechaev exhibited a human side. Some of the sessions of the secret *kruzhki* were exceedingly tedious, since they consisted primarily of reading long lists of names, commenting on the character traits of those listed, and judging their potential as recruits. Likhutin noticed that Nechaev slept soundly at one such session. Anna Uspenskaia noted in her memoirs that Nechaev enjoyed practical jokes and recounted an incident in which Pryzhov and Nechaev had gone off together to a bathhouse, where Nechaev had doused him with cold water and in general—according to Pryzhov—had had a great deal of childish fun at his expense. Uspenskaia took it upon herself to rehabilitate Nechaev's personal reputation in the face of memoirs—including her own sister's—which made him out to be an unmitigated villain. Zasulich had intimated in her memoirs of Nechaev that he had a reputation for combining revolutionary activity with romantic conquest. Uspenskaia denied this, but the evidence tends to support Zasulich.

In addition to the episode with Zasulich herself, there are others involving Elizaveta Beliaeva, Ekaterina Likhutina, Varvara Aleksandrovskaia, Natalie Herzen, and a young Frenchwoman named Albertine Hottin. Beliaeva, from a poor urban family, was about twenty-six when she met Nechaev. The parents did not permit either her or her sister to study. Early in 1868 they began to learn bookbinding and left home later that year. Uspenskii found them work, and they became typical urban dependents of the nihilist subculture in Moscow.[29] When the students left for the holidays, the two sisters barely survived. Beliaeva's lover and tutor was Viktor Lunin, an associate of Dolgov's circle who moved to St. Petersburg. According to Lunin's testimony, Nechaev visited Beliaeva daily before his departure and stayed long after midnight.[30] This seems odd in view of Beliaeva's character and level of development. Lunin claimed she was barely literate, while her sister described her as timid and unsociable. She evidently fell head over heels in love with Nechaev soon after Lunin's departure, for she wrote to her sister (who had also moved to St. Petersburg) that "she loved Pavlov [Nechaev], was ready to go with him through fire and water, and to endure any sacrifices for him."[31] Pryzhov testified that Nechaev, while proposing that Beliaeva go abroad with him, assigned her a totally passive role and told Pryzhov that she was completely expendable. She wasn't to know where and why they were going, and when they arrived in Geneva, she was to stay in her room.[32] Nechaev suggested something similar to Uspenskii, who felt that Nechaev's attitude toward Beliaeva was peculiarly calloused.[33] Generally, Nechaev preferred to travel in the company of women, and when he fled Russia in December 1869, he took another female member of the conspiracy, Varvara Aleksandrovskaia, with him. She was fourteen years Nechaev's senior and had been involved in the revolutionary movement since 1862. Aleksandrovskaia evidently had abandoned her husband—an official in St. Petersburg—and had been living with Aleksei De Teil's, another member of the conspiracy in St. Petersburg, by whom she had a daughter.

When he visited St. Petersburg at the end of September and stayed with the Likhutins, Nechaev spent most of his time with their twenty-four-year-old sister Ekaterina.[34] He asked her to accompany him to Moscow and Geneva at different times. Three days after Ivanov's murder, he went to see her and gave her a long red scarf as a souvenir. Nechaev told her that the scarf had been given to him as a token of friendship by the *ataman* (chieftain) of a gang of brigands.[35] After the arrest of her brothers, two other members of the St. Petersburg group took the scarf from her and burned it. One can hardly imagine that Nechaev's gesture was merely an attempt to strengthen his mystique. His awkward romanticism with women is even more evident in his correspondence and behavior with Natalie Herzen and Albertine Hottin. During his second flight abroad, along with a collection of Robespierre's memoirs Nechaev carried a copy of Rousseau's *Confessions*; and during his long imprisonment in the fortress after 1873, he worked on a novel entitled "Georgette," whose heroine may have been modeled on Albertine. She falls in love with a young ringleader of the International but denies him sexual fulfillment until the republican cause triumphs. Meanwhile, the young hero satisfies his lust in a love affair with a prominent (and lecherous) noblewoman of the Second Empire. The hero dies on the barricades during Marshal MacMahon's conquest of the Paris Commune. Unfortunately, the manuscript was burned with the rest of Nechaev's prison writings. (The impulse to incinerate evidence of Nechaev's existence was apparently shared by the police and Nechaev's comrades.) However, a brief résumé by a prison inspector survives. The inspector noted:

> Prominent on this canvas are the rather numerous erotic scenes upon which the author lavishes special care . . . The idea that people who love one another should not waste their energies on the gratification of their feelings while they are needed to help solve social problems is developed with great fervor and at great length both in this novel and in the fragment "To Whom Does the Future Belong?" But in the latter work, the heroine finally decides that indulgence in the delights of eroticism will not enfeeble the energetic man and sets off to visit him in his bedroom. In both novels, women of higher social standing are portrayed as monsters of depravity.[36]

The author of "The Catechism of a Revolutionary" continued to observe its rules, even in his novel. But there is no doubting the strong sexual interest and callow romanticism in his real relations with women and in his prison fantasies. They were incongruous with his revolutionary purpose—however much he tried to make them appear to be part of his totalistic rules of behavior. And precisely because he protested so vehemently against sentimentality and tenderness, his own expressions of them take on a comic, albeit sinister, character. In *The Devils* Dostoevsky achieves the comic effect partly by giving the demonic Verkhovenskii a gluttonous streak.

Despite the ineptness and immaturity displayed by Nechaev and his comrades, the sheer energy with which they threw themselves into their work and the self-sacrifice displayed by some of them are truly impressive. Nikolai Nikolaev is perhaps the most striking case. A teenager, he gave himself completely to the cause, first working with delinquent boys and following his preceptor Orlov's teachings by establishing a bookbindery in a house of detention. Nikolaev abandoned his job to do Nechaev's bidding in March 1869. He had offered to marry Aleksandra Dement'eva, Tkachev's common-law wife, so that she could obtain money denied her as a minor, but Nikolaev was no older than Dement'eva and the priest refused to marry them. Instead, Dement'eva bought the press with money that she borrowed from Tkachev, the young man who sold her the press having been willing to accept a down payment of 200 rubles instead of the full sum of 1,000. Since Nechaev had his passport, Nikolaev stayed ahead of a police search by spending several weeks traveling back and forth between Moscow, Ivanovo, and Vladimir, where various members of the movement helped him. He traveled much of the way on foot and peddled books and other merchandise. His health broke down, and Pryzhov found a bed for him in the Mariinskaia Hospital in Moscow—where by coincidence both Pryzhov's and Dostoevsky's fathers had worked, the former as clerk and the latter as doctor. After a two-week recuperation in June 1869, he traveled to Tula, a center of munitions manufacture 150 kilometers south of Moscow. There under the name Aleksandr Vasil'evich Belkov he worked as a carpenter until Pryzhov called him back to Moscow in late October to join the conspiracy.[37] Nechaev gave him copying tasks, and used him as an "observer" from the Committee. In addition to being a member of the section of the organization that killed Ivanov on November 21, 1869, Nikolaev participated in Nechaev's unsuccessful effort to stir up an insurrection among the arms workers in Tula. Cherkezov—who worked as a railway engineer—Aleksandrovskaia and De Teil's were also involved. Nechaev had scouted the territory and had given Cherkezov the names of local people who might help them.[38] But nothing came of the Tula affair—except Nechaev's acquaintance with Aleksandrovskaia.

Throughout the autumn of 1869 Nechaev wrote virtually nothing. He produced one proclamation at the beginning of November in response to the Polunin affair and had copies distributed in the auditoriums of Moscow University in hopes of reviving the student movement. Entitled "From Those Who Have United to Those in Disarray," it is a typically Nechaevist appeal, with demands for self-sacrifice followed by threats that the people would avenge themselves against those who would not join the struggle immediately. He tried to manipulate the students' feelings of isolation, idleness, and uselessness. "Come . . . to our ranks and put aside all of those lonely personal goals and strivings," he wrote.[39] Meanwhile, other proclamations from the émigrés in Geneva added to the literature of the conspiracy. During October 1869, the first proclamations appealing explicitly to specific social strata in the name of fraudulent committees or brotherhoods began to arrive at postal stations—notably, one with the imprimatur of The Descendants of Riurik, a second version of which appeared in 1870.[40] The émigrés printed Pryzhov's leaflet, "Until the Storm." It appealed to Ukrainian nationalism just as the proclamations to the gentry appealed to Russian nationalism. Nechaev had worked over Pryzhov's proclamation, altering the middle portion and adding his own conclusion.[41] Ogarev sent an anticlerical poem, "An Encounter," another appeal to the students to organize a massive revolutionary front, "Parting Words,"[42] and three agitational pieces aimed at the peasants.[43]

All of these were part of the master plan worked out by Nechaev and the émigrés to prepare the way for an uprising of all social groups. The anticipated revolutionary front itself was to be organized and led by the youthful radical underground. To all appearances, the preliminary work for the uprising of February 19, 1870, had been completed. According to the "Program of Revolutionary Actions," in October:

> members from all of the provinces must assemble, and all of the problems that have been theoretically solved must be discussed and accepted by a majority. From this moment the organization must begin systematic revolutionary activity embracing all of Russia.[44]

In keeping with the timetable of the "Program" Nechaev planned to leave Moscow for St. Petersburg in November to organize the coup, but events intervened.

Nechaev had created a section in early October comprised of Uspenskii, Pryzhov, Beliaeva, Kuznetsov, and Ivanov. Each carried on a specialized task. Beliaeva was to conduct propaganda among woman students, who had recently been granted permission to enroll in higher courses. Uspenskii was responsible for clerical work and kept all of the society's printed matter. The functions of the others have already been described. But Ivanov began to bridle at the decisions made by the Committee and at the petty duties assigned to the members. Each objection, of course, was a challenge to Nechaev, and the two men frequently argued. Each time that Ivanov questioned the Committee, Nechaev brought back word that the Committee had decided against him, and Ivanov noticed that the Committee's decisions always coincided with Nechaev's position in a dispute. On November 4, they had a violent argument over the distribution of proclamations in the Petrov Academy. Nechaev proposed that they paste copies of his proclamation "From Those Who Have United to Those in Disarray" in the student-organized dining rooms and libraries of the Academy. Ivanov, who was responsible for propaganda in the Academy, feared clashes with the authorities which might lead to expulsions and arrests.[45] Nechaev, of course, welcomed any and all forms of trouble between the students and the authorities. This time Ivanov said that he would not yield, even if the Committee decided against him, and it became clear that he was challenging the principle of complete subordination. The other members of the section stood behind Nechaev, and Ivanov had no choice but to yield or to leave the society. He decided to leave.

Nechaev learned on the eve of his planned departure for Moscow that Ivanov could not be trusted. Uspenskii carried word that he had left the society and might turn police informer. At his own trial, Uspenskii implicated himself as Nechaev's accomplice in conceiving Ivanov's murder.[46] According to Uspenskii, Nechaev first discussed this possibility on Sunday, November 16. During the next few days Nechaev had to convince Uspenskii, Kuznetsov, and Pryzhov that Ivanov's death was necessary and get them to agree to a method. They and Nikolaev (who did not participate in the discussions) acceded to Nechaev's plan of execution on Thursday evening, November 20. Nechaev had been wavering between poison and strangulation, and Kuznetsov, once he realized there was no point in further protests, suggested that they strangle Ivanov in the grotto in the park belonging to the Petrov Academy.[47] There was a pond next to the grotto where they might dispose of the body. Ivanov would be lured there by the story that a printing apparatus had been buried in the grotto by Ishutin and that they needed his help to recover it.[48] On Friday morning November 21, 1869, the group assembled in Kuznetsov's apartment. Pryzhov now realized that they intended to carry out the murder that very day and raised objections, but Nechaev told him that the decision had been made—it was too late now to back out. Pryzhov tried to fortify himself with vodka, but the others took it away from him. Nechaev assigned each man a task. Nikolaev would bring Ivanov to the apartment, where Pryzhov would be waiting. They would detain the victim while Nechaev, Kuznetsov, and Uspenskii went on to the grotto.

After spending a good part of the afternoon at Ivanov's apartment waiting for him, Nikolaev returned empty handed. Nechaev considered going back with Nikolaev and killing Ivanov in his apartment but decided against it and hit on the idea that Ivanov might be at a friend's. Nikolaev found him at Eduard Lau's at about 4:30 P.M. and gave him a summons with the Committee's seal. Kuznetsov waited out of sight on the street and when he saw Nikolaev and Ivanov emerge together ran ahead to warn the others. All but Pryzhov left for the park. When Ivanov and Nikolaev arrived, Pryzhov told Ivanov about the plan to recover the printing apparatus, and Ivanov agreed to help them. Pryzhov decided to serve his own purposes while detaining Ivanov, so they stopped at a tavern along the way for some vodka. While Pryzhov, Nikolaev, and Ivanov drank, Nechaev made ready for the execution. He checked the two exits to the grotto and with a cudgel opened a hole in the ice of the pond. Uspenskii prepared the cords and bricks which were to be used to weight down the body, and Kuznetsov acted as lookout.

At about 5:30 P.M. a hooded Kuznetsov intercepted Ivanov, Pryzhov, and Nikolaev a short distance from the grotto but was so flustered that he could not lead them directly to the entrance. Kuznetsov and Ivanov went ahead with Nikolaev and Pryzhov—Pryzhov remaining outside—behind them. Kuznetsov shouted: "Gentlemen, where are you?" and received the reply, "Here." Then Kuznetsov hung back at the entrance while Ivanov went into the grotto with Nikolaev following. Nikolaev seized him from behind and tried to pin his arms. They struggled in the dark, banging up against the sides of the grotto. Then Nechaev shouted: "Where is he?" and in the dark grabbed Nikolaev by mistake, clutching at his face and throat. Nikolaev screamed: "What are you strangling me for, it's me, Nikolaev," and lost his grip on Ivanov, who ran to the entrance of the grotto. Uspenskii shouted: "He's running away, catch him!" Kuznetsov intercepted him at the entrance, where Nechaev, Nikolaev, and Uspenskii all dragged him to the ground. Nechaev sat on his chest and began to beat and strangle him while Kuznetsov pinned his legs. The others watched, paralyzed. Meanwhile, Nechaev kept up a stream of curses and shouts at them and at Ivanov, who was inflicting painful bites on Nechaev's right hand. Ivanov was able to scream a few times: "Why are you beating me up, what did I do?" He evidently did not at first understand what was happening to him. Then Nechaev told Nikolaev to give him Kuznetsov's hood and shouted: "Strangle him." Nikolaev groped for Ivanov's throat but dislodged Nechaev's hand in the process, permitting Ivanov to turn his face to the ground and groan loudly. After a little while the struggling ceased, but Ivanov's body continued to twitch. Nechaev, still cursing, asked Nikolaev for his revolver and shot Ivanov in the back of the head, so that the bullet emerged through his left eye.

Spurred by more of Nechaev's curses, the others overcame their paralysis and helped him strip the body of its overcoat. Nechaev emptied the pockets of Ivanov's trousers, taking a few coins, cigars, a notebook, and a purse. The others were to tie bricks to Ivanov's body but proved too slow for Nechaev, who did almost all the work himself in a fury. He tied a red woolen scarf with a brick bound up in its ends around Ivanov's neck, secured the legs above the ankles with a cord which was also tied to a brick, and wrapped a hood around the legs above the knees. Then Nechaev commanded them to help him drag the body to the pond and push it under the ice. They all helped, slipping and struggling, stamping to widen the hole in the ice, Nechaev accidentally knocking Nikolaev into the water. Although more self-possessed than the others, Nechaev was not in control of himself: He pressed the coins he had taken from Ivanov into Kuznetsov's hand. He mistakenly put on Ivanov's hat and left his own in the grotto. Furthermore, he botched the job of weighting down the body, for it floated to the surface very soon after the murder and was discovered on November 25 by a group of peasants. A watch on the body (Nechaev had not searched all of the pockets) showed 5:40, helping to establish the precise time of immersion and to rule out robbery as a motive. There were some receipts from Cherkesov's bookstore in Kuznetsov's name in one of the pockets. For some reason Nechaev carried off Ivanov's bloody overcoat and gave it to Uspenskii to hold. When Uspenskii complained that it was a useless burden, Nechaev threw it alongside a haystack on a side road leading away from the park. The other three left by different routes, but all returned to Kuznetsov's apartment.

When they took stock, they realized that Nechaev had left behind his hat and Uspenskii his hood. Nechaev's clothes and his bitten hands were all bloody. He stripped off his clothes and gave them to Kuznetsov to burn, except for his trousers and overcoat. Kuznetsov used a towel soaked in vodka to clean off the coat and then threw the towel into the wood stove. Nikolaev put on Nechaev's trousers, which, though bloodstained, were drier than his own. There was blood and water on the floor where Nechaev had undressed. He tended to his wounds in the next room while Kuznetsov burned the evidence of the crime. When Uspenskii asked him something about the revolver, he cocked and accidentally released the firing pin, narrowly missing Pryzhov. He claimed that it was an accident—that his hand was weak from the wounds inflicted by Ivanov—but joked that it might have been a good idea to kill Pryzhov and blame the crime on him. Later that evening, when Pryzhov got ready to go, Nechaev embraced and kissed him, but the suspicion remained that the shot may not have been accidental. After discussing alibis, they dispersed. It had not been a neat job.[49]

Nechaev and Kuznetsov left Moscow for St. Petersburg the very next day and arrived the evening of November 23. Nechaev was dressed in an engineer's uniform and wore white gloves to conceal his wounded hand. Acting as Nechaev's scout, Kuznetsov contacted Liubov' Vorontsova, the married sister of Dmitrii Kovediaev, who belonged to the Moscow conspiracy, but she would have nothing to do with him. He also received a cool reception from Pavel Mikhailov. Nechaev, on the other hand, quickly found lodging with Ivan Likhutin's help, first with Konstantin Rosliakov and then with Vladimir Kovalevskii.[50] He and Kuznetsov spent the days following their arrival recruiting. Everything was done in haste. They would read the rules of the organization to the potential recruits and show them several of Bakunin's and Nechaev's pamphlets and documents stamped with the seal of The People's Revenge and Ogarev's poem to Nechaev.[51] Evidently, few people were sympathetic to Nechaev in St. Petersburg. The most enthusiastic response came from a circle of Siberian students recruited by Kuznetsov: Aleksandr Dolgushin, Petr Koshkin, and Petr Toporkov, who later became proponents of a conspiracy in most respects identical to Nechaev's. In Dolgushin, Nechaev found a kindred spirit, someone who had virtually memorized the first issue of *Narodnaia rasprava*. Dolgushin set as his goal the recruitment of 200 members organized into circles of ten with rules similar to those of The People's Revenge. They would annihilate the Tsar, his family, and "the entire Imperial party" as their contribution to a mass insurrection.[52] The recruitment of the individuals who later formed the Dolgushin circle was the only notable achievement of Nechaev's and Kuznetsov's journey to St. Petersburg. In general, Nechaev was less successful there than he had been in Moscow, although one should take into account the very important fact that he remained in St. Petersburg only a few days before Cherkezov and Nikolaev brought word that arrests had begun in Moscow.

What Nechaev might have done, given more time, is of course a matter of speculation. There is considerable evidence that resistance to Nechaev's ideas would have developed faster than any organization he might have built up, and that his methods of recruitment and conspiratorial techniques were so slipshod that The People's Revenge was destined in any case to be an ephemeral phenomenon. Only the recognition that Nechaev's commitment made him one of theirs prevented some members of the revolutionary underground from taking drastic action against him. His opponents were based mainly in St. Petersburg. To be sure, as noted above, Nechaev did find sympathetic listeners and recruits, and Dolgushin and his circle carried on Nechaev's tradition in modified form during the 1870s. At the same time, though, the Chaikovskii circle continued an anti-Nechaevist current in the student underground. Mark Natanson, one of the most distinguished revolutionary organizers in the entire history of the movement, had begun as early as the spring of 1869 to organize others against Nechaev's millenarianism. Though revolutionary, they were less sanguine than Nechaev. In retrospect, Natanson called his group "researchers"—that is, revolutionary socialists who did not believe they were ready to lead a revolution but had to study the possibilities and prepare themselves for spreading propaganda among the people. They did not take it on faith, as did Nechaev and his followers, that the peasants were ready to revolt and that revolutionaries should be prepared to lead the uprising on February 19, 1870. Natanson and his followers wanted students to gather accurate information in the countryside and the cities during their vacations. In 1869 their incipient organization called itself the Vul'fovskaia commune (named for the street where their apartment was located). During the autumn of 1869, they debated with Nechaev's followers in St. Petersburg and possibly with Nechaev himself at the end of November, although Natanson never admitted that he knew Nechaev personally. As able proponents of alternative revolutionary strategies emerged, Nechaev and his followers found themselves at an increasing disadvantage.[53]

Another respected member of the revolutionary underground, Mikhail Negreskul, son-in-law of Peter Lavrov (the outstanding theoretician of the "preparationist" phase of the *narodnik* movement), had opposed Nechaev during the student movement of 1868–1869. He had then encountered him in Switzerland. Nechaev, with his usual crudity, stole some of Negreskul's belongings—an overcoat, a frock coat and a plaid blanket—and evidently planned to use them at some opportune moment to implicate Negreskul in an intrigue. After his return to Russia, Negreskul did everything possible to warn Uspenskii away from Nechaev. Nechaev tried to involve Negreskul in the Kolachevskii affair by having Likhutin give Kolachevskii a parcel (presumably Nechaev's notebook but actually Orlov's) for delivery to Negreskul.[54] Kolachevskii told Negreskul the story of the extortion of the 6,000 rubles. Negreskul immediately divined what had happened to Kolachevskii and warned Likhutin not to try to cash the check. Although Negreskul was not able to save his friend Uspenskii from Nechaev's clutches, he was able to spread the word about the Kolachevskii affair and Nechaev's methods. Thus, when Nechaev arrived in late November he found that his mystique, such as it was, had worn thin. All of the stories, proclamations, and seals could take him only so far. Threats and fraud yielded negative results. The "researchers" or "preparationists" were no closer to the revolutionary truth than Nechaev, but they were closer to the morality of the young radicals of the time.

While Nechaev and Kuznetsov pursued their relatively futile project in St. Petersburg, the police began a series of searches of Cherkesov's bookstores and shop assistants in St. Petersburg and Moscow. The searches were completely unconnected with the discovery of Ivanov's corpse on November 25, and it is a complete coincidence that the agents of the Third Section searched Uspenskii's apartment on that day.[55] There they found, hidden in a sofa and armchair, blanks stamped with the seal of The People's Revenge, Nikolaev's foreign passport which Nechaev had used in March, the coded booklet with "The Catechism," the rules of organization of the society, the minutes of several meetings, and copies of the first issue of *Narodnaia rasprava*. In a trousers pocket they found a plan of the Moscow organization. In the bookstore itself they discovered some copies of "From Those Who Have United to Those in Disarray," some more of the society's blanks, and other materials addressed to the students.[56] After these discoveries, it was relatively simple for the police to round up most of the members of the conspiracy. Nechaev and Kuznetsov were warned by Cherkezov and Nikolaev about Uspenskii's arrest, and Nechaev returned to Moscow. Systematic arrests had begun, and the Third Section caught up with Kuznetsov on December 3, shortly after Nechaev's departure. He completely broke down and confessed to the murder.[57] On December 12, 1869, Uspenskii confessed and implicated the others.[58]

For a short time Nechaev tried to keep up the morale of his followers who remained at large by telling them that the Moscow organization was not very important, that the organizers from Geneva were still at work, and that the Tula arms workers were ripe for insurrection. As if to convince them (and possibly himself), he sent them on a last round of futile conspiratorial errands. Cherkezov, Nikolaev, De Teil's, and Aleksandrovskaia shuttled back and forth between St. Petersburg, Moscow, and Tula, presumably readying the uprising there—but also procuring passports.[59] For some reason, Nechaev used the name of a Geneva émigré, Elpidin, during his stay in Tula with Aleksandrovskaia. Nikolaev's faith in Nechaev had begun to waver during the last days in Moscow and Tula, and he asked him if the Committee really existed. Nechaev's answer approached candor—and shocked Nikolaev. He said that all means were permitted to bring people into the cause, that Bakunin and others followed that rule, and so did he. Although he did not admit that the Committee had never existed, he did not answer the question affirmatively.[60] However dispirited he was, Nechaev never stopped trying to twist events to his purposes. But he decided that it was time to leave the country again. Cherkezov and Aleksandrovskaia contributed 300 rubles toward the trip, and she and Nechaev left Tula sometime between December 15 and 17. They traveled through Orel, Dinaburg, and Verzhbolovo. Five days after their departure Cherkezov received a telegram saying that they had arrived safely in Königsberg.

Aleksandrovskaia's emigration proved to be a brief one. After a short stay in Geneva, Nechaev decided to send her back with more proclamations. She was detained and searched at the town of Verzhbolovo on

January 11, 1870. The guards found a number of proclamations concealed in her clothes, including a new one by Ogarev addressed to the Russian troops, entitled: "What Now Brothers!"[61] Aleksandrovskaia told the Third Section that Nechaev and Cherkezov had threatened her with Ivanov's fate if she didn't go abroad with Nechaev and fulfill his commissions.[62] Like all the others—with the exception of Uspenskii—she tried to appear the innocent victim. Aleksandrovskaia's arrest marked the end of The People's Revenge as a functioning organization.

As the facts of the conspiracy began to accumulate, the Russian government realized that they had a complex set of problems indeed. As early as December 16, 1869, the authorities began to entertain the idea of seeking Nechaev's extradition. Kuznetsov's and Uspenskii's confessions had given them the basis for accusing Nechaev of murder, a common crime.[63] An inordinate amount of government machinery moved into motion in late December 1869. The preliminary investigation of the conspiracy began with the appointment of Senator Chemadurov.[64] He conducted a second search of Cherkesov's Moscow bookstore on January 12 and 13, 1870, and this time turned up the "Program of Revolutionary Actions." Eventually, the investigators recovered all of the paraphernalia of the conspiracy—including the copper die with the society's seal. Chemadurov completed his preliminary investigation in May, 1871.[65] We will not examine the legal complexities in detail here. Suffice it to say that the Third Section, the investigating commission, the Ministry of Internal Affairs, the Ministry of Foreign Affairs, and the Ministry of Justice often worked at cross purposes. Eventually, the government sacrificed a large number of convictions in order to make Ivanov's murder the central issue and prepare the way for Nechaev's extradition. In this way some of the most important conspirators escaped harsh penalties with astonishing ease. Several other factors worked in their favor. The Russian court reform of 1864 and the ability of the defense lawyers, among whom were able trial lawyers known for their political liberalism, like Spasovich, Urusov, and Arsen'ev, no doubt affected the outcome. Furthermore, the youth and idealism of the defendants, and in this case, their seeming innocence by comparison with Nechaev, influenced public opinion and the court. It should be noted that some of those accused in the Nechaev conspiracy had been in jail since the spring of 1869.

In all, 152 people were arrested for involvement in The People's Revenge, but less than half that number remained in prison at the time of the trial. Among those released were Vera Zasulich, Enisherlov, the Ametistov brothers, the Mavritskii brothers, Antonova, Prokopenko, and Nadezhda Uspenskaia. Mikhail Negreskul was one of four who died in prison. Sobeshchanskii was adjudged mentally incompetent. Only sixty-four people were tried between July 1, 1871, and August 27, 1871, in the St. Petersburg Judicial Chamber. Chemadurov concluded that the conspiracy was too small, too incipient, and too local to warrant trial before the Supreme Criminal Court, thereby playing down its political importance.[66] The government did what it could to manipulate public opinion by proper staging and controlled coverage of the trial. Count S. I. Pahlen (the minister of justice), the police authorities, and A. E. Timashev, the minister of internal affairs, all agreed that the frankest and fullest exposure of the Nechaev affair in the newspapers would strike a blow against the revolutionary cause.[67] Alexander II was not so certain. When he received news of their plans he commented: "God grant it!" Although at first they entertained the idea of restricting coverage to the official organ, *The Government Herald*, they feared that they would be accused of censorship and distortion. They decided instead to forbid all newspaper editors from printing accounts of the trial sessions until the official stenographic account in *The Government Herald*, issued the day after each session, had appeared.[68] Sessions began daily at 11:00 A.M. and usually ended at 5:00 P.M.

Despite these measures, the government failed to control the atmosphere at the trial or to satisfy the defense attorneys that the stenographic accounts were accurate and unbiased. Among the factors they had neglected to take into account were the sympathy of the court bailiff, Postnikov, for the "nihilists," and the determination of the students to pack the courtroom. The memoirs of M. F. Frolenko, later one of the most militant members of The People's Will, describe the scene at the courthouse:

> The students . . . sometimes stayed the whole night long in the courtyard of the judicial chamber in order to get into the trial session. The courtroom was unbelievably crowded. People grabbed up newspapers and raptly read every word in the speeches of the defense attorneys and the accused—more so than if they had been reading novels.[69]

At the trial Spasovich's eloquence and Dement'eva's and Tkachev's brave defense of their convictions produced the strongest impressions. Courtroom gossip had it that the sentences were predetermined. Groups of nihilists attended dressed in dirty working clothes, which seemed to confirm the general line of the defendants that student poverty had been the most important stimulus to their actions. Agents of the Third

Section who were sometimes excluded by Postnikov, despite their passes, noted numerous gestures of sympathy toward the accused in the courtroom and overheard openly sympathetic conversations at the buffet in the court building.[70] The general atmosphere at the trial no doubt influenced the court in the direction of leniency. In spite of the government's careful planning, Russia's first public political trial did not have the anticipated effect on public opinion.

Reactions to the trial of the Nechaevists reveal the extent to which the radical subculture had taken root in Russia during the 1860s. Educated Russians had so far lost confidence in the Russian government and the young had been so deeply converted to a radical world view that even Nechaevism could not discredit the motives and outlook of the defendants. To future recruits to the movement like Frolenko, the Petrov Academy, instead of appearing to be the sordid nest of a vicious schemer, took on a romantic revolutionary aura. Frolenko and five comrades actually decided to go there because of the trial and sought out the grotto as one would a shrine.[71] The printing of censored documents, like the "Program of Revolutionary Actions" and all or part of several proclamations, did not repel young readers; quite the contrary, it excited their imaginations. Although they repudiated Nechaev himself, they reaffirmed his cause, and the stenographic account of the trial of his followers became a kind of short course in radicalism.[72]

The prosecution divided the Nechaevists into four groups of defendants. The first group included Nechaev's accomplices in the murder of Ivanov (Uspenskii, Kuznetsov, Pryzhov, and Nikolaev) and seven others who had played central roles during the first period of Nechaev's activity: Orlov, Volkhovskii, Tkachev, Dement'eva, Tomilova, Ivan Florinskii, and Mikhail Korinfskii. The murderers were deprived of all civil rights and sentenced to forced labor in Siberia. Uspenskii received the severest sentence and ended the most tragically. He was sentenced to fifteen years at hard labor in the mines.[73] In 1875 he attempted suicide but survived,[74] only to be murdered by his fellow prisoners in December 1881, as a suspected informer. (They proved to be wrong.)[75] Kuznetsov made the most of his ten-year sentence at forced labor. He became an ethnographer of the Siberian tribes and founded two museums, one in Nerchinsk and one in Chita. He reasserted his commitment to the revolution in 1905, when he joined the Socialist-Revolutionary Party. In 1906 he was sentenced to death, but the sentence was commuted to ten years more of forced labor in Siberia.[76] Pryzhov received a sentence of twelve years and died in 1885. Nikolaev was sentenced to seven years and four months and after 1880 lived on as a permanent settler in the Amur region. Orlov, Volkhovskii, and Tomilova were acquitted, and, as noted earlier, all of them continued revolutionary careers during the 1870s. Orlov's position was curious. Because of his ill health he became for a while a virtual dependent of the Third Section. (They gave him handouts and then, beginning in January 1872, an allowance of five rubles a month to defray the costs of his meat extract, goat's milk, and fish oil.)[77] Korinfskii was also acquitted and dropped out of the movement. Florinskii received the second-lightest sentence of the first group—six months in prison and five years of strict police surveillance. Tkachev and Dement'eva rejoined the movement, the former after serving a sentence of one year and four months and the latter a term of four months. They married in 1873. She followed him to France, acquired a medical degree at Montpellier in 1888, and in 1903 returned to Russia to practice medicine. In 1905 she was arrested for propagandizing the troops while serving as an army doctor in the Russo-Japanese War but after a year in prison returned to medical practice. She died in 1922 at the age of seventy-two.[78]

Tkachev, of course, carried on the Jacobin-Blanquist tradition as a revolutionary émigré, although he had relatively little influence during his lifetime. Much has been written about Tkachev's influence on Lenin and the continuity between Bolshevism and the spirit of the 1860s. Without attempting to examine the question in all its complexity here, we can at least note that in Tkachev—and Nechaev—Lenin found a revolutionary point of view close to his own. At least partly because of Lenin's frank admiration of Tkachev's writings, Tkachev is more of a figure in the history of the revolutionary intelligentsia than any of the other Nechaevists—except perhaps Nechaev himself.

The resolution of the trial of the first group reveals much about Alexander II's Russia. The government, though fearing revolution, had committed itself to some measure of liberalism and had created a legal system with which it could not live comfortably. Yet there was no way it could appear fair either, given the brutal system of detention and the conditions in Russian prisons. Senator A. S. Liubimov, the presiding officer of the St. Petersburg Judicial Chamber on July 15, 1871, greeted the four exonerated defendants with genuine enthusiasm: "You are liberated from trial and from imprisonment. Gentlemen, from this moment you no longer belong on the bench of disgrace, but out in the world, among all of us."[79] Liubimov's congratulatory speech shocked General Slezkin, chief of the Moscow gendarmerie, and Alexander II privately expressed disappointment about the outcome of the trial as a whole.[80]

The second group of defendants consisted of thirty-three associates of the main organization in Moscow, nineteen of them students in the Petrov Agricultural Academy and eight former students at Moscow University. Cherkezov and Beliaeva were tried in this group. The court acquitted ten of the defendants. Cherkezov received the severest sentence—six and one-half years of Siberian exile. The remaining twenty-two defendants received sentences ranging from one year to three weeks in prison, but all were placed under police surveillance for a period of five years after their imprisonment.[81] The sad stories of many of the students in the second group—almost all were in their early twenties—and the pathetic figure of Beliaeva could not but elicit sympathy. Only Dolgov and Cherkezov in the second group proved themselves as revolutionaries. Cherkezov escaped Siberian exile in 1876, joined the staff of Peter Lavrov's revolutionary journal *Forward!* in London, and became a prominent anarchist in European exile. Dolgov was arrested many times because of his association with The People's Will and the Socialist-Revolutionary Party.[82]

The third group of defendants was made up primarily of Nechaev's sympathizers in St. Petersburg, including those who had harbored him during his trips there and those involved in the Kolachevskii extortion attempt. Ten of the fifteen were students, with the largest group (four) enrolled in the Technological Institute. Three were from the Medical-Surgical Academy. This group also contained four women—only three had appeared before the court in the first two groups. Varvara Aleksandrovskaia, at the age of thirty-eight the oldest defendant, was sentenced to lifelong Siberian exile, the severest penalty in the third group. Other penalties ranged from sixteen months (Ivan Likhutin's) down to four months. Ten of the fifteen were acquitted.[83] Several of those acquitted had interesting, though nonrevolutionary, careers. Vladimir Kovalevskii served Count Witte in the Ministry of Finance between 1900 and 1902. Petr Popov emigrated to the United States, received a medical degree from New York University, and practiced medicine in Florida before returning to Russia in 1880. Viktor Lunin was elected to Russia's First Duma in 1906 as a Trudovik. Only Aleksei De Teil's tried to escape to Europe (like most, he had been placed under surveillance for five years) but was caught. He drowned in 1875, at the age of thirty-one. Two other members of the third group died in prison before the trial.

The fourth and final group of defendants was tried on August 27, 1871. These were five Siberian students in St. Petersburg, three of whom formed the nucleus of the Dolgushin circle after their release from prison. Petr Koshkin received a nominal sentence and, in view of the length of his detention and his youth, the prosecution requested full pardon from Alexander II. The others were acquitted.[84] Dolgushin remained a committed revolutionary, launched his own proclamations campaign in 1873, and was arrested in September of that year. After a trial and long detention, he began serving a ten-year sentence at hard labor in Siberia. He remained an agitator even in exile, and the prison authorities dealt with him severely. In 1881, he helped a fellow prisoner escape and assaulted the warden of the prison during the aftermath, for which fifteen years were added to his ten-year sentence. But he proved to be an incorrigible rebel, and the authorities transferred him first to the Peter and Paul Fortress in 1883 and then to Schlusselburg, where he died of tuberculosis in 1885.

Roughly two-thirds of those involved in the Nechaev conspiracy, whether tried or not, were students or had been enrolled in institutions of higher education within a short time of their involvement in the conspiracy. Of those who were tried, fifty-one (80 percent) were between nineteen and twenty-five years old in 1869; only seven were over twenty-five, and six were under nineteen. The median age of the conspirators in 1869 was twenty-two—Nechaev's own age.[85] Although the information on the social origins of the conspirators is not as accurate as that for their ages and occupations at the time of their involvement, it permits one to draw a profile of the average conspirator. He would be a twenty-two-year-old male, the son of a member of the military-administrative gentry elite enrolled in one of the prestigious academies, institutes, or universities in St. Petersburg or Moscow. Representation of social groups other than gentry is considerably lower. Kuznetsov's recruitment of several of his classmates from the Moscow Commercial School and Orlov's of his comrades from the Vladimir Religious Seminary account for a large percentage of their respective social categories. Roughly 52 percent of 116 people for whom social origins can be determined were from the gentry, 10 percent from the upper merchant class, 5 percent from the *meshchane*, 12 percent from the clerical class, and 8 percent were nongentry bureaucrats. The remaining 13 percent are distributed among nongentry military, lower professional strata, and peasants.[86]

The unusually high percentage of persons who were actually students in higher education at the time of the conspiracy distinguishes Nechaev's group from the revolutionary cohort of the 1870s. It is also more heavily weighted on the side of the privileged strata than the revolutionary group of 1873–1879, when more women, persons of clerical background, *meshchane*, peasants, and proletarians engaged in revolutionary activity. Nechaev's group is somewhat more concentrated in the twenty-one-to-twenty-five-year-old range (55 percent as opposed to 38.4 percent) than the group of revolutionaries arrested in 1873–1879, and there are even fewer persons over thirty years old (3 percent compared to approximately 13 percent) in his conspiracy. The figure for participants below the age of twenty-one is approximately the same—29 percent for the Nechaevists and 27.5 percent for those arrested in 1873–1879.[87] During the later period, the Medical-Surgical Academy and the Technological Institute in St. Petersburg and the Petrov Academy in Moscow continued to be centers of radical recruitment out of proportion to their size. Thus, the Nechaev conspiracy was one of privileged, highly educated youth, many of whom, to be sure, did not possess wealth commensurate with their opportunities, but most of whom had been readying themselves for entry into the elite structure. They repudiated elite status, led on by a domineering young man who made them feel childlike, parasitic, or degenerate if they did not act in the cause he had defined and in the manner he dictated.

Some of Nechaev's extraordinary power over them can be attributed to his unusual personal capacity for simultaneously terrifying and fascinating. It is best captured in Maria Negreskul's account of a visit Nechaev made to her husband Mikhail. The daughter of Peter Lavrov, and at eighteen already a person of unusual toughness of character and commitment, Maria wrote of Nechaev in her memoirs:

> Someone knocked at the door. A young man entered, introduced himself to my husband (I didn't catch the surname), from a distance bowed to me, and sat down on a chair near the window, with his back to the light. My husband sat down opposite him, and they began to talk. The young man seemed unattractive and uninteresting to me—thin, broad shouldered, with short-cropped hair and an almost round face. I sat off to the side on a sofa, but since they conducted their conversation in an undertone, out of decorum I picked up a book and ceased to pay attention to him. After a short time my husband left the room for some reason. I put down the book, lifted my eyes and met the eyes of the unknown visitor. Small dark eyes looked at me with such cold inquiry, with such implacable power, that I felt myself grow pale . . . and fear, animal fear seized me like steel pincers. Never, neither before nor after in my life did I ever experience anything

> similar . . . I mechanically turned the pages and felt weak and exhausted . . . I never spoke with this unusual man, saw him altogether three times in my life and then only in passing, but even now after forty years, I remember his eyes, I understand how people could slavishly subordinate themselves to him.[88]

Those who did not experience anything quite as acute nonetheless felt Nechaev's power. Some of the affectionate or admiring sobriquets applied to Nechaev—"tiger cub" by Bakunin and "eagle" by the guards in the Peter and Paul Fortress—reflect a similar impact. One of Nechaev's pseudonyms was Volkov—derived from the Russian word for wolf. Herzen called him a reptile (though not to his face). In *The Devils* Dostoevsky introduced Petr Verkhovenskii in a chapter entitled "The Subtle Serpent" and gave him the appearance and verbal cunning of a preternatural creature. Nechaev would have been no more troubled by this image of uncanny cunning than he was by the term "terrorist." He expressed something similar, though with a self-justifying preface, about himself.

> In the midst of the masses completely deprived of any kind of education—even elementary learning—illiterate, sunk in the deepest ignorance, bound by superstitions and religious nonsense, crushed by a terrible despotism, there formed, and continued to grow, bands of new people, coming out of the darkest backstreets of folk poverty, having deeply experienced all of the sorrows of the workers' life.
>
> These people with clenched fists forced their way into the light through all of the obstacles created by absolutism to keep the light of knowledge and truth from the *narod*. Thousands perished along the way, mangled by the sharp teeth of a grim existence. Only the staunchest survived hunger and cold, humiliation and insult, wriggling like snakes among the tyrants.[89]

Nechaev could and did use his relatively unusual background to explain and justify both the attractive and repellent aspects of his personality. His privileged converts tended to accept his self-analysis. Tyranny had created creatures suited for the task of destroying tyranny. Since no one had a clear picture of what a popular avenger should look like, Nechaev with Bakunin's help could reshape the "new man" in his own image. The guilt of the privileged and the malice of the self-made young man from the people explain some aspects of Nechaev's relationship to his recruits, but other aspects transcended the boundaries of social strata. Nechaev correctly assumed that sheer action and total dedication to the cause were his most appealing qualities. These were the qualities expected of a live and developed person. When asked about Nechaev's ability to dominate others Nikolaev said at his trial:

> I considered him a person more developed than me. . . . I explain this by his strong character. Since he was extraordinarily energetic, I completely subordinated myself to him. . . . Everyone obeyed him unquestioningly. I never heard anyone object to him or contradict him.[90]

Nechaev exploited adolescent anxieties as well as feelings of guilt associated with social position. He evidently understood that while aspiring to the "rigorism" of Chernyshevskii's Rakhmetov, his peers were actually afraid of giving in to the dreamy inactivity and passive dependency of an Oblomov or the license of a Cherevanin. Uprooted from their families, they still longed for the family's protection on the one hand and on the other sought complete emancipation from it. Striving for the ideal in relationships between the sexes, they were disturbed by the power of their sexual desires. Longing for a cause to which they could give themselves, they feared the irreversible consequences of total commitment. In the tradition of all *simplificateurs terribles*, Nechaev exploited their anxiety and guilt, gave them brutally simple solutions to their ambivalences, and provided a form of leadership satisfying both the urge to rebellion and the need for commitment.

Perhaps the most striking surviving evidence for his techniques of psychological manipulation appears in his letter to Natalie Herzen in May 1870, when he importuned the recently orphaned daughter of Alexander Herzen to work for the cause:

> During the first days after our meeting you expressed dissatisfaction with your petty life, but you did dimly realize what the reasons were for that pettiness. Life is petty when there is no aim to it, when a person is conscious that his existence is unnecessary to all except people of the same trivial ilk, when a person has so little faith in himself and in his powers that he cannot bring himself to make any decision to take any active step on his own initiative, but waits for fate (that most foolish of notions) sooner or later to give him a push. And sure enough, people like these are jogged along by fate in the guise of papas and mamas and various guardian-angel-custodians. . . .
>
> As long as a person moves only in such a milieu . . . he is a corpse. . . . But once he has encountered *other* people, once he has caught a glimpse of independence in someone, he can no longer live the life of *contented ease*, he must either leap boldly out of the mire or, con-

> sciously sinking into it, despise himself more and more until his powers of thought finally cease and the person turns into a vegetable.[91]

Nechaev has already conveniently translated his psychological probe into Freudian terms. To throw off the power of fate is indeed to throw off the power of parents internalized in the form of the superego, to alter the passive, masochistic posture of the ego, and (in this case) simultaneously to deny it a regressive, dependent orientation. Nechaev did not stop with childhood but even evoked the nursery:

> So whence that despair of a moribund person; that fear of casting off your fetters? Here we have the fruit of foolish cares and worries which have surrounded you ever since your childhood and so accustomed you to being in swaddling-clothes that even now you feel yourself, as it were, bound.[92]

In the letter to Natalie Herzen, Nechaev appealed to *her* presumed anxieties about failure to achieve full growth and independence, about regression and a deathlike or subhuman existence. While exposing to his audience the dangers of their own past, the inner brakes upon their further development, he promoted himself as the model of a person who had "leaped boldly out of the mire." This was not mere rhetoric, given what we know about Nechaev's childhood and early adolescence and especially about his last years as a drone in his struggling family. Nechaev did not acquire his insights into the anxieties of others painlessly. Undoubtedly, departure from home and family, followed by the freedom and demands of life in the student milieu of the capital, had increased his own anxieties. But in the context of the revolutionary subculture Nechaev could give his behavior a special meaning. He could offer his symptoms, pressed into the service of the revolutionary cause, as appropriate responses to Russian life—and to the ambivalences and anxieties of adolescence. In psychological terms, he offered his peers a defense mechanism against ambivalence, a radical solution in the form of a reaction formation to tender and regressive feelings.

> Stern with himself, he must be stern with others as well. All tender, effeminizing feelings of kinship, friendship, love, gratitude and even of honor itself must be suppressed in him by a total cold passion for the revolutionary cause. For him there exists only one comfort, one consolation, reward and satisfaction—the success of the revolution. Day and night he must have one thought, one goal—merciless destruction.

> Striving coldbloodedly and tirelessly toward this goal, he must always be ready to perish himself, and to destroy with his own hands everything that hinders its realization.
>
> The nature of a true revolutionary precludes any kind of romanticism, any kind of sensitivity, enthusiasm and excitement. It precludes even personal hate and vindictiveness. Revolutionary passion, having become in him normal and constant, must be united with cold calculation. Always and everywhere he must be not a person guided by personal inclinations, but the kind of person prescribed by the general interest of the revolution.

The words are probably Bakunin's, and he shared some of the ideas, but the code was far too severe for the aging romantic. Indeed, it was too severe for Nechaev. He wrote this little note to his sister Anna on April 13/25 1870; that is, several months after he had murdered Ivanov:

> It's been a long time since I've sent news about myself, although I've always known quite well how things have been with you. I wish you the best and strongly embrace everyone. If daddy will be in Moscow in the fall we might see each other.
>
> Your loving
> Sergei
>
> Pardon me
> Kisses to grandma and grandpa[93]

Nechaev could not suppress in himself filial and sibling affection, and he sometimes appealed to family feeling in his proclamations and journal articles. He placed himself in jeopardy by communicating with his family. Indeed, flamboyant romantic gestures punctuate his career—gestures of self-sacrifice, love, and honor—while his uncontrollable hatred and desire for vengeance ruined whatever chances he might have had for becoming a genuine revolutionary leader. Nechaev's rage for revenge reflected not only his sense of personal victimization but the victimization of his family. Family slaughter is a major theme in a proclamation to Russian officers, which he probably wrote jointly with Bakunin (though signed by Bakunin, some of the second half probably belongs to Nechaev). The proclamation exculpates the simple soldier and accuses the officers of carrying out the commands of their superiors:

> The officer usually takes refuge in the superior's command. Well, what if his superior commands him to kill his father, rape his mother, or

> hand over his sister so some general can have fun with her, or some great prince or perhaps even the Tsar. Does the officer have to obey that?[94]

The following passage contains a similar message about the victimization of the family: "Before our eyes our brothers perished from hunger; the blows of the knout with which they beat our fathers resounded in our ears, and the screams of our sisters, sold into prostitution for a crust of bread by our mothers."[95] Despite the studied pathos and exaggeration in these passages, we can be certain that they reflect Nechaev's authentic feelings about his own family.

Revolutionary ideology divided the world into exploited and exploiter: involuntary criminals—the peasant soldiers who killed their own kind, the crushed fathers who beat their sons, the starving mothers who sold their daughters or themselves into prostitution—and a voluntarily evil ruling class of high court figures, military officers, and their underlings. Nechaev could forgive his own kin for beating him, exploiting him, driving him into an inferior career, and tricking his favorite sister into marriage against her will by means of a revolutionary vision that permitted him to displace his pent-up rage onto the Tsar, his family, and his minions. He ascribed the utmost depravity and cruelty to the ruling family: "The dissolute Tsar Alexander II, dissipated in his very family life, debauches himself in monstrous luxury with concubines and lackeys."[96] Count Adlerberg, minister of the court, is described as chief procurer to the Tsar and organizer of palace orgies, while, as noted above, General Mezentsev, head of the Third Section, is accused of giving his sister to the drunken Tsar to advance his career. Sometimes Nechaev makes Alexander II a semicomic figure, a helpless drunk fallen into idiocy from his debauchery. At other times, he is depicted as a dangerous madman, a Diocletian. Even more striking are Nechaev's images of bloodthirsty, raging beasts.

> We come from the people, our skins wounded by the teeth of the present regime.[97]
>
> Out of fear for its very existence, and simultaneously intoxicated with rage, a crowd of high officials . . . now hurls itself with the bloodthirstiness of tigers on everything that is young, fresh, and new . . . But by no means did the government exhaust its bestial ferocity on the present younger generation, fated to pay for true, popular freedom, and like Samson, fated to fall under the ruins of this hateful, dark force.[98]

This is a brief comment on the politics of the empire: "Thus the injudicious master feeds a bloodthirsty bulldog raw meat, not supposing that this bulldog, at the first opportunity will not fail to chew up his very own calf."[99] There are also vivid descriptions of bloodthirsty officials gnashing their teeth, numerous references to beatings, whippings, and a general picture of the authorities giving themselves up to their "wild instincts." There are images of parasitic sucking as well, the following passage—already cited—being perhaps the most vivid example:

> But now we must pursue without delay the extermination of his Arakcheevs, that is, of those monsters in splendid court uniforms who, spattered with the people's blood, are considered to be the pillars of the state; those who organized and still organize the slaughter of the rebelling peasant folk; those administrative bloodsuckers ceaselessly sucking away at the yearning breast of the people who have shown and will show special zeal in devising measures and means for squeezing the last vital juices out of the people in order to dull their incipient understanding.[100]

All these statements, of course, suggest infantile anxieties, but even more important, a reservoir of primitive aggression, which Nechaev tried to dispose of by means of projection. But he was not really successful at fending off his sadistic and masochistic impulses. Though he had access to a pistol at all times during Ivanov's murder, he first beat and strangled his victim. This gratuitous violence, accompanied by Nechaev's furious cursing, reveals something other than the cold-blooded, businesslike disposal of a traitor to the cause. His stories about the attempts of the secret police to strangle him were both projections of sadistic impulses and masochistic anticipations of his own martyrdom. Generally, when dealing with external authority, Nechaev used two defensive strategies. On the one hand, he pictured it as powerful, bestial, a "dark force," projecting upon it his own aggressive impulses. On the other hand, he denied its power, picturing it as weak, confused, easily toppled by a disciplined conspiracy combined with a peasant uprising. In either case, Nechaev exhibited an irrepressible need to confront the dark forces and wild instincts in himself and in the external world. His murder of Ivanov, his participation in the campaign to kill the Tsar, both before and after imprisonment, were expressions of that need. But he simultaneously prepared himself for martyrdom.

Nechaev quite consciously understood the value of the rhetoric of martyrdom for an idealistic, adolescent audience, whose deepest cultural symbols contained the idea of redemptive suffering. In one of his few signed pieces, "To Russian Students," he appropriated the greatest martyr of all for the revolutionary cause. He wrote: "Follow the words of the first revolutionary agitator, Christ: 'Do not cast pearls before swine.' "[101] In another article, Nechaev closely identified heroism with self-sacrifice—martyrdom:

> Catholics, the Orthodox, atheists—all alike respect the heroic martyrs of the Reformation, if they are not blinded by fanaticism.
>
> Fanaticism, wild fanaticism has, however, in this instance its self-justification. It, so to speak, purchases for itself the right to remain indifferent to the heroism of its opponents, because it is ready at any instant to undertake the same kind of heroism. Reading in the lives of the saints about the archpriest Avvakum, about the horrors and unutterable tortures which he endured—and how he endured them!—we can only weep over the sad fate of a people in which such enormous energy was always wasted on such a harmful cause. . . . In such fanaticism there is a species of greatness and valor, and if from one perspective it insults reason by the absurdity of its cause, from another it provides an excellent model of personal self-sacrifice and firmness.[102]

Throughout his revolutionary career, Nechaev carried with him a vision of self-sacrifice, martyrdom for his chosen cause. His acts of external aggression both real and contemplated, although undertaken in the name of the cause, served his own psychological economy, and both the anticipation and ultimate realization of martyrdom were part of the accounting.

While serving himself, Nechaev served the cause convincingly, though not well. It is, of course, impossible to say precisely how he affected the psyches of his followers, but it is reasonable to assume that his ability to dominate or manipulate his peers issued from his grasp of modes of action, symbols, and rhetoric that could activate in them both the aggression and the impulse toward self-sacrifice that drove him. Perhaps this is what Uspenskii meant when he tried to explain the conspiracy: "I must add to what I have said one powerful cause, an undefined force dragging us forward. I refer to that psychological state in which we found ourselves at that time, to that nervous agitation which possessed us."

Chapter V

Nechaev's Second Flight Abroad

Soon after his arrival abroad, Nechaev renewed contact with Ogarev and Bakunin and began a second proclamations campaign. For approximately two and one-half years the Russian émigré community in Switzerland—and indeed the entire European socialist community—suffered Nechaev's intrigues and mystifications. Most of his conspiratorial and publicistic activity was compressed into the seven months between January and July of 1870. During this time Nechaev lived in or around Geneva, aided mainly by Russian, Swiss, and Italian revolutionaries associated with the older émigrés. He remained in hiding continuously under a variety of pseudonyms: Neville, Laendley, Barsov, Baron, Volkov, Liders, and Grazhdanov. Bakunin affectionately called him "Boy," punning on the Russian word for battle.

Most of what Nechaev wrote during this period—and of what Ogarev and Bakunin wrote at his behest—perpetuated the myth of a Russian revolutionary Committee surrounded by a powerful movement; some of their writings glorified Nechaev and later defended him against detractors; others tried to stir up sentiment against the police agencies pursuing Nechaev and against Swiss cooperation with the Russian government. Above all, the three men tried to inflame all segments of Russian society against autocracy and the imperial system. In addition, Nechaev either engaged in or contemplated extortion, blackmail, seduction, counterfeiting, and theft in his efforts to finance his campaign. Most of this activity was sheer bravado. As one familiar of Bakunin and Nechaev noted in his memoirs, Nechaev unsuccessfully tried to play the role of Karl Moor.[1] Nechaev could not function well outside the émigré community. Inside the community—largely concentrated in Switzerland—it was always possible to find a safe haven, some means of support, and sympathy for the cause. Furthermore, Alexander Herzen's death on January 21, 1870, removed one possible obstacle to his activities. To be sure, even during Herzen's lifetime Ogarev and Bakunin had run with the bit in their teeth when enticed by revolutionary youth. Now, they fell almost completely under Nechaev's control, and through them he tried to control the ample resources of the Herzen family. Nechaev's behavior and Bakunin's association with him (hardly anyone took Ogarev seriously anymore) scandalized the leaders of European socialism, virtually destroyed Bakunin's position as a leader in the movement, and thereby affected the course of the socialist movement. After the Nechaev affair, Marx was all too ready to indulge his Russophobia and to see in every Russian revolutionary émigré an agent provocateur.

Nechaev's activities in London, Paris, Lyons, Brussels, and Zurich between the summers of 1870 and 1872, when he returned to Switzerland for the last time, remain relatively obscure. He virtually dropped out of sight after July 1870, and his statements to the Swiss police after his capture did little to clarify his movements. He most certainly lied about how long he had stayed in Switzerland and Paris. He claimed to have lived in Brussels during the Paris Commune, but one source places him in Zurich at that time.[2] Several sources attest to his presence in Lyons in September and early October 1870. Given the brevity of his revolutionary career and its frenzied character from the winter of 1868 until the summer of 1870, an apparent hiatus of almost two years is all the more mysterious. His attempts to evade police agents, his growing notoriety after June 1870, and his dwindling resources no doubt partly explain his relative invisibility after he left Switzerland for London in July 1870. The story of Nechaev's second flight abroad is therefore largely the story of his adventures in Switzerland and his relationship with Bakunin and Ogarev.

After he entered Switzerland in early January, Nechaev followed a procedure similar to that he had followed in March 1869. He contacted Ogarev first and Ogarev on January 5, 1870, informed Herzen (who was to die sixteen days later) that Nechaev had returned. Herzen at first refused to see Nechaev, but relented five days later.[3] Ogarev's account of Nechaev's courage—a credulous recounting of Nechaev's fabrications—had swayed him. But the meeting never took place, and to the very end Herzen opposed collaboration with him: "I could very well see the young man and give his courage its full measure of recognition—but his actions and those of the two senior partners I consider positively harmful and inopportune."[4] Bakunin's reaction was predictably more enthusiastic. On January 12 he wrote to Ogarev and Nechaev from Locarno:

> My dear ones. When I received your note I jumped so for joy that I almost shattered the ceiling with my old head. [Bakunin was over six feet tall.] Luckily, the ceiling is very high. . . . Here shelter, a bed, a table, and room await him and also the most profound secrecy. He should come, whether by vehicle or on foot, under an assumed—for example a Polish—name.[5]

During the ensuing weeks, however, he worked instead with Ogarev in or near Geneva, simply taking up where they had left off in the summer of 1869. Nechaev wrote four proclamations, collaborated on two more,[6] and produced a second issue of *Narodnaia rasprava*; Ogarev wrote two agitational pieces and a leaflet;[7] and Bakunin contributed three pamphlets.[8] They rushed several of the pamphlets through Ludwik Czerniecki's Geneva press so that Varvara Aleksandrovskaia, Nechaev's companion during his flight from Russia, could smuggle them into Russia. As noted above, she was searched at the border on January 23/11 and the proclamations were found. The Russian postal authorities first mention receipt of the new proclamations on April 10/March 29, when Nechaev's "To Russian Students" (in packets addressed to Kiev and Ivanovo) began to arrive.[9] It carried a false London publication mark. "To the Students" continued Nechaev's self-glorification campaign, which reached the height of absurdity during his second stay abroad. It is pure Nechaev.

> Comrades,
> Fate has preserved me yet another time.
> Amidst the havoc of the bloody reaction of recent days,
> I was spared with the few survivors.
> The enraged governmental tigers failed to capture me.
> They have become rabid to the point of mindlessness, to the point of absurdity: they have rushed to hunt me in Europe.
> But I am out of their clutches. Apparently I am fated to survive this foul government!
> The youth has once again offered up in sacrifice the best people from its midst.

We say that this is the last sacrifice!
Still another rank of our brothers has fallen in battle.
We say—this is the last rank.[10]

The following is perhaps the most interesting sentence in the entire proclamation: "We sacrificed many comrades in order to reach an understanding of our position, of our inevitable assignment and essential vocation."[11] Nechaev used the verb *otdat'*, which can mean many things, including "to sacrifice." It can also connote handing persons over to legal authority, or giving someone his due—itself ambiguous. Furthermore, he used the active construction "We sacrificed" instead of a passive construction. As is frequently the case in Nechaev's writings, the compulsion to confess, to tell all, breaks through the mystifications. The ambiguity of expression betrays tension and ambivalence. The idea of redemptive suffering, the repeated use of the word "sacred," the fatalistic rhetoric, and finally, the injunction: "Follow the words of the first revolutionary agitator, Christ: 'Do not cast pearls before swine!' "[12] give the proclamation a distinctly religious character. The language is rich in sexual imagery as well: "By means of a dense, invisible network we will envelop [seize, embrace] the sufferer [feminine], the Russian Land; we will penetrate everywhere and everywhere we will sow good seed."[13]

Like most of the proclamations, "To Russian Students" was designed to appeal to the special interests, resentments, and passions of the group to which it was addressed; however, Nechaev appealed to the youth (*molodezh'*) as the force of the future and not to the youth in their role as students. The true allies of youth were not those who remained within the universities as "philistines of science," but:

> new fresh people, to whom the future belongs. It is the world of the worker, divided neither by the boundaries of states, nor by tribal distinctions. Here are the people who will understand us. Because, our cause—the cause of the people, is their cause.[14]

This last brief statement virtually exhausts the programmatic substance of the proclamation.

Most of the proclamations exposed the evils suffered by a particular group and identified its enemies without offering a positive program. The proclamation "From the Russian Revolutionary Society to Women" contains the clearest positive program—to all appearances, federative anarcho-syndicalism:

> All of the land, all factories and plants, all workshops, all of the instruments of labor, all of the paths of communication, telegraphs, etc., will belong to associations (*arteli*) of workingmen and women who will enjoy equal rights. These producers' associations will be constructed according to the geographic and ethnographic conditions of each locale, and all of them will be bound together by federative solidarity.[15]

It is difficult to know who wrote which parts of the proclamations and the articles in *Kolokol.* Nechaev almost certainly had a hand in the composition of most of them. At best, one can identify some characteristic Nechaevist themes and rhetoric. Nechaev's personal vision—his fully developed program—appeared only in the journals he controlled completely: the second issue of *Narodnaia rasprava* and the single issue of *Obshchina.* Until the appearance of the article, "The Chief Foundations of the Social Structure of the Future" in *Narodnaia rasprava,* Nechaev had concerned himself almost exclusively with the means for achieving revolution and the immediate aims of an uprising and had derided the attempts of others to prescribe the future social order. Now he left no doubt that his vision of means and ends were all of a piece. He revealed himself to be one of socialism's *simplifacateurs terribles.* He reduced the economic, political, social, and cultural phenomena that had distorted human nature and fouled the human condition into four principal forms: Capital, the State, the Family, and Religion.[16] Only the proper organization of labor and the proper distribution of wealth would prevent these distortions. The Committee (still, one assumes, guided by Nechaev) is identified as the only means for destroying the old system and building the new; thus, all power and wealth had to be concentrated in the hands of the Committee.[17]

After the destruction of the old order (only in his prison writings did he describe precisely how this would occur), the Committee would organize workers' associations. Although they would be able to choose the *artel'* in which they would work, all citizens would be forced to produce according to their capabilities. Those who refused would be deprived of food, shelter, materials, tools, and the right to travel. In short, they would be condemned to death.[18] Each workers' association would elect its own leaders, who would manage the affairs of the *arteli* and serve as intermediaries between them and a central institution called the "Office" (*Kontora*). The Office would serve as a regional center for the exchange of manufactured products and raw materials. All of the essentials of commune living would be acquired through the Office. It would regulate regional production and consumption by means of an elected body of deputies from its constituent *arteli.* They would gather labor statistics and (here the author is rather vague) by means of periodically published data provide for the regulation and evaluation of labor and processes of production.[19]

In addition, the Office would control all social institutions (dormitories, dining rooms, schools, hospitals) and direct all major construction projects, such as canal or road building. Nechaev paid special attention to child rearing. Generally, the intellectual and physical development of children would take place without maternal care, although mothers who wished to raise their own children could do so, provided they fulfilled the regional work norm (determined by the Office on the basis of scientific data). Individuals might develop special projects and receive exemptions from the usual work norms in order to devote themselves to projects whose utility had been determined. The Office would help develop and translate into projects serving the general welfare of a locality all types of scientific inquiry and technological invention. Individuals who had otherwise fulfilled their work norms could dispose of their time freely in a variety of recreational, educational, and creative pursuits.[20]

Under these conditions, human beings might realize their full intellectual, physical, and moral capacities. Egoism would disappear; individual striving would not run counter to the welfare of the collectivity; human development would accelerate rapidly; and all of the old institutions, which had divided human beings and turned them against each other, would survive only as bad dreams. Legal institutions and the police would be superfluous. There would be no need for contractual relationships. Relations between the sexes would be based on mutual agreement and dissolved without difficulty, since children would be raised collectively.[21]

Nechaev reiterated his positive vision several months later in the journal *Obshchina* in the article "Our General Program." He even more clearly identified the communist vanguard: the youth and the proletariat. Like several Russian émigré socialists, Nechaev considered himself a Marxist of some sort and he tried to incorporate aspects of Marxist communism into his program. The strategy of revolution sketched in paragraph twenty-two of the program in *Obshchina* adds a strategic dimension that had been absent in the earlier version in *Narodnaia rasprava:*

> 22. The chief bases of the Commune described here can result from a social revolution carefully prepared and led by a rigorously solidary

force comprised of those elements of Russian youth which, having come forth from the people, unite in themselves, together with theoretical development and practical knowledge, strength of will as well, the latter having been achieved in the struggle for existence of the proletariat. These principles can be introduced at once into the life of the working class population of the large cities, from which the *arteli* will send out emissaries, whether groups or individuals, to the provinces to conduct propaganda and gradually to construct a life based on those very same principles, of course in keeping with the conditions of the locale and the degree of receptivity of the masses.[22]

Marx was appalled by what he termed the "barracks communism" of Nechaev's full program. Between the printing of the first version of his program in *Narodnaia rasprava* and the second in *Obshchina*, Nechaev had the opportunity to hear and react to criticisms. He replied to them, characteristically, with a threat in a footnote, quoting the alleged response of members of the radical community to the idea of collective dining rooms:

"I would shoot myself if they ordered me to sit down at such a table!" Another, also radical and still fresher and younger said: "And I would shoot the persons who would order me to do it." Oh, wretched naiveté. Is it possible that people belonging to the cause do not know that during the first days of the insurrection a vast multitude of similarly inclined gentlemen, who cannot eat without a silver service and other such comforts, will die a heroic death. People belonging to the cause are deeply convinced that a number of them will conspire and attempt to return to the good old days. This knowledge forces the social party to prepare itself to repel any reaction, and at the first necessity to sacrifice such individuals to the welfare of the masses.[23]

To be fair to Nechaev, what some of his contemporaries called "barracks communism" should be compared to the positive program of Russia's leading socialist thinkers of the 1860s and 1870s. Although the idea will horrify Soviet historians—who try to preserve an apostolic succession from Chernyshevskii to Lenin, and for whom Nechaev is persona non grata—his positive program is reasonably close to Chernyshevskii's Fourierist tradition; and although the foremost Russian socialist theoretician of the 1870s, Peter Lavrov, condemned Nechaev, Lavrov's vision of the communal system of the future resembled Nechaev's in several important respects. However, Nechaev's simplistic vision of human nature, his reductionism, his authoritarianism, and above all, his savage vindictiveness toward those who could not or would not adapt themselves to his imperatives, clearly distinguish him from most Russian socialist publicists of that era. He was a man full of rage, and whatever the positive content of his program or his cause, his psychological makeup determined his choice of means.

There were other disturbing aspects to Nechaev's publicistic activities. His feverish attempts to create a cult did not abate during his second stay abroad. Although the revolutionary movement attracted a variety of personalities, including braggarts and picaresque types, it is impossible to find anyone else who lied so systematically about himself in order to build a mystique. Sometimes Nechaev would describe and identify himself with an ideal revolutionary type whose personal background had endowed him with special fighting qualities and leadership ability. But he did not rest content with a description of the new type of revolutionary. Shortly after his arrival in Switzerland he began, with Bakunin's help, a propaganda campaign in his own behalf. They placed letters in socialist journals of several nations. The campaign, to be sure, served larger purposes as well. Nechaev and Bakunin agitated against the Russian government, its police agents, and the cooperation of foreign governments with the Russian secret police. However, Nechaev also used the major organs of European socialism to spread false stories about his arrest and escape from Siberia. The first such story, entitled "Russian Events," appeared in French in *Le Progrès*, a Swiss socialist journal, on February 5, 1870. Nechaev had published a slightly different version of it in January in the second issue of *Narodnaia rasprava*, but the two versions agreed in all essentials. A young man dressed like a factory worker had been seized in a tavern in the city of Tambov and carted off. That evening the high officials of Tambov province whispered about Nechaev, Bakunin, and a secret revolutionary society. Numerous arrests were made. Ten days later in the vicinity of Perm', on the road to Siberia, three gendarmes entered a lonely inn. They traveled by cart; a fourth person, bound and gagged, was strapped to it. The senior gendarme commandeered the hotel, while the others untied the prisoner. Then they took him into a room and closed the door. Almost instantly, sounds of a terrific struggle issued from the room—heavy blows, loud moans. An hour later the cart turned back to Perm', but now there were only the three gendarmes. In the cart there lay a long object wrapped in cloth and tightly bound with ropes. The next morning the governor of Perm' sent a telegram to St. Petersburg to "higher spheres" and informed them that the political criminal who had been sent to Nerchinsk had died en route; however, the chief of the Third Section, General Mezentsev, received another telegram to the effect that his orders with respect to Number . . . had been carried out in all details, whereupon he leaped from his chair and spent the entire evening "joyously licking his thin, Jesuitical lips, and smiling a foul smile."[24]

Having disposed of himself, Nechaev went on to describe cowardice and fear in high places, a veritable orgy of spying, arrests, police cruelty, and deportations. He reported Ivanov's murder (hinting that Ivanov had been killed for dereliction from the cause) and the ensuing police panic in Moscow.[25] A reader would infer that Russia was on the verge of revolution.

Nechaev then presented the happy news of his own rescue without explanation in the proclamation "To the Students," but two weeks after the appearance of "Russian Events" he provided European readers with an account of his escape and reprinted it in *Kolokol* several weeks later. Building on his previous story, he simply claimed that his revolutionary comrades had bribed the gendarmes, and that they had strangled their own officer![26] It might be helpful to summarize here the string of falsehoods Nechaev concocted about himself: an arrest and escape from the Peter and Paul Fortress in St. Petersburg during January–February 1869; death in Siberia, celebrated in poetry by Ogarev; death at the hands of three gendarmes on the way to forced labor in Nerchinsk, Siberia; and finally, the escape described above. Nechaev had a bad case of "nostalgia for the supreme sacrifice," to borrow Camus's phrase. But he also wanted real power. So he worked out a compromise in which he acquired the mystique of the martyr-hero only to abandon it for that of the survivor-hero. All the while he exploited the idea of redemptive suffering and openly fantasized about his final self-sacrifice:

> Those tortures, those agonies and torments which I would have to endure at the hands of the St. Petersburg Tsar-monster and his hangmen-officials, would be easy for me! I am ready to endure them gladly and to lay down my head, if my last words would be a signal for the beginning of an open worldwide struggle with this despicable social order! . . .
>
> This is all that I want to say to the European public.
>
> Nechaev.[27]

In the end, Nechaev proved that he meant what he said. Much of his power resided in his ability to communicate genuine fanaticism, to convince those around him that he was indeed capable of the supreme sacrifice.

Bakunin added to these mystifications by suggesting for a time that Nechaev was a "monstrous myth" created by the Russian government. He wrote to several Swiss radicals and asked them to agitate against any move by the Swiss Federal Council to aid the Russian government in the pursuit and extradition of political criminals. (On February 18, 1870, Bakunin had read in a French newspaper, *La Presse*, February 16, that the Russian government had tracked Nechaev to Switzerland and asked the Federal Council to extradite Nechaev. It had indeed.)[28] Even after he had "admitted" that he had been wrong in supposing that Nechaev was a myth, Bakunin still pretended that he did not know him and took up his defense in the name of liberty and the honor of Swiss republicanism, writing a lengthy pamphlet entitled "The Bears of Bern and the Bear of St. Petersburg," which appeared in March 1870. In it he not only affirmed Nechaev's existence and perpetuated the myth of Nechaev's frightful trials and two escapes, but defended political assassination.[29]

The odd character of the stories about Nechaev's adventures did not go unnoticed. Sigismund Borkheim, a friend of Marx's who shared his Russophobia, seized the opportunity afforded by these tales to impugn the integrity of Russian revolutionaries in general and Bakunin in particular. An article entitled "Nechaev's Letter" appeared in *Volksstaat* (Leipzig) on March 16, 1870. Nechaev replied to Borkheim's insinuations in a letter to the editor of *Volksstaat* dated April 15, which appeared in two installments on May 14 and June 4, 1870. Although only Nechaev signed it, Bakunin presumably collaborated, since Nechaev could not have written it in German, and the astute argumentation of the first installment suggests that Bakunin played the primary role in its composition. The second installment displays more Nechaevist rhetoric. Each side in this little controversy was guilty of contempt for the other's nationality, of innuendo about the other's real intentions, and of general nastiness. Borkheim had gratuitously insulted the Russian revolutionary tradition and got what he deserved. Nonetheless, Marx vented his spleen on Wilhelm Liebknecht, the editor of *Volksstaat*, for printing Nechaev's reply. In a letter to Engels dated May 17, 1870, he wrote:

> How he [Liebknecht] could print Nechaev's vile letter, comprised of nothing but abuse and containing nothing more than the stupidest Russian banalities in the spirit of Herzen—is still incomprehensible to everyone. Only colossal laziness, which forces him to fill up the newspaper with whatever comes to hand just so he doesn't have to work at it, might somehow explain this.[30]

In early July, Marx learned from German Lopatin, the young Russian revolutionary who took upon himself the task of exposing Nechaev to the émigrés, that the entire Nechaev affair was a hoax. Both Marx and Engels accepted Lopatin's version of Nechaev's murder of Ivanov. On July 6, 1870, Engels wrote to Marx: "It's quite nice that Nechaev turned out to be simply a scoundrel."[31]

During the course of the campaign to build up his reputation and to fight Swiss-Russian cooperation, Nechaev learned some new lessons from Bakunin. The reasoning about legality and criminality in "The Bears of Bern and the Bear of St. Petersburg" struck a chord in the younger man, who was still capable of appropriating serviceable ideas from the older generation. In his article Bakunin had written:

> It is therefore impossible to be either a revolutionary or a true reactionary without committing acts which, from the point of view of criminal and civil codes are incontestably delinquencies or even crimes, but which, from the point of view of actual and serious practice, whether reactionary or revolutionary, appear as inevitable misfortunes.[32]

This statement in itself added nothing to Nechaev's arsenal, but Bakunin expanded the argument from his anarchist perspective and after providing historical examples concluded:

> But that which is permitted to the state is denied to the individual. Such is the governmental maxim. Machiavelli said it, and history, and the practice of all actual governments alike prove him right: Crime is a necessary condition of the very existence of the State, which therefore creates an exclusive monopoly of it, from which it follows that the individual who dares to commit a crime is twice guilty: first of all, against human conscience, but then and above all against the State, in arrogating to himself one of its most precious privileges.[33]

Several months later in his journal *Obshchina* Nechaev, in his own unmistakable style, presented a Nechaevist version of Bakunin's ideas:

> Aristotle called man a political animal; he might have called him a criminal brute. . . . Law, so to speak, organizes murder and mutual devourment, brings about plundering; law is that talisman, which permits a small band of cheats and parasites to exploit and savagely beat masses of people—with impunity! You can be the worst son of a bitch, the vilest scum, and you are an inviolable and sacred person, if you are outside the law (to be outside the law means to make the laws) and if you are the most virtuous subject, the law all the same can christen

> you a scoundrel! . . . Force gave birth to law; the instinct for exploitation of those nearby, the instinct of parasitism, the instinct for plunder gave birth to law. . . . Mankind must recognize that to the present moment law, having given birth to crime, itself was the greatest crime, and the criminals were not the ones who were punished, but those who punished.[34]

Though only one issue of *Obshchina* appeared, it did not escape the notice of later revolutionaries. More than thirty years later Lenin showed strong interest in Nechaev's writings, and after the revolution of 1917 he named *Obshchina* as one of the revolutionary journals worthy of republication.[35]

Had Nechaev contented himself with publicistic activity, his career might easily have taken a different course. Eventually, he alienated those who would have forgiven him his past actions and foolish words. But he apparently felt compelled to expand his arena of activity and could not do so without more money. Furthermore, he tried to keep alive the myth of a powerful organization and evidently felt that the best way to do this was to threaten people in the name of The People's Revenge. Finally, he could not overcome his need to undermine the authority of people with better reputations than his own. The twenty-two-year-old adventurer had made himself an object of international attention through a series of deceptions and a murder—all in less than two years. His aliases reveal a touch of megalomania: Baron; Barsov, containing the root for "lordliness"; Liders, taken from the English, "leader." During his second stay abroad he seemed to resent the fact that he was not recognized as the supreme leader. Within a few months he felt that he could publicly denigrate his revolutionary ancestors, his present revolutionary colleagues of the older generation, and the leaders of the International. Soon after his arrival in Switzerland, Nechaev began a series of intrigues: thefts, extortions, and attempts at blackmail. He acquired of the remaining half—10,000 francs—of the Bakhmetev fund, but in this case there was no need for threats, thanks to the compliance of the Herzen family and, with Bakunin's prodding, Ogarev's zealous cooperation. Bakunin and Ogarev evidently believed that they were transferring the money to the Russian Committee via Nechaev. There is little record of how Nechaev spent the thousands of francs he took. Some of the money financed the publication of *Kolokol* in April and May. Ogarev possessed more than 1,000 francs in June 1870, after *Kolokol* ceased publication.[36]

Although Nechaev did not threaten Herzen's heirs about the money, he did try to prevent them from publishing Herzen's reproaches to his former comrades in a posthumous collection of his last essays. On March 7, 1870, Nechaev sent a letter to Herzen's widow with the imprimatur of the Bureau of the Foreign Agents of the Russian Revolutionary Society Narodnaia Rasprava. As usual, he dignified the form with a bogus number (N° 108). The letter ends with this grim warning:

> Having expressed our opinions to messrs. editors we are quite certain that they, knowing with whom they are dealing and understanding the position of the Russian movement, will not force us to the sad necessity of acting in a less delicate manner.[37]

Tuchkova-Ogareva (Herzen's widow) transmitted the letter to Herzen's son, who refused to be intimidated by Nechaev. The collection appeared later that year. It included Herzen's "Letter to an Old Comrade" and an unflattering essay on the new generation of revolutionary émigrés. Nothing came of Nechaev's threats.

The above incidents seem like mere trifles. Nechaev was merely perpetuating the methods he had employed in Russia, where he had committed much worse crimes. But in the context of socialist émigré politics, his actions took on added significance. Marx's enmity for Bakunin and his struggle with him over the ideology and structure of the First International gave Nechaev's petty intrigues historical significance. They permitted Marx to build a case against Bakunin—a case of guilt by association—and served as the pretext for expelling Bakunin from the International. The central incident, the Liubavin affair, involved Marx—or more precisely—involved Bakunin's translation of Marx's *Das Kapital*.[38] N. N. Liubavin had been associated with German Lopatin, Mikhail Negreskul, and other young students of socialism before he went abroad in 1868. Negreskul followed in 1869 and in the course of his stay abroad learned that Bakunin was leading a hand-to-mouth existence. He conceived a plan whereby both socialism and Bakunin might be served and asked his friend Liubavin to help. During the summer of 1869 Liubavin sent Bakunin a small sum of money and wrote to N. F. Daniel'son (another member of the group mentioned above and future translator of *Das Kapital*) and N. P. Poliakov, a publisher in St. Petersburg, to arrange for a translation of the first volumes of *Das Kapital*. Bakunin was promised 1,200 rubles for the job, a quite substantial sum for a man in his position. Liubavin, who lived in Germany, forwarded the 300 rubles Bakunin had asked for in advance on

September 28, 1869. Though Bakunin acknowledged receipt of the money and told Liubavin on November 2, 1869, that he had begun work on the translation, Liubavin did not receive a page of it during the remainder of the month. After some pressure from Liubavin, in December 1869, Bakunin sent the first pages of the manuscript.[39] In all, Liubavin received very little. Within a few weeks, of course, Nechaev interrupted Bakunin's routine (such as it was). He told him that there were more important things to do, and Bakunin, who evidently found the work agonizing and referred to *Das Kapital* as "Marx's economic metaphysics," happily commissioned Nechaev to terminate the arrangement. Nechaev did so in his own way. On February 25, 1870, he wrote a letter to Liubavin, once again in the name of the Bureau of the Foreign Agents of the Russian Revolutionary Society Narodnaia Rasprava. It accused Liubavin of exploiting Bakunin, called him a "kulak-bourgeois" among other things, and commanded him to release Bakunin from "any moral obligation to continue the translation." It also threatened Liubavin with rough treatment if he failed to carry out a series of instructions, which were obviously designed to prove to Bakunin and others the power of the Bureau.[40] The incident proved only Nechaev's unscrupulousness and Bakunin's irresponsibility, for which he paid dearly more than two years later when Marx produced Nechaev's letter at the Hague Congress of the First International in September 1872. Furthermore, the Liubavin incident brought German Lopatin to Switzerland in May 1870, and Lopatin played the major role in exposing Nechaev to the émigré community.

In addition to making threats of the sort described above, Nechaev filched letters and other papers in the hope that he might blackmail their owners. Neither practice yielded anything but additional evidence for the accusations eventually compiled by his and Bakunin's opponents. Nechaev also used his followers as spies. Most notably, he employed his faithful lieutenant, Vladimir Serebrennikov, as a spy in the Russian section of the First International, headed by Marx's Russian ally, Nikolai Utin. Utin's group strenuously opposed Bakunin's and Nechaev's machinations in their journal, *Narodnoe delo,* and Utin helped Marx in his campaign to destroy Bakunin's anarchist Alliance. The Serebrennikov incident, revealed in a letter of July 24, 1870, from Utin to Marx, was a typically Nechaevist fraud. Serebrennikov asked the Russian section to protect him from Nechaev and Bakunin and showed them letters in which Nechaev threatened to kill him unless he joined their conspiracy.[41] The ruse worked, and Serebrennikov became secretary of the section, but Nechaev could not refrain from boasting about his infiltration of the Russian section to M. P. Sazhin, a Bakuninist. Sazhin told Utin, and Serebrennikov was expelled from the group.[42] Of all Nechaev's erstwhile comrades, only Serebrennikov (three years Nechaev's junior) remained loyal to him after the damaging picture of Nechaev emerged in devastating fullness in the stenographic accounts of the trial of the Nechaevists, printed in July and August 1871.

The activities described above are aspects of the obsessive behavior described earlier. Taken together, they constitute *Nechaevshchina,* the Russian suffix connoting evil or wrongdoing. When one surveys petty and ineffectual mystifications of this sort, it is difficult to take Nechaev seriously. But however ineffectual he was, it would be a mistake not to take Nechaevism seriously. History has yielded, and continues to yield, leaders cast in his mold. If Nechaev had possessed greater self-control and maturity, he might have gone much further; but, of course, he would not have been Nechaev.

The centerpiece of Nechaev's second stay abroad was the publication of *Kolokol.* The story of the new *Kolokol* is inextricably tied to Nechaev's relationship with Natalie Herzen, and understanding their relationship, in turn, is singularly valuable for understanding his methods. Most of what we know about Nechaev's techniques of manipulation and coercion comes from depositions to the Russian police, testimony at the trial of the Nechaevists, letters written by his unmaskers, and memoirs written long after the events. Natalie Herzen's diary and correspondence with Nechaev add detail and color to the picture and exhibit Nechaev's sentimentality as well. Nechaev's clumsy efforts to seduce Natalie inject a comic element into Nechaev's story, although, as always, there is a sickly and even sinister aspect.

Natalie Herzen was Alexander Herzen's eldest daughter—twenty-five years old in 1870 when she met Nechaev. Shortly after her father's death she traveled from Paris to Geneva to see Ogarev. Raised in an oddly bohemian but simultaneously aristocratic environment, she had been exposed to all of the cross-currents of revolutionary politics and émigré life. The Herzen children had grown up in a complex emotional and cultural mélange of governesses, teachers, family retainers, and revolutionary writers and politicians of several nationalities. Nonetheless, to all appearances Natalie, an attractive young woman with a Napoleonic brow and aquiline nose, had grown up a properly repressed Victorian. She had suffered a psychotic episode after a brief relationship with a blind Italian nobelman.[43] Under her father's care, she began to recover, and after his death on January 21, 1870, had recovered sufficiently to want to travel to Switzerland to console Ogarev. Given the virtual amalgamation of the Herzen and Ogarev families, Natalie had a distinctly filial attitude toward Ogarev, who regarded her as his own child Yet under pressure from Nechaev and Bakunin he became their accomplice in an intrigue to acquire her share of the Herzen family fortune and to add her prestigious family name to a resurrected *Kolokol*. Nechaev, Bakunin, and Ogarev had to fight off a coalition of Natalie's family and friends who tried to protect her from involvement in revolutionary affairs and who opposed the scheme to resurrect *Kolokol*. Bakunin argued in a letter of February 22, 1870, to Ogarev that it was they who had to rescue her from them. He put forward both therapeutic and ethical reasons for asking Natalie to stay in Switzerland:

> My dear old friend. Thank you for your confidence. The matter is sufficiently straightforward. It appears that they want neither the renewal of *Kolokol* nor the participation of your elder daughter in the Russian cause—in your cause. . . . not understanding that if she remains longer in their aimless, hopeless and idle desert, she may indeed lose her mind and that her health, as much as her heart, demands that she live with you and help you. . . .
>
> You must—and you alone are able to save your elder daughter. Whether or not she'll be in any condition to work for the Russian cause, or will retain a desire to—we will see later on. . . . I believe, and indeed you also believe, that she will find a new life for herself in the Russian cause; *they* believe the opposite. The future will show who is right, and who is not. But first of all you must save her. Because, Ogarev, I am certain *that if she remains with them, she will lose her mind*. You must *liberate her from their unconscious but instinctive egoism*, which they conceal from themselves under the guise of golden prudence and quotidian bourgeois wisdom. Surely poor, dear Tata [Natalie's nickname] must do better in life than end up as a nanny to Aleksandr Aleksandrovich's [her brother, Alexander Herzen's son] children or Natalie Alekeseevna's [Ogarev's wife, who had left him for Herzen] sidekick, or a comrade to that truly insane Wagnerian-Germanizing Pomeranian Old Maid [Maria Reichel], consoling herself by making little paintings ins Blaue hinein.[44]

No thanks to Bakunin and Ogarev, Natalie Herzen did retain her sanity. Bakunin's behavior toward Natalie and the Herzen entourage during the months following Herzen's death can only be described as vile, although Nechaev so far outstripped him that he appeared a harmless old eccentric by comparison. Bakunin enthusiastically and Ogarev unwillingly delivered up Natalie Herzen into Nechaev's hands.

While visiting Ogarev during her trip to Geneva in early February she first encountered Nechaev, who was introduced to her as Mr. Volkov. She saw before her a very Russian type wearing dark spectacles, which did not entirely conceal his penetrating glance. The rude young man paced theatrically back and forth with his right hand thrust into his jacket, à la Napoleon.[45] Their first interview was inconsequential—little more than a preliminary psychological probe by Nechaev, but enough to reveal to him that she was interested in "the Russian cause" and enough for her to sense his arrogance and authoritarianism. Later, Nechaev began to play his usual game of assigning potential recruits small tasks. He asked about her drawing ability (she had studied painting), which put her immediately on the defensive, for she had heard a rumor that he was planning to counterfeit banknotes. Nechaev actually wanted a series of drawings designed to agitate Russian peasants:

> "In one drawing you will show, for instance, a crowd of *muzhiks*, armed with whatever they can lay hands on, scythes, sticks, and so on. In front, there's a young fellow who's lost his hat. He's straining to rush over to one side, pointing at the soldiers standing there. But he's stopped by a priest who is beating him over the head with his cross. Do you understand?"
>
> "I understand. But the task is a difficult one, it is too much for me. I am very sorry."
>
> "It's no use giving up before you have tried; start with one figure, and then we'll see. For example, a gentleman-landowner, as they used to be—fat, rich, sprawling drunkenly on a couch, and then a landowner as they look nowadays—thin, dressed in rags."
>
> "Now *that* I *could* do."[46]

Nechaev also wanted her to draw some peasants setting fire to a manor house. When she indignantly refused—

> An ironic smile appeared on Volkov's face, and still pacing up and down, he shouted to Ogarev, who was sitting in the dining-room: "Hey, listen what 'they' say here! They refuse to draw, because, you see, it's contrary to their way of thinking to teach *muzhiks* to set fire to things."[47]

They also initiated Natalie into revolutionary work by having her address their numerous envelopes and packets of leaflets and pamphlets. She did not stay long in Geneva but left for Paris on February 11, and given the discrepancy between her diary and memoirs it is not clear whether all of this occurred in early February or after her second trip to Geneva later that month.

During the brief interval between the two trips Natalie and Nechaev wrote each other several times.[48] This fact in itself suggests that she was something less than candid when she hurriedly passed over her initial contact with him in her memoirs. Both her diary and the contents of her letters (signed "Reginald Wilson" at Nechaev's request) reveal that Natalie had become a nervously willing accomplice, fulfilled Nechaev's commissions, and braved the wrath and dismay of the Herzen entourage in Paris to return to him and Ogarev in Switzerland. Nechaev had convinced her that the cause needed her. Both before and after her departure he had impressed upon her Ogarev's alcoholic helplessness and the need for a trustworthy and accurate helper in Geneva. She believed that her cooperation was a matter of life and death for imperiled revolutionaries and was evidently fascinated by this righteous fanatic. She must have heard all the tales about Nechaev, yet, in February committed herself to helping him. Not all of his letters to her have been preserved, but like his conversations, they had a powerful impact.

While Ogarev played his role somewhat reluctantly and sadly, Bakunin, not content to bring pressure upon Natalie through Ogarev (both he and Nechaev exploited her concern for Ogarev to keep her in their camp), wrote directly to her and to Herzen's widow,[49] who accompanied Natalie to Switzerland and even became involved in Nechaev's adventures. Once Natalie arrived in Geneva, Ogarev presented her with her first new commission from Nechaev, for which she had to travel to Neûchatel and Le Locle. What happened in Le Locle must be pieced together from her diary and memoirs, each of which provides different (and sometimes contradictory) details of her adventures.[50] Outside Le Locle she found Nechaev hidden in a little chalet in the care of a hunchbacked man and a dwarf woman. As usual, he was autocratic, self-assured, and quick to show exasperation and anger at the slightest opposition. She carried with her a manuscript, whose contents were unknown to her. Ogarev had instructed her to tell Nechaev that two offending paragraphs would have to be removed, or else he could not endorse the manuscript. Nechaev flew into a rage. The incident reveals Ogarev's unwillingness to subordinate himself completely to Nechaev.[51]

The commission was probably a pretext to give Nechaev the opportunity of putting pressure on Natalie to help them revive *Kolokol.* All the while he pretended to act in the name of the Committee. She was naturally reluctant to let the name of her father's journal be used by people he despised. While fascinated by Nechaev and acting for a while like a rabbit hypnotized by a snake, Natalie tended to see things from a defensive point of view. She had to defend her family, her personal honor, and her fortune. Nechaev blundered badly, believing that he could overwhelm her (as he had so many others) by revealing to her inner secrets of the Committee—alleged instructions about the line of the new journal. If her diary is correct, Nechaev might have been contemplating for a while a truly radical *Kolokol* devoted to the most extreme terroristic and egalitarian traditions of the French revolution, the traditions of Marat and Babeuf, with whom Nechaev genuinely sympathized.[52] He also impulsively showed her the Committee's "instructions" to set up secret editorial offices, a counterfeiting enterprise, and other illegal operations. All of this only repelled and frightened her, although not sufficiently to deter her from undertaking the modest commission of helping Ogarev put his papers in order when she returned to Geneva.

During March, Bakunin and Nechaev went to Geneva to put more pressure on Natalie. Bakunin's lack of scruples in this enterprise yielded nothing to Nechaev's. At one point he suggested to the fastidious young woman that she serve the cause with her feminine charms. They tried unsuccessfully to name her the editor of the planned journal, another obvious ploy to exploit the Herzen name. Bakunin's resentment toward Herzen's children, their way of life, and their wealth burst out, and like Nechaev he tested her with insult, near intimidation, and every possible psychological lever—especially her loyalty to Ogarev. Nechaev and Bakunin hoped they could frighten her with the prospect of an unfulfilled life as a parasite and hanger-on in her brother's household and entice her with the image of the strong, revolutionary woman—free in her personal life but dedicated to a meaningful cause; fully developed as a woman but disciplined as a comrade. While Natalie remained open to the idea that a revolution was brewing, she was genuinely repelled by the revolutionary methods they discussed. It appears, however, that their psychological manipulations affected her, for it is otherwise impossible to explain the fact that after the unpleasant scenes described in her diary she continued to associate herself with their enterprise.[53]

Both her diary and reminiscences tell much about her state of mind during the late winter and spring of 1870. At one point she writes that "they almost succeeded in driving me completely out of my mind." During March, Nechaev made several mistakes in his campaign to make Natalie Herzen his obedient instrument. He tried to make love to her and, in an awkward way, proposed.[54] Only her fundamental commitment to aiding the revolutionaries, her loyalty to Ogarev, and her curiosity about the entire mystery surrounding Nechaev kept her from bolting. Like all the others who found Nechaev's personal behavior repugnant or embarrassing, Natalie Herzen tolerated it for the sake of his cause. But only up to a point. On March 13, 1870, she wrote him a note to the effect that she would not go to Ogarev's apartment (where she often encountered Nechaev) unless he gave her his word of honor that he would not kiss her.[55] Although Nechaev gave his word, an apparently psychosomatic illness often kept her from appearing at Ogarev's to do her addressing work. In a series of eloquent letters written in May and June, Nechaev desperately tried to repair the damage done to their relationship by his conduct at Ogarev's but failed. Nechaev's campaign of the spring of 1870 succeeded to this extent: He prevailed in his effort to revive *Kolokol;* won out over Ogarev's and Bakunin's objections in setting the course of the journal; and won Natalie Herzen's cooperation, however limited.

The new *Kolokol*'s first issue appeared on April 2, 1870, and the sixth and last on May 9, 1870. It showed occasional traces of Nechaev's extremist rhetoric, but the lead articles breathed an irenic spirit of reasonableness and moderation beyond anything one might expect of the older generation of radical émigrés, not to mention Nechaev. The most radical political statement in the journal appears in the very last issue, in a brief article signed by Ogarev.[56] The reasons for this moderation are clear enough. Having failed to rally the most radical groups in Russian society, Nechaev intended to revive the relatively united opposition to autocracy which had appeared after the Crimean War and had split up decisively only after 1861. Some articles try to evoke again anger for Alexander II's failure to grant a constitution. Others appeal to liberal nationalism and anti-imperialism. Several of them—articles on censorship, corruption, the brutal treatment of peasant rebels and political prisoners, the plight of youth in the face of unenlightened but arrogant professors and priests—show Nechaev's touch. The journal exposed in lavish detail official cruelty and depravity and paraded before the reader exemplary figures, most often peasants or students, who had resisted arbitrary and unjust treatment, only to suffer greater punishment at the hands of bestial authority. The journal also contained articles designed especially for Ukrainian and Baltic nationalists and for the Catholic population in the western part of the empire. In other words, Nechaev and his helpers dramatized for the readers of *Kolokol* the fate of the victims of imperial authority and appealed to a variety of liberal sentiments.

Although revolutionary in aim, the journal failed to present a clear strategy for organizing a coalition of all opposition groups against the monarchy or a set of ultimate political, economic, and social goals.

Such vagueness may have suited the liberal mentality, but socialist revolutionaries could only scoff. Bakunin, who had actually agreed to the journal's line, out of pride could not restrain himself from reproaching the editors of *Kolokol* for their lack of a program in a letter to the editors published in the second issue. Nonetheless, Nechaev refused to give in. Only in the last issue did he and Ogarev give a clearer indication of what they had in mind. There, Ogarev's statement about the organization of a secret society lifted the curtain a bit higher—brief glimpses had appeared in preceding issues—to reveal the organizational principle he and Nechaev shared. It was, after all, Ogarev who had helped introduce the centralist, conspiratorial tendency into the revolutionary movement.

Although Nechaev undoubtedly dictated the journal's general line, it is difficult to determine his precise contribution. In addition to the articles and letters devoted to stories of his escape, he probably wrote much of the "correspondence" from Russia appearing in the column entitled "News from Russia." The stories in this column apparently were drawn from Russian newspapers and periodicals, but Nechaev almost certainly fabricated many details to give the information inside color. The editorial comment on an agitational leaflet for Ukrainian peasants (written by Pryzhov and Nechaev) includes a statement to the effect that only conspiratorial methods inspired by popular ideas could save the oppressed, a clearly Nechaevist attitude.[57] The sadistic imagery of the article "The Naiveté of the Liflanders" suggests Nechaev's hand, although Vladimir Serebrennikov was probably the primary author.[58] Another article, "Misfortune from Tsarist Caresses . . . ," was signed by N. I. Zhukovskii, but the attitude toward heroism and self-sacrifice and, more specifically, toward the archpriest Avvakum's fanaticism was certainly shared by Nechaev, if not inspired by him.[59]

Nechaev's only signed piece in *Kolokol* is a Russian translation of his letter about his incredible escape from agents of the Third Section while being transported to Siberia. In a preface to Nechaev's letter (and to two others concerning the manhunt in Romania and Germany) in the first issue, the editors of *Kolokol* engaged in a bit of mystification, reproaching Nechaev for his "youthful exaltation" and his desire to sacrifice himself for the cause, but commending him for his patriotic fervor. "The time for heroes has passed," they wrote.[60] Yet Nechaev's letter and other pieces in *Kolokol* contradicted the call for "shadowy, nameless actors." Heroism was central to Nechaev's self-image, and he knew very well that Russian revolutionary youth thirsted for stories of hideous trials, insane courage, and self-sacrifice. He therefore treated the readers of *Kolokol* to a double mystification—the pretense of editorial sobriety and maturity alongside still another fraudulent heroic episode in the life of the student revolutionary, Nechaev. In addition to reprinting in Russian translation the letter about his second arrest and escape (printed in French in *L'Internationale*, *Marseillaise*, *Le Progrès*, and *Volksstaat*), Nechaev printed replies to Borkheim's attack in *Volksstaat*.

Nechaev and his young colleagues scattered throughout the journal crude comments about the sexual misbehavior of high officials, sensual images of police brutality (whippings on the silken divans of the Third Section,[61] the white bodies of Baltic barons under the whips of the secret police[62]), innuendoes that the Tsar was insane, and numerous accusations of official corruption. Although Herzen had not been completely innocent of this type of journalism in the original *Kolokol*, the new version of the journal lacked his grace and literary skill, not to mention his intellect. Bakunin and Ogarev finally understood what had befallen the journal—and them.

It is not clear, however, that Ogarev ever broke with Nechaev over the journal's basic line. Like Herzen, Ogarev enjoys a relatively good reputation among historians, and they commonly seek a way to disassociate him from Nechaev. For example, one of Ogarev's recent biographers claims that the older man broke with Nechaev because he could no longer tolerate Nechaev's hostility toward theory and his amorality in revolutionary practice,[63] but the evidence adduced refers to a situation that developed several weeks after the appearance of the last issue of *Kolokol*. On the other hand, a letter from the publisher of the journal, L. Czerniecki, to Ogarev reveals that bad relations had developed between him (Czerniecki) and Nechaev.[64] Their disagreement, rather than any conflict between Ogarev and Nechaev, may have led to the cessation of publication. Ogarev had cooperated, however reluctantly, with Nechaev. There is no way to avoid the conclusion that both Bakunin and Ogarev displayed weakness of will and lack of principle in their relationship with Nechaev. The brief history of this most undistinguished journal illustrates the point, although less dramatically than other episodes in the relationship between Nechaev and the émigrés.

During May 1870, Nechaev's precarious situation began to worsen. The police search continued, and on May 7 the émigrés gathered in Geneva to fight the rumored extradition treaty. No single source provides a clear picture of the events of that evening.[65] Among those present was German Lopatin, but he did not use the occasion to attack Nechaev. The only consequence of the meeting was a petition protesting any attempt at extradition. Two days later the Swiss police arrested Semen Serebrennikov on the streets of Geneva and detained him for almost two weeks until witnesses established that he was not Nechaev.[66] Nechaev had to flee his hitherto safe apartment at 12 rue de la Cluse. Toward the end of his stay in Geneva, Natalie Herzen provided him with one last service. She and Tuchkova-Ogareva hid him in their rooms, spirited him out several days later dressed as a woman, having instructed him minimally in feminine comportment, and transported him to his point of embarkation on Lake Geneva.[67]

It turned out that Nechaev had less to fear from the Swiss police than from his own compatriots. The appearance of German Lopatin in Geneva marked the beginning of the end for Nechaev. Lopatin acted on behalf of his friends Liubavin and Daniel'son, both of whom feared that Nechaev would use the documents in Bakunin's possession concerning the translation of *Das Kapital* to compromise or blackmail them. Moreover, Lopatin came armed with tales of Nechaev's activities in Russia. A man of unusual courage and self-confidence, he could not be intimidated by the likes of Nechaev.

Lopatin tried to arrange a series of conversations with Bakunin and Nechaev so there could be no question of unfairness. In Nechaev's presence he told Bakunin the truth about Nechaev's "escape" and his grandiose "Committee." True to form, when confronted by someone stronger than he, Nechaev remained silent. Lopatin (against his better judgment) held a separate meeting with Nechaev, providing Nechaev with the opportunity to give Bakunin a distorted version of their conversation, for Lopatin had to leave for Paris immediately after the meeting. Nechaev's attempt to discredit Lopatin precipitated a correspondence between Bakunin and Lopatin which settled the matter. Although Bakunin's insulting letter to Lopatin has not been preserved, Lopatin's reply of May 26, 1870 has.[68] Lopatin sensed that something was odd about Bakunin's reaction to the revelations. It was as if Bakunin had known all along that Nechaev had been deceiving everyone, yet had chosen to believe Nechaev's grotesque lies. This only made matters worse for Nechaev and Bakunin. Whereas Lopatin had been interested mainly in helping Liubavin and Daniel'son escape blackmail, he now developed such powerful contempt for Nechaev that he felt obliged to pursue the matter to the very end.

In his lengthy letter to Bakunin, Lopatin quoted back to him words that Nechaev had attributed to Lopatin: "The old fellow [Bakunin] couldn't hold out, gave up the letters, and now he's in *our* hands: *we* can do anything with him: even if he is against *us*—it's of no account!"[69]

Lopatin very astutely grasped the type of mentality that could fabricate such tales:

> I can only shrug my shoulders in the face of such an unbridgeable abyss of insolence. "What kind of language is this!" I exclaimed together with you. And why does this Nechaev imagine that every person must, like him, always refer to himself as "*we*." I make bold to assure him that besides him, only empresses express themselves so stupidly! And furthermore, why does Nechaev imagine that everyone, like him, only thinks about somehow holding other people "in their hands?" Once again I make bold to assure Nechaev that this too is in the imperial manner.[70]

Others had noticed Nechaev's despotic character but, unlike Lopatin, had not understood the joint workings of the defense mechanisms of projection and identification that Nechaev employed to justify his harshness and his search for power. Lopatin, albeit in passing and ironically, had hit upon Nechaev's identification with imperial power and aggression. As long as Nechaev employed his defense mechanisms in direct conflict with authority, his fellow revolutionaries might tolerate their unpleasant aspects; but his identification with the aggressor profoundly affected his relationships with revolutionary colleagues. He became a danger to all of them. Nechaev's inability to channel his aggression toward appropriate objects—a pathological tendency he exhibited from the very beginning of his career—could no longer be tolerated. Even Bakunin had to yield to the astuteness of Lopatin's perceptions, though not without a struggle.

Since Lopatin did not trust Bakunin, he sent the letter to Natalie Herzen with a copy of Bakunin's letter to him and asked her to read both. She should then organize a meeting with Bakunin, Nechaev (if possible), and a small group of trustworthy people, in whose presence Bakunin would read the reply. Natalie Herzen was not able to arrange the meeting, since Bakunin had left Geneva for Locarno, and Lopatin had to resort to an awkward arrangement to ensure sufficient publicity in the émigré community. In a letter of June 1, 1870, he asked Natalie Herzen to read his reply to Bakunin, Ogarev, and Vladimir Ozerov, a staunch Bakuninist—the last two were privy to the contents of Bakunin's letter—and then send it to Bakunin.[71] Lopatin wanted Bakunin to share the letter with Nechaev. It is clear from Lopatin's two letters to Natalie Herzen that for the sake of his own reputation, he wanted to follow rational and fair procedures. He had little confidence that Bakunin would admit the truth about Nechaev.

Bakunin received Lopatin's letter of May 26 sometime between June 2 and June 9 and replied to him on the latter date. In his letter Bakunin agreed that Nechaev had lied about their conversation of late May and apologized for his letter to Lopatin.[72] (The remainder of the letter is a lot of pettifoggery about Lopatin's unfairness to Bakunin.) Although Bakunin accused Nechaev of an insolent lie, he refused to discuss the more important issues raised by Lopatin. Furthermore, he reproached Lopatin for presuming to have sensed something odd in his reactions to Lopatin's accusations against Nechaev. In a letter written on the same day, June 9, to Ogarev, Natalie Herzen, Ozerov, and Semen Serebrennikov, Bakunin revealed that he would try to save Nechaev.[73] Lopatin had forced Bakunin's hand. As noted above, Lopatin had told Marx, among others, about Nechaev's lies and had also begun to disseminate a story that Nechaev had murdered Ivanov because Ivanov was a wealthy supporter of Nechaev's enterprise and had refused to give him any more money. Although Marx's recounting of Lopatin's story of Ivanov's murder to Engels in a letter of July 5, 1870, (based on a conversation held in London shortly before) differs slightly from the version Lopatin sent to Natalie Herzen in a letter of August 1, 1870, the implications are similar: Ivanov had not been a spy; Nechaev had acted out of wounded pride and despotism.[74] All of this occurred approximately one year before the details of the crime and the stories of the participants became public knowledge, but Lopatin claimed access to inside knowledge. In spite of the fact that he had several of the details of the murder wrong, Lopatin quite clearly had communicated with people who knew some of the most important facts.[75] In view of all that had happened, all that had been brought to light, how would Bakunin save Nechaev? Indeed, why should he save Nechaev?

There is every reason to believe that Lopatin had correctly analyzed Bakunin's behavior and that Bakunin was not as naive as he made himself out to be. One of the pamphlets written during the first proclamations campaign, "The Posing of the Revolutionary Question," had expressed contempt for "conspirator-socialists." In March 1870, Bakunin's pamphlet "Science and the Vital Revolutionary Cause" had raised the problem again in a typology of reformers and revolutionaries. In the course of discussing doctrinaire revolutionists, who approached the revolution from books rather than from life, Bakunin had developed a subtype:

> In other, less serious, and therefore all the more dramatic and vain ones, reading the history of past revolutions stimulated their youthful

> imagination; the example of famous revolutionary heroes inspired the desire to become, or, at the very least, to appear to be heroes of that sort. They dream of violent revolutions in which they themselves play, it goes without saying, the very last role, of struggle on the barricades, of terror and of salvational decrees, issued by them, and they themselves are terrified at the thought of how terrible they will be. . . .
>
> It is useless to expend any talk on these people. Their business is not the cause, but themselves. Forever speaking in the name of the people, they never troubled to and don't want to learn about the people. The people are for them only a pretext, a pawn, a prop, a mindless and dead mass, waiting for life, thought, happiness, and freedom from them and them only. They feel in themselves the dictator's calling and have no doubts that the people will move, like a stupid herd, by their magic. Their ceaseless self-infatuation brings them to the point of madness. No object, no incident, no matter how vast, can force them to forget about themselves: in everything they see only themselves.[76]

Is it possible that Bakunin did not recognize his "Boy" in these lines? After many conversations and a reading of Nechaev's agitational pieces, could Nechaev's dictatorial character and his megalomania have passed unnoticed? Hardly. But Bakunin showed great restraint in dealing with Nechaev; he attacked him in print only obliquely—as in the letter to *Kolokol.* What passed between them in private conversation is revealed —though only in glimpses—in a letter to Nechaev to be discussed later. What is certain is that Bakunin found it virtually impossible to give up on Nechaev, or to give him up. The reasons were more personal than ideological. Nechaev's sadistic forcefulness attracted Bakunin, and he had probably anticipated that he would be humiliated by Nechaev. Nechaev served Bakunin well at a personal level, though in this instance, the personal and public could not be separated. Bakunin's need to subordinate himself to Nechaev and to be humiliated—a need that can be inferred from the entire pattern of their relationship—did not dull the older man's understanding. He simply was helpless, and when the day of reckoning arrived, Bakunin's ambivalence prevented him from dealing with Nechaev unequivocally.

One final factor should be mentioned. Bakunin was virtually a pauper. Having resolved the Liubavin affair through Lopatin, he remained without means of support. The Bakhmetev fund had passed into Nechaev's and Ogarev's hands, and Bakunin received a little of it in the form of doles from them, but no substantial support. Nechaev had proven himself an energetic (though unscrupulous) fund raiser, and Bakunin had counted on him for material support, although he had been frustrated by Nechaev's stinginess. Nechaev's complete destruction would cut off a possible source of funds. At the age of fifty-six Bakunin had to be concerned with matters of this sort, and his correspondence leaves no doubt that he was.

Bakunin's effort to save Nechaev took the form of a voluminous letter, presumably begun on June 2 and completed on or before June 9, 1870.[77] The letter is a strange mixture of confession and tenacious refusal to see the whole truth. It is Bakunin's apologia to his friends for his grotesque position, and by its very nature circles around the truth, sometimes touches it, but fails to embrace it fully. Bakunin admits that he had detected contradictions in Nechaev's presentation of the state of affairs in Russia and that he had "consciously and systematically refused to believe" that Nechaev was a deceiver despite instincts that told him otherwise.[78] Early in the letter he admits that Nechaev had been using him for "immediate aims" which were unknown to him.[79] As the letter progresses, it appears that he had sensed not only this but also had divined that Nechaev had used his name to create the organization in Russia.[80] In other words, Bakunin had knowingly permitted Nechaev to use him; he had even approved of Nechaev's contemptuous attitude toward the émigrés—including himself. Unless Bakunin is lying in the letter to Nechaev, the conversations with Lopatin—not Lopatin's letter of May 26—had convinced him of the truth of the charges against Nechaev.[81] If this is true, then in order to have believed Nechaev's slander of Lopatin, he would have had to have been an utter imbecile, or simply irrational; and given everything he had tolerated in Nechaev, it is difficult to understand how he could have reproached Lopatin for unfairness. He had chosen the reptilian Nechaev over a young man who *had* been arrested, *had* escaped from exile—a person who, to all appearances, had all the virtues of the practical revolutionary. Bakunin hated to hear the truth and hated to see Lopatin triumph over Nechaev. He claimed to believe Lopatin, yet in the letter continued to entertain the possibility that Nechaev's Committee existed. Rather than give up Nechaev, he chose to persist in his error, to continue to refer to the Committee, to believe, against all odds, that Nechaev could change his ways. Bakunin finally did produce a plausible, though psychologically shallow, explanation for his tolerance of Nechaev's naive Jesuitism:

> While denying your truthfulness and your rationality, I not only do not deny your energy and your unconditional devotion to the cause, but believe that with respect to both, few people can be found in Russia who are your equal; this, I repeat to you still another time, was

> the chief, indeed the only basis for my love for You and my faith in You—and to this moment I remain convinced that it is a guarantee that You more than all of the other Russians with whom I am acquainted, have the ability and the calling to serve the revolutionary cause in Russia—of course, only under the condition that You wish to and are able to change the entire mode of your activities in Russia and abroad.[82]

Bakunin's statement does not tell the whole psychological truth, but it does confirm Nechaev's extraordinary power to project passionate, self-effacing commitment. Somehow Nechaev could convince others that all of his Jesuitical, despotic methods, all of his self-glorification had only one end: the triumph of the people's cause.

Bakunin believed Nechaev to be a man of genuine passion and courage, a selfless man who could work without gloves in the "all-encompassing Russian filth";[83] and Bakunin knew that he himself could not do this. Bakunin's youthful idealistic Romanticism, his Hamletism, and their relationship to his personal development have been mentioned already. Suffice it to say that the materialistic Romanticism of his middle age was not merely a reaction to his Hamletism; it was a grotesque inversion of it, one consequence of which was a commitment—perhaps a desire—to take the filth as he might.

In his letter to Nechaev, Bakunin presented a set of conditions for their future collaboration. They amounted to a demand that Nechaev renounce his methods and organizational principles for Bakunin's methods (set forth in the letter) and program—the anarchist program of the first issue of *Narodnoe delo*. Nechaev would also have to clear Bakunin's reputation by revealing the truth about the Liubavin affair, by clearing up Bakunin's relationship to the Bakhmetev fund, and by abandoning any design to cooperate with Bakunin's archenemy, Utin. Bakunin had so completely put his reputation into Nechaev's hands that an immediate and complete rupture was impossible even if he could have mastered his fascination with Nechaev, which is doubtful. The maneuvers that followed in June and July led to a complete break, although Bakunin wrote what amounted to an apologia for Nechaev in a letter of June 20, 1870, addressed to the same group to which he had sent the letter containing his conditions to Nechaev.[84] The last negotiations occurred early in July, when Nechaev came to Geneva for discussions with Bakunin and Ogarev.[85] It appears that Nechaev made a final effort to subordinate Bakunin to him but this time failed.[86] Henceforth Bakunin was to act defensively. Nechaev's departure for England (probably in mid-July) signaled a complete break. After that time, Bakunin was willing to use some of Nechaev's own methods against him. In a letter of July 24, 1870, he asked his ally Valerian Mroczkowski (at that time in London) to try to steal back from Nechaev the letters Nechaev had stolen from him, Ogarev, and the Herzen family.[87] Semen Serebrennikov, who had broken with Nechaev, claims in his memoirs that Bakunin was ready to label Nechaev an agent provocateur,[88] but there is no evidence that Bakunin was willing to go further than sending warning letters to friends, telling them exactly what to expect of Nechaev.

In London, Nechaev discovered what Bakunin had done and immediately sent Bakunin and Ogarev a little note:

> Why, when we parted and you kissed me like Judases, did you not tell me you were going to write to your acquaintances? Your last letter to Talandier, and the warning to Guillaume about the danger of participating in a cause of which you have always been the theoretical instigators, are acts of the most dishonourable and despicable kind, committed out of petty spite. With total disregard of common sense and the interests of the cause you are bent on wallowing in the mire—well, then, wallow!
>
> Farewell[89]

However, this was not Nechaev's parting word. In an open letter to Bakunin and Ogarev dated August 1870, and printed in *Obshchina,* Nechaev had the gall to demand the remainder of the Bakhmetev fund, which he had calculated to be significantly greater than the sum given to him.[90] The open letter, obviously written in a more reflective moment than the note, impugned Bakunin's and Ogarev's motives and thereby cast doubt on anything they might say or write about him.

There is a long epilogue to the Bakunin-Nechaev relationship, but it belongs more to Bakunin's biography than to Nechaev's and will not be told here. It is the story of Marx's successful use of the Nechaev affair to discredit Bakunin and expel him from the International. As for Nechaev, when Marx learned from the published accounts of the trial of the Nechaevists that Nechaev had claimed to have belonged to a section of the International in Brussels and to have been sent by the section to Geneva, he saw to it that the General Council of the International publicly exposed Nechaev's lie in an announcement of October 14, 1871.[91] Nechaev had become a kind of pariah. Nonetheless,

Bakunin remained confident in Nechaev's passionate commitment. His letter of November 2, 1872, written to Ogarev more than two months after Nechaev's arrest, testifies to Bakunin's largeness of spirit and once again displays his capacity to protect his original conception of Nechaev.

> And so, old friend, the unheard of has come to pass. The republic has extradited the unfortunate Nechaev. Saddest of all, this will undoubtedly be the occasion for our government to revive the trial of the Nechaevists, and there will be new sacrifices. However, some kind of inner voice tells me that Nechaev, who has perished irretrievably and who undoubtedly knows that he has perished, on this occasion will call forth from the depths of his being—confused, soiled, but far from vulgar—all of his primitive energy and valor. He will perish a hero, and this time will betray nothing and no one.[92]

Bakunin's profession of faith is an appropriate epitaph to their relationship.

Nechaev's activities between his departure for London in July 1870, and his final return to Zurich in June 1872, can be faintly sketched, but the details are conjectural.[93] He spent about three weeks of his London period in an unsuccessful effort to involve himself in the Lyons uprising of September 1870. Nechaev's lack of confidence in European socialist leaders and the International, expressed in the lead article (untitled) of *Obshchina*, marked his participation in the Lyons uprising as well. There is undoubtedly more than a little pique in his attitude, since his efforts to establish ties with the leaders of European socialism were hindered by his notoriety. In Lyons he told a Polish revolutionary (who noticed that he carried a great deal of money with him) that he had lost confidence in the French revolution and refused to take part in it. Nechaev's interlocutor was impressed mainly by his bombast.[94] Before his departure from Lyons in early October, Nechaev left a letter, the contents of which are not known, and several copies of *Obshchina* for Bakunin. Then he left for Marseilles, presumably on the way back to London.[95]

Nechaev's life in London is a complete mystery. When he traveled to Lyons in mid-September, he carried with him a letter of recommendation from a London-based member of the International to Louis Palix, one of the Lyonnaise Bakuninists, but the identity of the recommender is not known. Some of the names and addresses in Nechaev's notebooks are those of Londoners, but given Nechaev's habit of keeping lengthy lists of this sort, one cannot attach any significance to the names. One can be certain that he did not know enough English (if, indeed, he knew any at all) to circulate freely. Vladimir Serebrennikov accompanied him to London to collaborate on *Obshchina*, and turned up in Paris in early August, probably on a commission from Nechaev. Peter Lavrov speculated in a letter of August 5, 1870, that Serebrennikov's presence in Paris might mean that Nechaev was in Paris as well but said nothing further on the subject in later letters.[96] Lopatin's comment to Lavrov, who had warned him to beware of Nechaev in England, is close to the mark: "I am completely indifferent to his fate; as for myself, I am not afraid, since these gentlemen abroad resemble bears whose teeth and claws have been pulled out."[97] Later, Lopatin reported that Serebrennikov had tried unsuccessfully to arrange a meeting with Marx for the purpose of gaining admission to the International. Marx followed Lopatin's advice, and in turn advised the General Council to be wary of Serebrennikov.[98]

Nechaev next tried to establish a base for his activities in Paris. His Paris addresses are known. He lived at rue St. André des Arts N° 56 and then moved to rue du Jardinet N° 5. While living in Paris under the name Stephan Grazdanowe, he may have tried to earn his living as a correspondent by writing about events in France for Russian newspapers.[99] In the spring of 1872 he tried to place articles about politics in *Birzhevye vedomosti* (*The Stock Exchange Gazette*, St. Petersburg) but was urged by an editor to send articles about Parisian cultural life instead.[100] Nechaev evidently pursued a similar course with *Nedelia* (*The Week*, St. Petersburg) in 1871.[101]

According to M. P. Sazhin, Nechaev had lived in Paris during the Prussian siege of the city and had left on foot sometime after the armistice of January 28, 1871. They first met in Zurich early in March. Nechaev and Sazhin spent nearly two weeks in close companionship. When Sazhin heard of the Paris Commune of March 18, he decided to go to Paris. He returned to Zurich after the destruction of the Commune—presumably some time after May 29, 1871—and found Nechaev still there.[102] Nechaev had gotten work as a sign painter, and lived on the outskirts of Zurich under his Serbian name.[103] Though Sazhin tried to help Nechaev make connections with the large Russian colony in Zurich, Nechaev's reputation frightened off most of them. Nechaev had not abandoned his old methods and managed to convince Ivan

Ponomarev, one of the Russian students there, to sign a contract with The People's Revenge, promising the usual horrible results if he failed to obey the Committee's dictates.[104] In addition, Sazhin got Nechaev in touch with V. N. Smirnov,[105] who had fled Russia and settled in Zurich during the summer of 1871. Nechaev revealed to Sazhin and Smirnov his calculations of the true value of the Bakhmetev fund and showed them excerpts from compromising letters that he had stolen from Bakunin, Ogarev, and the Herzen family. He planned to blackmail them in the event they refused to transfer the presumed sum to him.[106] Meanwhile, Sazhin had written to Bakunin and told him about Nechaev's efforts to establish ties. In a long reply Bakunin catalogued Nechaev's sins, firmly refused to act jointly with Nechaev, and told Sazhin, in effect, that he would have to choose between him and Nechaev. Sazhin and Smirnov immediately decided to break off relations with Nechaev and did so after reading him excepts from Bakunin's letter.[107]

Nechaev, however, refused to give up. The large colony of Russian, Polish, and Serbian students in Zurich proved to be the most fertile ground for his style of revolutionary activity. He found among these students several who would shelter him, defend him against his opponents, and even try to perpetuate—though not in precisely the same form—his centralist, conspiratorial mode of revolutionary strategy. During the course of 1871 Nechaev established ties with a group of Slavic students—predominantly Polish, but with Russian and Serbian members as well—who sympathized with the Jacobin-Blanquist tradition.[108] Members of this group later joined Petr Tkachev, who fled Russia in December 1873, and in 1875, created a journal in Paris devoted to the Blanquist strategy, *Nabat* (*The Tocsin*).[109]

Kaspar Turskii, a young man of Nechaev's age, the son of a wealthy Polish landowner, had begun his revolutionary activity in 1863, during the Polish uprising. After several years of schooling in southern Russia, and several arrests, Turskii escaped from the province of Arkhangel in 1869. In 1871, he fought for the Communards in Paris and settled in Zurich after the fall of the Commune. In Turskii, Nechaev found a kindred spirit, and if Nechaev had a direct heir, it was Turskii.[110] Another Polish student in Zurich, Karl Janicki, helped Turskii in his efforts to organize a Blanquist organization, first in Zurich and later in Russia. A Serbian student named Manuilo Hrvachanin also belonged to the group and might have been one of several people in Zurich who harbored Nechaev in 1871–1872.[111] Elizabeta Iuzhakova, a young Russian student of the natural sciences in Zurich, and another veteran of the Paris Commune, became one of Nechaev's close confidants. Around this nucleus, Nechaev hoped to revive his organization. During the autumn of 1871, they tried to organize a Zurich-based section of the International and may have tried to sneak Nechaev in under the pseudonym A. Dubov.[112] The General Council did not approve their application.

The circle that had formed around Turskii and Nechaev intersected with another, larger organization founded in May 1872—the Polish Social Democratic Association in Zurich. Turskii introduced Nechaev to the secretary of the organization, a Pole named Adolf Stempkowski, who also served as secretary of the Zurich section of the International headed by Hermann Greulich and, one should add, worked for the Third Section as well.[113] The enmities and mutual distrust of Slavs and Germans and the petty factionalism within the Slavic socialist community reflected the general malaise of the International in 1872. Nechaev, perfectly at home in this atmosphere, participated as fully as his situation permitted.[114] He moved back to Paris for the last two weeks of December 1871, and the early part of January and spent much of the spring of 1872 there before returning to Zurich in the latter part of June. His tiny faction had little time to develop before the Third Section tracked him down during the summer of 1872. The manhunt and capture will be described in the next chapter.

During his imprisonment, three of Nechaev's new associates in Zurich—Iuzhakova, Sazhin, and Ponomarev—learned from him the location of his "archive" in Paris. After a long search, Sazhin and Ponomarev retrieved it with the help of Peter Lavrov and the wife of Henri Brissac, the French socialist publicist and Communard, and brought the trunkful of papers to Zurich. A group of Bakuninists, including Sazhin, Zemfiri Ralli, Vladimir Gol'shtein, and Aleksandr El'snits, examined the documents. Among them they found some letters from Herzen to Ogarev, in which Herzen critically examined his own revolutionary career and revealed unpleasant aspects of his domestic life; Natalie Herzen's letters to Nechaev, which Sazhin returned to her; Ponomarev's and two other recruits' contracts with The People's Revenge; a number of letters, including several of Ivan Turgenev's; drafts of Nechaev's correspondence to *Nedelia;* a receipt from Bakunin to The People's Revenge for 500 rubles; and, in Bakunin's hand, a copy of the "Catechism of a Revolutionary." When Sazhin showed Bakunin the last document, the old revolutionary showed little reaction and had no comment. All of the materials in the Paris archive, except for Natalie

Herzen's letters,[115] were burned by Ralli, Sazhin, and Bakunin.[116] Evidently, Vladimir Serebrennikov kept some of Nechaev's papers and tried to sell them to Ralli for 400 francs—an interesting sidelight on the character of Nechaev's bosom companion—but Ralli took them from him by force. All of Nechaev's intrigues from more than two years were thus reduced to ashes, but the long and astonishing denouement of his career had just begun.

Chapter VI

Capture, Imprisonment, Death

The Russian government's pursuit of the elusive Nechaev between December 1869, and August 1872, remains unparalleled in the history of the Russian revolutionary movement. As months passed, his ability to keep at bay both Russian and foreign agents while conducting his revolutionary propaganda and agitation inspired alarm. Concern about the progress of the manhunt extended beyond the Third Section to several ministries and to the court itself. Eventually, the ministries of Justice and Foreign Affairs joined the Third Section in a series of complex maneuvers to ensure that once found, Nechaev could be captured on foreign soil and handed over to Russian justice. The Russian government's complex diplomatic and legal game occurred against a background of war and political upheaval: the Franco-Prussian War, the fall of Napoleon III, the Third Republic, the Paris Commune, and the disintegration of the First International. In a prison novel, Nechaev later dramatized some of these events, but peaceful Switzerland rather than revolutionary France was the stage for the main action of the drama of his pursuit and capture.

By December 16, 1869, the Russian police realized that Kuznetsov's and Uspenskii's depositions provided them with a basis for pursuing Nechaev as a common criminal—a murderer—and having him extradited on these grounds.[1] Police officials urged the government to establish diplomatic and police relationships that would simultaneously prevent Nechaev from crossing national borders and facilitate his extradition. In February 1870, Count P. A. Shuvalov, the chief of gendarmes, sent word to Russian ambassadors in Europe to take appropriate measures to apprehend Nechaev. The first Russian agent to pursue Nechaev abroad, A. F. Shul'ts, alerted the Prussian police and arranged for Nechaev's transfer into Russian hands should he be apprehended in Prussia. Colonel A. N. Nikiforaki followed Shul'ts abroad in February 1870.[2] K. F. Filippeus, a Baltic German from Courland with a distinguished military and bureaucratic past, proved to be the most zealous and creative of the Third Section officials involved in the case. Filippeus employed Karl-Arvid Roman as an agent provocateur, mainly in Switzerland, and Roman, having assumed the identity of a radical sympathizer of ample means and the name Postnikov, proceeded to ingratiate himself with Ogarev and Bakunin.[3] He believed that Bakunin was the key figure and never suspected that the sodden, absent-minded Ogarev could have led him to Nechaev. In April 1870, Roman made friends with Bakunin, a friendship that cost him more than a little travel and Filippeus and the Third Section several hundred rubles. Bakunin not only borrowed money from Roman; in August 1870, he sent him to the Bakunin family estate at Priamukhino carrying a letter in which Bakunin demanded his share of the estate and threatened to force its sale.[4] On September 28, 1870, Roman traveled from Geneva to Lyons at Bakunin's behest in the belief (inspired by Bakunin, who was evidently mistaken) that Nechaev had enrolled in a legion of volunteers to fight in the Lyons uprising.[5] The unfortunate Roman not only failed to find Nechaev, he found that Bakunin had been arrested and returned to Geneva. Two weeks later he himself was arrested as a revolutionary during a second trip to Lyons. Nechaev had indeed spent three weeks in Lyons between September 14, 1870, and early October, but the agent only learned about it after Nechaev had returned to London.[6] Word reached Roman about Nechaev's whereabouts from time to time, but always too late. After months of fruitless hunting, he gave up the search.

Filippeus, however, refused to accept defeat. In a report of January 19, 1872, to an unidentified higher authority (probably N. V. Levashev, second in command to P. A. Shuvalov, who was simultaneously head of the Third Section and head of the gendarmerie), Filippeus expressed succinctly the immediate anxieties of the Third Section:

> The interests of justice, extremely important in themselves, demand that the chief perpetrator of the crime not escape punishment. But aside from that, from the perspective of public safety and the personal security of the Emperor, Nechaev's agitational activity warrants extremely serious attention and it is necessary to end it, since it is capable of inspiring fantasies in young people, and it is impossible to remain

> confident that from among these fantasy-ridden youths another Karakozov will not come forth.[7]

Filippeus outlined what he would need to effect Nechaev's capture: utmost secrecy about the manhunt, with only the Emperor, P. A. Shuvalov, and (presumably) Levashev informed about the plan; a six-to-eight-month period in which he would not be rushed or asked for punctual progress reports; unrestricted credit up to 6,000 rubles, and no bookkeeping for 3,000 of them; the right to promise Russians and foreigners rewards (to a total of 6,000 rubles) for their services in the event of Nechaev's capture; permission for a three-week trip to Moscow and abroad to select agents, examine local conditions, and map out a detailed plan of action.[8] In retrospect, Filippeus's preparations—especially the proposed budget—seem quite modest. Budgetary constraints may well have helped Nechaev win more than two years of freedom.

There is surprisingly little information in the files of the Third Section about Nechaev's whereabouts in 1871—mainly rumors about his hiding places. In August 1871, for example, it was reported that he or someone resembling him was in the United States, on the West Coast.[9] Rumors circulated in the student underground that he was in Constantinople. In October, Nechaev's former employer, Iakov Garelin, reported that one of his workers had seen Nechaev in Ivanovo and that he had disguised himself either by dyeing his hair blond or by wearing a long, blond wig.[10] During much of 1871 Nechaev was in Paris, but there is no evidence that he was pursued by French secret agents until July 1872.[11] At about that time, Count Levashev and the Préfecture de Police—Levashev having been alerted by an agent in Switzerland that Nechaev was in Paris in June and was planning to leave for Zurich—arranged for two French agents to observe Nechaev in Zurich; for close surveillance of the Paris-Lyons railways; and for Nechaev's arrest and transfer to Russian agents in France, should he return there from Switzerland.[12] The French agents coordinated (though badly) their efforts with the Russian agent who organized the last, successful stage of the manhunt, Major Nikolich-Serbogradskii.

Nechaev did indeed return to Zurich by way of Basel in late June 1872, and entrusted himself to the care of the Polish revolutionaries there—mainly Turskii and Adolf Stempkowski.[13] Stempkowski and several other Polish émigrés worked in the paint shop of one Kafel, who employed Nechaev as a sign painter. In August 1872, the French agents in Zurich finally spotted Nechaev and provided their superior with a description of him.[14] Evidently, however, they had acted imprudently, for the Russian ambassador to Switzerland, Prince Mihail Aleksandrovich Gorchakov, who had replaced N. K. Giers in 1872, sent an urgent telegram to Paris to the Préfecture de Police to replace them.[15] Eventually, the Russian agents proved to be most effective when they were most liberal with bribes. The large colony of Slavic émigrés in Switzerland at last yielded an informer. A Swiss named Zega acted as go-between for Nikolich and Stempkowski. Although the Russian agent had been receiving information about Nechaev's machinations in the spring of 1872, he had never actually seen him. Zega reported to Nikolich that with Stempkowski's help he had seen Nechaev on August 5 twice, in two cafés in Zurich.[16] On August 8, Nikolich asked Gorchakov to inform St. Petersburg that they should send Kolyshkin, a police official who had interviewed Nechaev in January 1869, to identify Nechaev for the Swiss police. Meanwhile Nikolich offered Stempkowski 5,000 rubles in gold, and Stempkowski told him that he and Nechaev would be in the Café Muller at 1:00 P.M. on August 14.[17] Nikolich, who was known to the Swiss police by the code name Konevich, arranged an ambush with the chief of police in Zurich, J. J. Pfenninger. The Zurich police provided eight men dressed in civilian clothes under the command of Major Noetzli. Five of them staked out the café, while three others waited outside. Nechaev arrived at 2:00 P.M. and joined Stempkowski and two Swiss members of the International, Greulich and Remy.[18] While Nechaev sipped his beer, one of the Swiss police agents (Hangartner) approached him and asked him to come outside the café for a few words. Nechaev was barely outside when the other agents seized him and bound his arms. He called out to Stempkowski for help, and he, playing his role of comrade to the end, feigned intervention, while Greulich and Remy looked on. As they took him away, Nechaev shouted: "Tell the Russians that Liders has been arrested."[19] The police divested Nechaev of a six-shooter and a pocket knife.[20] Nikolich confronted him at the jail with these words: "Ah! Hello, Mister Nechaev, at last I have the opportunity to make your acquaintance at first hand." According to Nikolich, Nechaev blanched and said in Russian: "I don't understand you, dear sir."[21] To Pfenninger he said in French that he was Stefan Grazhdanov, a Serbian citizen, and gave his age as twenty-two. However, when Nikolich asked him a question in Serbian, Nechaev could not answer and lamely replied that he had lived in Russia for so long he had forgotten Serbian. In Russian, Nikolich told him that he had been arrested for Ivanov's murder.[22] Several months later, after Nechaev had been extradited, tried, and imprisoned, the Russian government, highly pleased, distributed generous rewards. Each member of Major Noetzli's convoy received one hundred Swiss francs, while Noetzli himself received 2,000.[23] Pfenninger, who played a significant role in both the capture and the extradition, received 4,000 Swiss francs.[24]

The Russian government used a combination of tough diplomacy and legal sleight of hand to achieve the extradition. As noted before, Russian officials had entertained the idea of extradition since December 1869. On January 14, 1870, Gerakov, who had interrogated Uspenskii and Kuznetsov in connection with his investigation of the Ivanov case, reported that he had determined that Nechaev had conceived the crime five days before it had been carried out.[25] The testimony of all four accomplices supported his finding. On this basis, Nechaev could be tried under paragraph three of article 1453 of the penal code of 1866—the ambush clause—which provided for loss of all civil rights and a sentence of penal servitude. The first paragraph of article 339 and article 350 of the Code of Procedures justified the pursuit of the criminal on foreign soil.[26]

Russian diplomacy came into play almost immediately after the discovery of the crime and Nechaev's flight. In February 1870, Giers, the Russian ambassador in Switzerland, began to test the idea of extradition with the president of the Swiss Bundesrat, Jakob Dubs. Dubs wrote to the chief of police in Geneva on February 17, 1870, and his attitude is summarized quite well in the following remark to Camperio: "It therefore seems highly desirable that this Nechaev not be found in Switzerland!"[27] During the first two months of diplomatic maneuvering, Dubs fought the idea of extradition, although he told Giers that Nechaev's presence on Swiss soil would not be tolerated.[28] During February, March, and April, Russian-Swiss negotiations were complicated by Nechaev's elusiveness. On February 21, 1870, Camperio reported to the Bundesrat that Nechaev had left Genevan territory ten days earlier.[29] In April, Russian pressures increased, especially after April 10, when Giers informed Dubs that Nechaev had returned to Geneva.[30] On April 1, Camperio had reported to Dubs that Bakunin had appeared in Le Locle and that Nechaev must be with him. Meanwhile, the Slavic émigré community had mobilized against extradition, and Nechaev himself wrote a letter to the Swiss authorities on April 20, 1870, asking for final resolution of the question of asylum for him. It was falsely postmarked London, and Ogarev transmitted it with his own accompanying letter to the Bundesrat on April 24.[31] On April 25, 1870, the Bundesrat instructed the city council of Geneva "to arrest Sergei Nechaev provisionally if he is discovered on your territory, then to interrogate him about the crime of which he is accused, about the circumstances in which it was committed and the motives which had dictated it, and then to send the stenographic record of that hearing to the Bundesrat."[32]

In May 1870, rumors once again began to circulate that Nechaev was in Geneva and Semen Serebrennikov's mistaken arrest there on May 9 gave the émigrés an opportunity to attack Russian-Swiss cooperation. After two weeks of confusion involving the Geneva police, the president of the Bundesrat, M. J. M. Knusel of the Department of Justice and Police, Giers, Ogarev, and several witnesses, Serebrennikov was freed. The Swiss historian of the extradition process aptly describes the last incident as a fiasco, and indeed, the definitive end of the early period of diplomatic testing.[33] Though Russian agents continued the manhunt, a hiatus on the official diplomatic front began in May 1870, and continued until the summer of 1872. Giers remained pessimistic about the chances for arranging the extradition through Switzerland, as he revealed in a dispatch of June 1, 1870, to Shuvalov. And since Switzerland, with its large community of political émigrés and growing Russian colony, was the most attractive field of action for a political fugitive, the prospects for apprehending Nechaev looked fairly dim.

However, by July 1872, Gorchakov had secured the cooperation of Swiss officials. In a secret telegram of July 29, 1872, he revealed that Emil Welti, who had succeeded Dubs as president of the Bundesrat, would vigorously support efforts to arrest Nechaev but that final action would rest with the cantons.[34] On August 11, 1872, Knusel told Pfenninger to go ahead with the arrest and to use "Konevich's" services. The arrest, as noted above, occurred on August 14, 1872, and it initiated a new series of legal and diplomatic moves.[35] Identification remained a problem for the Swiss, for they did not want a repetition of the Serebrennikov scandal. Nechaev persistently maintained his story that he was a Serbian citizen named Stefan Grazhdanov, despite the fact that Kolyshkin on August 17 identified him as the student Nechaev, who had been arrested twice in St. Petersburg in 1869 "for unseemly behavior in public and for the designated student disturbances."[36] Kolyshkin also presented a photograph. On the same day, in a written statement (in French), Nechaev denied any acquaintance with Kolyshkin, accused him of lying, and claimed that the photograph was not of him.[37] The authorities in Zurich, by now convinced that the man held by them had a falsified passport, nonetheless felt that they could not positively identify him as Nechaev by means of Kolyshkin's testimony alone and wrote to this effect to Bern. T. S. Stoianovich, one of the several Serbian socialist students who were connected with Nechaev, identified him as Stefan Grazhdanov, but on August 21 when shown a photograph of Nechaev denied that it was the student he had known in Belgrade. However, the Zurich investigators found that their captive's appearance matched the description of Nechaev published by the Prussian police in January 1870, and the scars on Nechaev's hand looked like they had been caused by bites. On August 26, Ivan Smolian, who had examined Nechaev in 1866 and worked with him in the Andreevskii parochial school in 1866 and 1867, told the Zurich police that Nechaev had been in a group photograph taken at the school. He identified the person in the photographs Kolyshkin gave to the Zurich police as Nechaev, even though when he had known him, Nechaev had been beardless, or virtually so. Eventually the Swiss Department of Justice and Police asked to see the group photograph and received it in early October. All of this evidence convinced them that the person they had arrested on August 14, 1872, was indeed Sergei Nechaev.[38]

Meanwhile, "Grazhdanov" stubbornly clung to his story. He refused to speak or write Russian and communicated in French with the Swiss authorities. Relying on the Russian émigré community to protect him, on August 18, he wrote to Pfenninger and requested that members of the Russian émigré community in Zurich who knew Nechaev personally be asked to identify him.[39] On August 19, he presented Pfenninger with his *vita*. He stated that he had been born near Belgrade and claimed to have learned several trades while traveling through the Balkans as a teenager (waiter, sign painter, and typesetter) and to have served as a tutor for the children of Russians living in Romania. He also tried to explain the stamps in his passport—which told a puzzling story about his movements after 1869, when the passport was "issued" in Bucharest.[40] On August 25 and 29, he wrote to Pfenninger again. In the letter of August 25, he appealed to Pfenninger's pride as a member of the Swiss republic who might protect an innocent person from the Russian imperial police and referred to the precedent of Serebrennikov's case.[41] In the other letter, he advised Pfenninger to ask Stoianovich to search for other Serbs in Zurich who might identify him, knowing, of course, that Stoianovich would produce them.[42] In short, Nechaev lied systematically as long as he thought there was some chance to escape being identified, and, with his usual manipulativeness, appealed to his captor's sense of compassion, authority, and justice.

During the second half of August, Gorchakov began to bring considerable diplomatic pressure to bear on Welti. On August 28, 1872, he wrote to Vladimir Il'ich de Westmann, who ranked second only to his own father, Aleksandr Gorchakov, minister of foreign affairs:

> This morning I transmitted to Welti a declaration authorized by his majesty the Emperor, and I have informed him categorically that if after that declaration extradition is refused under the pretext that the reading of the documents which have been asked for, and which I have promised, implicates [Nechaev] in a political crime, the Swiss will bear responsibility for the relations with Russia which will result. The Bundesrat, in view of the gravity of the situation . . . will examine these documents itself . . . and will not transmit them to Zurich unaccompanied by its conclusions and its advice. The final decision still depends upon the canton.[43]

The legal materials requested by Welti became the crux of the matter. The Bundesrat asked to see the prosecutor's charges and the judgment of the court against Nechaev's coconspirators, an awkward request indeed, for the documents would show that Ivanov's murder was only an episode in the history of the political conspiracy. It would be possible to evade the Swiss request by basing the Russian position on the absence in Russian criminal law of any provision for trying a criminal in absentia. Instead, the Ministry of Justice decided to send materials prepared for Nechaev's trial which, of course, would be carefully selected to separate the murder from the conspiracy and to make it appear an independently motivated act. Under the guise of strict adherence to the letter of Russian law, the Ministry of Justice would not send criminal charges, since they could only be made after a formal interrogation, but only the points to be raised during the interrogation. Finally, they would send the Bundesrat excerpts from the trial relating to the action of Uspenskii, Pryzhov, Kuznetsov, and Nikolaev. The legal strategy of the Russian authorities is contained in the following edifying passages of legal-bureaucratic prose:

> The dispatch of these documents has one goal—to convince the Swiss authorities of the justice of our views, that independent of the political crime, which we do not deny, Nechaev, by virtue of the murder of Ivanov, committed in addition a common crime, since the necessity of this murder did not issue exclusively from the demands of a secret political society founded by Nechaev, but rather the former was sooner guided by personal motives, enmity to Ivanov, in whom he saw a rival whose intellect and character were a threat to his personal

> position. As a pretext for the murder, Nechaev presented to his accomplices the suspicion that Ivanov intended to inform the government about the secret society; but this suspicion is not borne out either by the depositions of the accused and witnesses or by the actions of Ivanov himself, who, although disagreeing with Nechaev in many areas, did not separate himself from the secret society, and to the contrary, continued until the end to consider himself one of the chief members of the society, which is proven by the pretext by means of which Ivanov was lured to the fatal grotto, a pretext which he would not have yielded to if he had before this moment left the society.
>
> The juridical distinctness of the murder from the political conspiracy is proven moreover by the fact that in the investigation the former . . . was at that time examined by the investigator separately. The essential aspects of this investigation will be translated into French, and made accessible in the event that it is needed by the Swiss authorities.[44]

As noted earlier, the idea of separating the murder from the political conspiracy had emerged in December 1869, and both the investigation and the trial that followed had laid the basis for the strategy pursued in 1872. In September 1872, the minister of justice sent one of his own men to Bern to help Gorchakov explain the case from the point of view of Russian legal theory and practice.[45]

On September 11, 1872, Gorchakov transmitted the documents prepared by the Ministry of Justice.[46] It would be wrong to assume that the Swiss were dependent on the Russian government for their information. The stenographic account of the trial published in the summer of 1871 was available to them, and a group of émigrés—Ralli, El'snits, Gol'shtein, Ozerov, Gol'denberg, and of course, Bakunin—had sent the Bundesrat other excerpts from the trial, which emphasized Nechaev's fanatic devotion to his political and social cause.[47] Furthermore, the Swiss authorities had Nechaev's own propaganda barrage of February 1870. Nonetheless, on September 14, 1872, the Bundesrat accepted the Russian government's theory of the crime. Their reasoning followed these lines: Ivanov's opposition to Nechaev was not of a political nature; he did not betray the group; his murder had nothing to do with any political action, either before, during, or after the fact.[48] During Nechaev's detention, the Swiss authorities acquired sufficient evidence to convince them that he was indeed the man sought by the Russian government. In addition, Gorchakov formally declared that Nechaev would not be judged or punished in Russia for any crime except the murder. Finally, if the Swiss government complied with the Russian request and extradited

Nechaev, the case would be seen as a precedent for which the Swiss government could claim reciprocity.[49] The matter now rested in the hands of the canton of Zurich. Even more conclusive evidence that "Grazhdanov" was Nechaev—testimony of the Serbian minister of foreign affairs and the group photograph mentioned above—reached Bern on October 4 and 5, 1872, respectively, and the federal authorities transmitted it to Zurich. When confronted by Pfenninger with this latest evidence, Nechaev realized that the game was up and confessed his true identity.[50] However, he made one last attempt to save himself by trying to convince the canton of Zurich that he was indeed a political criminal.

On October 14, 1872, Nechaev wrote out a deposition in which he presented his version of his career. The deposition contains the only account in Nechaev's own words of his motives for killing Ivanov.

> Three months before that day [February 19, 1870, the target date for the revolution], on which we had hoped to attain our goal, the more than equivocal conduct of one of the members of our society named Ivanov came to our attention. From day to day, as we approached February 19, Ivanov exhibited more and more ill will. It was soon clear to us that his indiscretions of all sorts, his rejections of the rules of our society, in a word, all of his conduct, were inspired by the intention to harm our cause. It was also evident that he was only waiting for a favorable moment to break his ties with us decisively and would not even adhere to the fundamental commitment of an honest person: to be discreet.
>
> After long reflection, I and four of my friends who headed the society agreed that this man was preparing to betray us on the decisive day, and that it was absolutely necessary and inevitable either to rid ourselves of Ivanov, or to permit our entire organization to perish, which had been built up with so much suffering and sacrifice.
>
> Almost on the very eve of an uprising, when each of us was ready to sacrifice his life for our cause, we could not evade the issue which remained, that is to kill Ivanov. Five of us (I and four of my friends) arrived at this decision, as a purely political matter.
>
> But it was too late. The government already had been informed about the existence of the plot and the goals of its members. Two or three days after the death of Ivanov, the political police, suddenly and without any pretext, searched the house of Uspenskii, a member of the society, and there found papers which compromised the principal members. The searches and arrests which followed permitted them to discover the secrets of the plot. Our enterprise was aborted, and the arrested patriots were thrown into the cells of the fortress. A few were

> able to escape abroad, and for those few, among which I count myself, it has since become clear that Ivanov was nothing more than an agent of the political police, and that before his punishment he had succeeded in denouncing the society.[51]

There is no evidence to support Nechaev's claim that Ivanov was an undercover agent, but Nechaev understood very well that if he could convince the Swiss government that Ivanov was an agent, the Russian government's contention that Ivanov's murder was a common crime would become problematic. It would be difficult, if not impossible, for the Swiss government to violate its traditional hospitality to political fugitives without considerable embarrassment to itself.

The delay between the Bundesrat's unanimous decision for extradition, its sending of its recommendation and the legal documents to Zurich, the decisive identifications and Nechaev's confession, and the decision of the Zurich cantonal council alarmed Russian agents and caused Gorchakov to bring more pressure to bear on Welti.[52] Fears that Swiss internal politics might affect the final decision in Zurich, however, proved to be without foundation. Welti, Knusel, and Pfenninger evidently had sufficient influence in the canton to overcome resistance, and on October 26, 1872, Zurich voted to accede to the recommendation of the Bundesrat.[53] Gorchakov triumphantly informed de Westmann and sent as well a telegram to Count Adlerberg, minister of the court and aide to Alexander II, with the request "déposer ce resultat aux pieds de notre Auguste Maître."[54] The Bundesrat formally transmitted the decision of the canton of Zurich to Gorchakov and informed him that Zurich had concurred that Nechaev should be tried in Moscow for a common crime, the premeditated murder of Ivan Ivanov—and for that alone—and sentenced according to paragraph 3, article 1453 of the penal code of 1866.[55] Meanwhile, arrangements had been made with Swiss, Bavarian, and Prussian authorities for Nechaev's safe transport to Russia.

Students in Zurich loyal to Nechaev, others who had little to do with Nechaev but who bitterly objected to any extradition agreement, and sympathetic Swiss pondered several plans of action, including a jailbreak. Apparently they chose bribery. Two women, whose identities have not been established, reportedly bribed a warden with 200 Swiss francs. He revealed to them the time scheduled for Nechaev's transfer from the jail late on October 26, only a few hours before the transfer actually occurred. The young people who wanted to liberate Nechaev gathered before the jail shortly after dawn on October 27. A droshky drove through the gates and then another with Nechaev seated in it, bound and surrounded by gendarmes. They drove off at a trot toward the railroad station. The students ran alongside Nechaev's droshky and arrived at the station simultaneously with it. There, Nechaev and the gendarmes got out. Nechaev was hobbled, so that he could take only small steps. A young Serb came up to him and tried to pull him away from the gendarmes, but after a brief struggle the gendarmes separated him from Nechaev. The Serb was arrested and expelled from the canton the next day.[56] The convoy successfully transferred their prisoner to the coach. Thus ended Nechaev's life as an émigré.[57]

The Russian government had arranged with Austria for four Bavarian gendarmes to meet Nechaev in Lindau. He traveled in their company across Austria and Germany,[58] entered Russian Imperial territory at Verzhbolovo, and arrived in St. Petersburg on October 19, 1872, at 8:00 A.M. One hour later he was delivered to General Korsakov, commandant of the St. Petersburg fortress, who incarcerated him in one of the cells of the Trubetskoi bastion, where he remained until December 22, 1872. On that evening, he was placed aboard an express train for Moscow. There, Major Remer took him into custody and placed him in a special cell guarded by twelve gendarmes.[59] Throughout this period, Nechaev had been held incommunicado. His request of December 7 to talk to his sister Anna had been refused by the Third Section.[60]

In Moscow, Nechaev exhibited the obstinate pride characteristic of all his activity. He refused to admit to anything but a political crime. On December 28 he rejected the charges placed before him by two officials of the Moscow judiciary and waived his right to a defense attorney. He announced that he would not defend himself either, since the accusation was a slander.[61] When the officials placed the document containing the formal charges against him on a table in his cell, he picked it up and threw it on the floor. The guard in the cell picked it up, and Nechaev shouted: "Do you want me to throw it down again?"[62] He continued to resist all attempts by his captors to dignify the situation with the full regalia of legal procedure. On January 4, 1873, he was informed that he would be brought to trial on January 8, 1873, and was given a summons and a list of the judges and jurors. Once again he refused the documents, saying that they did not concern him, since he was not a Russian citizen but an émigré and did not recognize Russian law and that just as he had been seized by force in Switzerland and taken to Russia, he would have to be taken forcibly to trial.[63]

Nechaev's trial took all of five hours. It began on January 8, 1873, at noon in the Moscow District Court. Both Russian police agents and newspaper correspondents in the courtroom have left vivid descriptions of the trial. Nechaev entered the courtroom with his hands thrust arrogantly into his trousers pockets and immediately sat down on the criminal's bench.[64] When P. A. Deier, the presiding judge, asked him his name, he replied that before he answered the question he wanted to announce that he did not recognize the right of the court to judge him and that he would explain the reasons, if the court desired. Deier outlined the procedures for appealing jurisdictional questions and tried to continue, but Nechaev loudly proclaimed:

> Mr. Chairman, I am an émigré, I have ceased to be a subject of the Russian Emperor, the procedures of your judiciary have no meaning for me. (At this point Deier commanded the gendarmes to take him outside the courtroom, but Nechaev continued, now shouting.) I consider it a disgrace to permit judgment of my conduct . . . (The doors closed behind him.)[65]

According to the stenographic account of the trial, the public assembled in the courtroom shouted several times: "Out with him! Take him away!"[66] whereupon Deier called for order and threatened to clear the courtroom. In a written complaint of January 10, 1873, to Count Levashev, Nechaev claimed that he was led out because of the crowd's applause. When he was outside the courtroom, the gendarmes dragged him along a corridor and into an empty room, where he was punched and kicked in the back, although he didn't resist in any way—indeed remained completely cool (*khladnokroven*) throughout the ordeal—and did not permit the incident to change his behavior in the courtroom.[67] A report of January 11 gave the police version of what happened outside the courtroom. Nechaev put up a struggle, shouting all the while, and was able to free one of his arms, so that he almost reached the revolver of one of the gendarmes. With both of his arms immobilized, Nechaev resisted by refusing to walk and had to be dragged and pushed into the room, where they shoved him onto a bench. He was so enraged that the features of his face were distorted, and he only regained his composure when they gave him a drink of water.[68] An unsympathetic reporter from the *Moscow Gazette* described Nechaev's reappearance in the courtroom.

> A moment of tense expectation began. Ten minutes passed between the order of the chairman to bring the accused into the courtroom and his appearance, and that only tightened the nerves of the public even more. At last, accompanied by two gendarmes with naked sabers, the defendant appeared.
>
> He entered with his head thrown back and with an unnatural, mechanical gait, just like that of a bad melodramatic actor . . . . His appearance is in no way remarkable—such faces appear quite frequently among the dandier shopkeepers. Rather thick, but not very long chestnut hair combed straight back; narrow, deep-set eyes, with darting pupils; a thin little mustache with a gap under the nose and twisted ends; a scanty beard, turning into even scantier sideburns on his cheeks. Both the mustache and the beard are lighter in color than the hair on the head. A fairly regular profile, but at full face the broad forehead and prominent cheekbones give his visage a squarish aspect and a vulgar appearance.[69]

Deier asked Nechaev if he wanted to exercise his right to challenge any of the jurors. Nechaev shouted: "All of the formalities of the Russian judiciary mean nothing to me. (He was led out again, still shouting) I am no longer a slave of your despot! Long live the *zemskii sobor* (national assembly)!"[70]

Nechaev was tried by a jury of five merchants, two officials, one artisan, one honorary citizen (these were often wealthy merchants), and one peasant.[71] After Deier read the charges of the court, Nechaev (who had been brought back to hear them) shouted: "The killing of Ivanov is a purely political matter. It comprises a part of the conspiracy which was examined in St. Petersburg."[72] Before he could continue, the presiding judge once again ordered the gendarmes to remove him, but they brought him back during the cross-examination of the witnesses. In fact, the prosecution brought forward only one witness, a student at the Petrov Agricultural Academy named Mukhortov, who had been with Ivanov a few days before the murder, and whose hood Kuznetsov had borrowed—the very hood that had been used to bind Ivanov's legs. Nechaev refused to exercise his right of cross-examination and repeated his earlier position, that he did not recognize the right of the court to judge him; he turned his back to the judge and instead faced the public, assuming various arrogant postures—leaning his elbows on the table, sitting arms akimbo, twisting his mustache, and nibbling his beard.[73]

The main witnesses could not appear for the simple reason that they were all in Siberia, though it is not clear why several others, whom the prosecution named, could not be found. Instead, their depositions were read—that is, statements given in November and December 1869, and January and February 1870. The court heard no testimony about the conspiracy or Ivanov's character. Uspenskii's statement at the trial of the Nechaevists, which suggested that he himself had pointed the finger at Ivanov as unreliable, was not mentioned. After the reading of each deposition, the judge asked Nechaev if he had any objections, but each time Nechaev remained silent. The prosecutor Zhukov's summary took approximately an hour. He presented the decision of the Bundesrat and the canton of Zurich as evidence of Nechaev's culpability. Zhukov argued that under paragraph 3, article 1453 of the criminal code it was not necessary to establish the motive for the crime—only that it had been premeditated and carried out by the accused—in order to try the accused. However, the prosecutor pointed out that the Swiss authorities extradited Nechaev only after they had been convinced that the crime was not a political one.[74] Later, Deier argued that the crime *had* been motivated by personal enmity—because Ivanov held other views than Nechaev and was evidently more developed than he and might outdo him.[75] The prosecutor and presiding judge had to fulfill the terms of the extradition agreement, which complicated their task. On the other hand, since after December 1869, the investigation of the crime had been carried out with extradition in view, Zhukov and Deier could rely on depositions that issued from procedures and interrogations designed to separate the murder from the political conspiracy. Perhaps the most ironic moment in the trial occurred when Deier dismissed Nechaev's contentions that he could only be tried as a political criminal and that he could not be tried by a Russian court:

> The first of these objections is not worthy of consideration because if he considered himself a political criminal, then nothing prevented him at the moment when this event occurred, from remaining in Russia and . . . to be judged for that, which in his opinion, he had to be judged. But now he has deprived himself of the possibility of being judged as a political criminal, because, not having returned by his own free will, he was delivered to the Russian government by the Swiss government under the condition that he would be subject to trial only for that weighty crime with which he is now accused.[76]

The hermetic character of the legal situation cannot be better summed up. The more fundamental issues of politics, violence, and the law were not admitted into the courtroom.

As the trial neared its end, the chairman referred to the legal reform of 1864 and its accompanying slogan: "Let mercy reign in the Courts."

Nechaev at this point interjected: "But a gendarme officer beat me up!"[77] Deier hurriedly continued his instructions to the jury. When asked by the judge whether he had anything to say in his defense, Nechaev replied:

> I consider it degrading to my name to defend myself from a slander, which is obvious to everybody. All Russia knows that I am a political criminal. I repeat what I said to Count Levashev: The government can take my life from me, but not my honor.[78]

According to a police agent's report, when he pronounced these words Nechaev dramatically struck his breast.[79] The jury retired about fifteen minutes after this last incident and returned twenty minutes later with the verdict—guilty. Zhukov read the penalty: loss of all ordinary rights and twenty years of hard labor in the Siberian mines followed by permanent settlement in Siberia. Deier asked whether Nechaev had any objections and received the reply: "This is a kangaroo court."[80] After Deier repeated the sentence in its full form, described the procedure for appealing the case, and asked the gendarmes to remove the prisoner from the courtroom, Nechaev got in a last word: "Long live the assembly! Down with despotism!" According to the police agent's report, this evoked only laughter in the courtroom.[81] Perhaps the Russian authorities had learned something about managing the courtroom atmosphere since the trial of the Nechaevists; perhaps Nechaev's trial was anticlimactic after the mass trial of 1871; or perhaps there was a genuine lack of sympathy for Nechaev. His trial sped past the public, apparently without arresting its attention.

During his incarceration in Moscow after the trial, Nechaev wrote a lengthy complaint and self-justification to Count Levashev. As noted above, he complained of police brutality, giving his version of what had happened after he had been taken out of the courtroom the first time. But most of the letter of January 10, 1873, is devoted to Nechaev's political views. In effect, it is his appeal to the authorities and is worth quoting at length, not only for this reason, but because it represents a logical continuation of one aspect of the strategy he pursued after his second flight abroad—an attempt to appeal to constitutional, liberal sentiments.

I am writing to you, Count, and permit myself to think that the behavior of the gendarme officer will not be condoned by you. I hope that I will not be subjected to a series of such insults in the future which are as useless as they are disgraceful to their perpetrators. I permit myself in view of this fact to express to you, Count, a few general reflections. My fate has been decided, or is almost decided—I am going to Siberia, my words cannot be anything but truthful, and you, probably, do not have frequent occasion to hear the truth in your high position. The state post which you occupy permits you to see the condition of contemporary affairs. Leaving aside dreamers and the proponents of utopias, it is nonetheless impossible not to recognize that Russia at the present moment—*is on the eve of a political revolution.* Everywhere and always there have been in society adherents of well-known, more or less advanced aspirations of a radical, destructive nature, there were always petty conspiracies, insignificant plots—but before all of this only led to ferment in a few minds, and for this reason could be suppressed by repressive measures from time to time. Things are different now: aspirations have formed in Russia which are now inherent in the entire society—aspirations far more definite, more persistent, and therefore more possible of realization. Such aspirations inevitably accompany a given degree of social development. Just as a growing child inevitably cuts teeth, a society which has reached a given stage of education will inevitably experience a need for political rights. A government, even if is comprised of geniuses, can only restrain, slow down the realization of these aspirations a little (and doing that, risking its own overthrow), but it has not the power to destroy the political ideas taking root in society. In a word, Russia finds itself on the eve of a *constitutional* revolution. This is clear to any developed person, who works very little at it, but attentively follows the condition of minds.

I will not decide beforehand here the question, how will the reconstruction of the state occur—exclusively by revolutionary means, or by initiative of the government itself, which will decide to renounce absolutism? Perhaps, the very person who announced with respect to the peasant question that "liberation from above is preferable to liberation from below," will take upon himself the initiative for a reconstruction of the structure of state, if he succeeds in convincing himself in time, that it is impossible to stand against the power of a maturing society.

It is inappropriate here to analyze how feasible state initiative is. One thing is certain—no matter how this occurs, it will be impossible to avoid social upheavals. I am a son of the people! My first and chief goal—is the happiness, the welfare of the masses. Knowing from life experience the class of simple people both in Russia and abroad, I also know that any kind of social upheaval, no matter what its outcome, will not only harm the interests of the upper classes of society, simultaneously at the outset it will lay a heavy burden on the people. If, on the one hand, Razin and Pugachev sent the gentry to the gallows in Russia, and in France they sent them to the guillotine, then on the other hand, both there and here the mass of people fell under grape-shot, villages were burned and so on; destruction and annihilation—the inevitable fellow travelers of any revolution, at least, of those which history has shown us—staggered with equal force both the higher class of society and the crowd. The task of any honest government in this stormy century, given the inevitability of social disturbances, is to prevent, at the very least, the repetition of miseries, similar to those which accompanied the bloody rebellions of Razin and Pugachev. And these miseries will most certainly follow, if the wild arbitrariness and bestial measures of the administration are not ended. A government permitting such measures plants the seeds for future revolutionary terror, it sharpens the blade for its own head. When political ideas find an echo in the farthest corner of the Russian land, then the cavaliers of the law of the fist can only zealously serve the government ill—they will heighten the malice in the mass of discontented people, who even without that are inflamed with passion.

Let the government deceive itself with the hope that the stormy days are still far off. Let it invent superficial reforms and hope by them to divert public attention. Society has already awakened and will soon demand an accounting. There may be in Russia naive people in state service, for whom any kind of social movement seems to be the result of a conspiracy of twenty or thirty agitators; there may be those who hope to stifle the new ideas by repressive measures, instead of standing under the banner of these ideas, leading society along the path of progress and receiving blessings instead of curses. Undoubtedly, among those who govern the great Russian people there are still many persons who hold to the saying of Louis XV: "Après nous le déluge." But for everyone without exception it must be clear that any kind of repression will evoke bitterness, create new enemies and that aimless barbarism is harmful, absurd, meaningless.

The émigré, Sergei Nechaev, transformed by Mr. Mezentsev from a political criminal into a common criminal.

I go to Siberia in the firm belief that soon millions of voices will repeat this cry: "Long live the National Assembly!"[82]

The letter to Levashev is extraordinary in several respects. It shows quite directly how Nechaev connected the history of the French revolution, and particularly the Terror, with the Russian tradition of brigandage, and how he tended to deceive even while revealing some of the truth. Everything we know about Nechaev tells us that he anticipated violence and destruction with relish and, rather than seeking to avoid them, exhibited extraordinary inventiveness in finding ways to provoke them. He detested liberal constitutionalism and the idea of reform from above. One need only turn some of the ideas around to see Nechaev's real position. He wanted to lead the gentry to the guillotine and the masses to the grapeshot. The patent attempt to manipulate Levashev by appealing to whatever liberalism Nechaev sensed in him (after a face-to-face interview in St. Petersburg before Nechaev's transfer to Moscow for trial) and by implying a distinction between him and barbarians like Mezentsev is a shrewd tactic. Finally, there is a certain rhetorical niceness about the combination of ideological self-justification, accusation of the authorities, largeness of spirit and vision, and wounded patriotism and personal dignity. While ostensibly a complaint about police brutality, Nechaev's letter is an apologia pro sua vita as well. It is only the beginning of his psychological sparring with his captors. There is some possibility that the letter affected the treatment he received as a prisoner.

The problem immediately facing Russian officials was the ceremony of public disgrace which, according to article 963 of the criminal code, had to be announced publicly. General Slezkin wanted to withhold the announcement and feared that the formal procedure, including transporting the prisoner through populated streets, might lead to serious disorders.[83] The governor general of Moscow, Prince V. A. Dolgorukov, in a note of January 19, 1873,[84] assured the gendarmes that order would be maintained. On January 25, 1873, at 8:00 A.M. Nechaev was placed in a cart. As they tied his hands to it, he shouted:

> "When they lead you to the guillotine, then I'll tie the straps on you. I go to Siberia in the firm conviction that millions of people sympathize with me. Down with the Tsar, down with despotism! Long live freedom! They've made me, a political criminal, a simple murderer! The new Russian judiciary is a disgrace. It's not a court but a crooked card game."

The drummers in the convoy tried to drown out his words, but he shouted so loudly that some of those accompanying him were visibly affected: "Down with the Tsar, he drinks our blood!" When he reached Konnaia Square and the pillory he refused to hear the traditional priestly exhortation and shouted: "There will soon be a guillotine here, and here they'll cut off the heads of those who brought me here!" After they tied him to the pillory he shouted with all his might, while turning from side to side: "Down with the Tsar! Long live freedom! Long live the free Russian people!" According to the official reports, he shouted in vain. Few people watched the ceremony, during either his trip to the square or the ten minutes he was pilloried. Someone in the crowd shouted: "He's got to be mad. Why not hang him right now?!"[85]

Actually, Nechaev was closer to the truth about Russian justice than even he knew on January 25. While officials of the judiciary did not know that the trial and sentencing were a charade, the Third Section and the Tsar himself were aware that Nechaev would not be sent to Siberia, but rather imprisoned in the Peter and Paul Fortress in St. Petersburg. After he read a report from General Slezkin describing the ceremony of public disgrace, Alexander II wrote:

> After this we had every right to try him again in a criminal court, as a political criminal, but I suppose that this would do little good and would only arouse passions, and therefore it is more prudent to imprison him *forever* in the fortress.[86]

Although it is not possible to determine exactly when the decision was made to violate the terms of the extradition treaty, there is no evidence that preparations were ever made to send Nechaev to Siberia. The decision is not difficult to understand. Escapes from exile, even from distant Siberia, were not infrequent, and a man of Nechaev's cunning and pertinacity would have been difficult to watch. The authorities took the prudent path. On January 26, 1873, Nechaev was placed in a special coach by Major Remer and six gendarmes. They did not go directly to St. Petersburg but took the Moscow-Brest line to Smolensk, Vitebsk, Dinaburg, and Tsarskoe Selo before arriving in St. Petersburg on the night of January 28. Nechaev was delivered to General N. D. Korsakov, with the instruction that the prisoner's identity was to be a strictly guarded secret. Nechaev became No. 5—the number of his prison cell in the Alekseevskii ravelin of the fortress on the island in the Neva River.[87] There was only one other prisoner in the entire ravelin, and his insane shrieks could be heard in Nechaev's cell.

More than fifty years ago, a prominent Soviet historian discovered a mass of materials that revealed the Third Section's extraordinary curiosity, even solicitude, about their prisoner. At first they received weekly bulletins about his health, both psychological and physical, his attitude —indeed, all aspects of his behavior. The reports tell us that Nechaev ate three meals a day: a light morning tea, a heavy dinner at midday, and an evening tea at 6:00 P.M. The budget for Nechaev's provisions went up from fifty to seventy kopecks a day—a quite respectable expenditure in Russia of that time. He wore his own clothes instead of a prison uniform. At first he had permission to read only the books and journals from the prison library. By early February he was begging the prison authorities for books and writing materials. He said that he was accustomed to intellectual work and would lose his mind if not permitted to exercise it. On February 9, 1873, the authorities received a request for eight books, among them John Stuart Mill's *Political Economy*, Solov'ev's *History of Russia*, and Louis Blanc's *History of the French Revolution*. Count Shuvalov refused him only Blanc's book and gave Korsakov permission to purchase books for Nechaev.[88] The prisoner claimed that he wanted to write a book about state law.

The first serious clash between No. 5 and the prison authorities occurred on February 19, 1873, when Nechaev refused to eat a Lenten meal and asked for the usual fare. In addition, he made some antireligious remarks, for which he was reprimanded, but nonetheless received what he asked for. The next incident occurred on March 14, several days after a change in the gendarmes assigned to guard him. He threatened to go on a hunger strike unless he could to talk to Korsakov. On April 1, 1873, he threw a chair at a gendarme officer and began a hunger strike which lasted from April 1 to April 5. Nechaev reputedly said that the Tsar was to grant a constitution and that he would be freed. He also threatened suicide.[89] The reasons for his behavior are not clear, although the changes in personnel that occurred at that time and possible dissatisfaction with the quality of his meals have been suggested. On April 4, 1873, he received medical attention and was given medicine regularly for an extended period.[90] As time passed, his behavior returned to normal. Beginning March 8, 1873, he received writing materials, which were brought to him every day at 9:00 A.M. and taken away after supper. Nechaev's insatiable appetite for reading material is evidenced in his requests for more books. Count Shuvalov sent him his own copies of *Revue des deux mondes* for 1872.[91] The only change in Nechaev's routine (it should be noted that he could take daily walks in the prison garden) occurred on October 2, 1873, when both prisoners in the ravelin were transferred for one day to the Trubetskoi bastion because of the danger of flooding.

After 1873, the commandant of the fortress ceased to issue regular bulletins about Nechaev's condition and behavior to the Third Section. One was issued in 1874 and one in 1875, and the only noteworthy fact in either is that in June 1875, Nechaev wrote a statement of his political goals to Alexander II which, however, was not passed on to him and has not survived. But on January 30, 1876, having just passed the third anniversary of his solitary confinement, Nechaev wrote a letter to Alexander II that was delivered. It is a voluminous letter, filling six folio pages (eleven sides).[92] In it, Nechaev asked the Tsar to review his case and presented the legal reasons the Russian court lacked jurisdiction over him. He also gave his version of what had happened in the courtroom, and the statements he attributes to himself are quite close to the stenographic record. In his letter, Nechaev emphasizes Deier's peremptoriness, which he explains was the cause of his own rude posture in the courtroom. He also explains his reasons for not exercising his right to appeal the decision of the Moscow District Court to the Court of Appeals of the Senate; they are the same reasons he had given for not accepting the jurisdiction of the Moscow court. It is clear from the letter that Nechaev was not aware of the details of the extradition agreement between Russia and Switzerland, nor that the Russian government had violated it by incarcerating him in the fortress. Nechaev had expected—or hoped—that the Swiss would eventually repudiate the extradition and had waited patiently, but after three years had abandoned these hopes and decided to ask Alexander II to review his case. He stated his terms for what he considered to be a fair trial:

> I, Nechaev, now as then in 1873, am prepared to recognize myself as a defendant not only in a Russian court, but even in a Turkish or Chinese one, if only there is prior observance of all of the legal conditions called for by public law:—if the government of the Swiss republic, on whose soil I was arrested, will take upon itself direct judicial responsibility for the correct outcome of the trial—that is: to announce to me beforehand (in the presence of an official of the Russian embassy)—on what bases and on what conditions they are extraditing me to Russia, and to supply me with a copy of its decision with respect to this—a copy formally attested to by the seal of the republic and the signatures of the appropriate members of the government.[93]

Nechaev shifts the blame from the Russian to the Swiss governments and courts—another attempt to manipulate by playing off one authority against the other and by appealing to the compassion, self-respect, and pride of his immediate oppressor:

> I remain in the isolation of a cell, in expectation of the decision of Your Imperial Highness with respect to this question, with hope for

the possibility of justice in my fatherland, in the second half of the nineteenth century.

A prisoner, by virtue of the illegality and scandalous arbitrariness of the Swiss oligarchs, languishing for the fourth year in a cell in the Peter and Paul Fortress.
The émigré
teacher Sergei Nechaev[94]

In a postscript, Nechaev asked permission to see his family.

General A. L. Potapov, who replaced Count Shuvalov as chief of the Third Section in 1874, replied in the name of Alexander II on February 7, 1876:

> His highness the Lord Emperor commands that he is pleased not to act on the request and to prohibit the criminal Nechaev from writing and to take from him what he has written up to the present moment and to examine them, but not to prohibit his reading.[95]

Nechaev's papers were seized, examined, and used as the basis for a psychological analysis by an anonymous official.[96] The report is one of the most interesting documents about Nechaev for two reasons: It describes, even if only in outline, Nechaev's prison writings, and it attempts a psychological analysis based mainly, if not entirely, on these writings. Nechaev had written in several genres: "letters" from London on the aims of modern democracy; other political reflections; personal reminiscences about his own activity; a memoir on the student movement of 1868–1869, which the official described as especially interesting; the novel "Georgette," which has already been described; another novel describing the student and émigré environment; recollections of Paris (the fall of the Second Empire); some literary sketches of the Paris Commune and the First International; a segment of still another novel describing his travels; and a short piece called "Milovzorov's School," describing the brutality of the Russian elementary schools. Nechaev had also accumulated a mass of notes on other writers' works, reflecting his ambition to master French, German, and English, as well as his interest in political and social questions. The inspector was impressed with Nechaev's achievement as an autodidact, but also remarked on the bilious resentment that pervaded the writings—the self-made man's resentment and hatred of the privileged. Nechaev trusted only people like himself and refused to admit that any others could truly serve the people. What is especially interesting, Nechaev recognized that violent upheaval caused reaction—his own study of history had evidently brought home that message—yet he believed in the inevitability and desirability of the total annihilation of the old system, leaving the task of reconstruction for the future. In addition to this seeming ambivalence, the inspector found in the writings Nechaev's tendency to deceive—perhaps even to deceive himself—about the motives for his actions by twisting the facts. The inspector's summary remarks are the most incisive:

> A tendency to revel in the contemplation of the force of his own loathing for all well-to-do people, the deliberate development in himself of instincts whose soundness and legitimacy he has not verified, that drive him to an almost blind hostility to the existing order—these are all features of one who is a revolutionary not by conviction but rather by temperament, as the author—not without a certain amount of satisfaction—admits to seeing himself. Perhaps the author is indebted to them for some of the influence he exerts over people who are even less cultured and less accustomed to take a critical view of their own opinions. But of course, these features would not increase the respect of an impartial person for the author—even the respect that one cannot deny a talented enemy.[97]

Nechaev's "blind hostility" to power, wealth, and authority overcame at moments the manipulativeness he cultivated in himself. Unquestionably, he assumed that the powerful and privileged were depraved and that any means of struggle against them were legitimate. The inspector, however, did not realize that Nechaev's rage was not channeled against the upper classes alone, but might burst out against his own comrades. Indeed, Nechaev's uncontrollable rage led to dire consequences in the ensuing months.

On February 9, the new regime began. When he received word on that day about the Tsar's decision, Nechaev uttered one word: "*khorosho*," which can be translated as "very well!" The inner anguish and rage he felt burst out at 4:00 A.M., when he broke the twelve panes in the window of his cell with a tin mug. The guards seized and straitjacketed him and tied him to his bed. The next morning they removed him from the bed, but he remained in the straitjacket until the morning of February 14.[98]

This, of course, was not Nechaev's first outburst of violence. As noted earlier, he had thrown a chair at a gendarme officer in April 1873. According to his own account, the general drift of which was later confirmed by V. K. von Plehve, during 1875 Potapov had visited him with the purpose of eliciting information about the revolutionary underground—just as Levashev had done, so Nechaev claimed, in 1873—and when Nechaev insulted the government, he threatened him with corporal punishment. Nechaev responded with a slap which drew blood from Potapov's nose and mouth. Potapov, a military officer with a distinguished record and a former Cossack Ataman, evidently replied with the comic gesture of falling on his knees and thanking Nechaev, but did not punish him. However, the outburst of February 1876, inaugurated a new period in Nechaev's imprisonment. On February 20, 1876, he was transferred to a cell with an iron grille in the window frame and put into chains.[99] This is his own description of his punishment:

> His hands and feet were put into heavy shackles, and the chains tying these shackles together were purposely shortened, so that the prisoner was bent into the shape of a yoke and could not stand up straight nor lie down fully stretched out, and so was forced to sit hunched up; for two years he dragged fetters; his hands and feet were covered with ulcers; he grew weak, death could only liberate the victim from the hands of the butchers, but the butchers didn't want to part with their victim, and the fetters were removed from Nechaev, but then only so they could threaten him constantly with new ones.[100]

Nechaev became the Avvakum of Peter and Paul Fortress.

The authorities' version has it that the foot fetters were removed on May 21, 1876. The act of generosity may be attributed to the new commandant of the fortress, Baron E. I. Maidel'.[101] Nechaev also regained his privilege of walking in the garden. However, his arms were still shackled, and he suffered from running sores. Perhaps more important, he now had access only to the books and journals in the prison library—materials he had already read repeatedly. In December 1877, Maidel' informed Mezentsev, who had replaced Potapov as head of the Third Section in 1877, about Nechaev's wounds. Mezentsev in turn informed the Tsar, and on December 14, 1877, they removed the shackles.[102] By the end of 1877, Nechaev's physical situation had returned to the status quo ante bellum.

The authorities, evidently fascinated with the idea of converting Nechaev, decided to place religious books in his cell. The campaign began in March 1878. On March 29 Nechaev found eighteen religious books and pamphlets in his cell when he returned from his walk in the garden. This drove him into a fury, expressed mainly by rapid pacing about the cell and jerky motions. He told the commandant that he was not a believer and would not be hypocritical, yet his guards informed the commandant that the books had been moved, and that Nechaev evidently was reading them.[103] (Later, it was discovered that Nechaev used religious arguments to convert his guards to his cause.) He continued to demand books, and the new commandant finally asked permission for a monthly book ration for Nechaev. From 1878 to 1880 A. R. Drentel'n headed the Third Section. Under his regime Nechaev received limited quantities of books, but not nearly enough to sustain him, and Drentel'n did not restore his writing privileges.

Drentel'n's appearance in 1878 followed the assassination of Mezentsev by Sergei Kravchinskii on August 8, 1878. The head of the Third Section had been stabbed in broad daylight on the streets of St. Petersburg. Mezentsev's assassination was only one of a series of attacks on officials conducted mainly by members of the revolutionary underground, who, during 1875–1876, began to organize into the first durable and effective revolutionary organizations—Land and Freedom and, after 1879, The People's Will. The first attempt on the life of an official had been carried out by Nechaev's former associate—Vera Zasulich—on January 24, 1878, against General F. F. Trepov. Gradually, the revolutionary organizations shifted their emphasis from "self-defense" to "disorganization" and finally to political terrorism. The move to a political strategy was the last step in a decade-long development in the revolutionary movement of the 1870s, an evolution that broadly repeated the phases of development of the nihilist 1860s: that is, a period of development or preparation, in which the revolutionary vanguard assimilated the latest "scientific" theories; a period of propaganda and agitation—in the 1860s expressed mainly through the idea of popular enlightenment and in the mid-1870s through the extraordinary "Going to the People"; and finally, a period of Jacobinism, in which a handful of committed revolutionaries, who wanted to give history a push, organized political conspiracies. However, it was the logic of commitment and failure—not a revival of Nechaevism—that underlay the reappearance of the centrally organized political conspiracy. Indeed, the idea of returning to Nechaevism repelled the leaders of The People's Will. Their attitudes had been formed after the full extent of Nechaev's deceptions and his ruthlessness within the movement itself had become common knowledge.

A prominent Soviet novelist, Iurii Trifonov, has written a historical novel about The People's Will based on a thorough reading of the historical documentation. He has imaginatively reconstructed a meeting held in Voronezh on June 24, 1879—the turning point in the evolution of Land and Freedom into a party devoted to political terror. Several members express fear of *Nechaevshchina*, but they are assured that the conspiracy will not be turned against the members of the organization itself. The doubters drag up all of Nechaev's sins:

> What do we have in common with that filthy deceiver and extortionist? To say this is to admit a total lack of understanding about the Russian liberation movement! He deceived the dying Herzen! He blackmailed Ogarev! Vera Zasulich has told about his unscrupulous swindles. Bakunin repudiated him! . . . He killed an innocent man! The revolutionary Jesuit! Everything he did came out of Machiavelli's *The Prince*.[104]

Yet as the novel unfolds, Nechaev's arguments are reiterated by the leaders of The People's Will:

> History moves too slowly, one needs to give it a push. A seizure of power is such a push. We act for the people. And as representatives of the people we will give them a constitution and a National Assembly.
>
> For the people! Isn't this *samozvanstvo* (pretendership)?
>
> No, because we are the flesh of the people. We—are the children of peasants, surveyors, priests, junior officers, the children of former slaves, emancipated serfs . . .
>
> Oi, Boris, how you love to make pretty speeches!—Ol'ga grimaced:—You ought to be a preacher, not a revolutionary.
>
> But revolution is preaching.[105]

The final discovery of the convergence of their general strategy and Nechaev's occurs toward the end of the novel, after they have received a note smuggled out of the fortress by a guard friendly to Nechaev. The time is January 1881, more than a year after the Executive Committee of The People's Will has decided to kill Alexander II. All of the methods for killing the Tsar discussed in Ishutin's "Hell" and by Nechaev and his followers have actually been tried: They have mined the railways and blown up a train; they have smuggled dynamite into the Winter Palace and set off an enormous explosion; they have been involved in three attempts on the life of the Tsar since November 1879. Now, unexpectedly they discover that Nechaev is alive and imprisoned in the Peter and Paul Fortress. Should they try to help him escape? All of Nechaev's past sins are discussed, but even those to whom the term "*Nechaevshchina*" is anathema agree that he should be helped. Andrei Zheliabov, the head of the terrorist organization, shocks his group by pointing out that they have moved quite close to Nechaev's position.

How!

What are you saying?

Present evidence! Such accusations cannot be thrown around idly!

Sirs, we are in the process of fulfilling the program of the "Catechism." There it was stated that the revolutionary has to penetrate everywhere in every layer of society, in the mansion of the nobleman, in the military world, in literature, in the Third Section, and even in the Winter Palace. I remember it quite well, because at the time it shocked me and seemed like such a fairy tale. Now we know that it was not a fairy tale at all, everything has been carried out: we have infiltrated the military, literary circles, we have an agent near the Chain Bridge [in the offices of the Third Section] and had one in the Winter Palace!

Taras [Zheliabov], can you kill a person?—asked Vera [Figner].—Not a traitor, not a spy, not an enemy, but simply—because his death gives you some kind of power?

What do you mean some kind of power for the killer? Suppose it's for the general good? Suppose—you get power and with its help put the world in order? Aren't we going to get together on some Sunday soon to execute the Tsar, but he—is not a spy, is not a traitor, is not a personal enemy. But we hope to acquire some kind of power over history by his execution, to reverse the course of Russia's fortunes. We are killing for the sake of Russia's welfare! In this one finds all of the tragic complexity; we dream about peaceful progress, and we are forced to kill, we strive for a national assembly where people can be convinced by words, but we ourselves are making bombs, in order to convince them by means of dynamite.

Just a minute, you're comparing different things; the killing of poor Ivanov and the Tsar . . . —Vera alone weakly protested. The men remained silent.

Different in magnitude. The same model. We also began with senseless murders; some Gorinovich, some fool of a Geiking . . . But if

> Sergei Gennad'evich were not in the ravelin today, he would be sitting with us and his hands would be as black from dynamite as Grisha Isaev's.[106]

Only Nechaev's peculiar motivations and indiscriminate abuse of his comrades distinguish him from the terrorists of the late 1870s and early 1880s. Ultimately, his goals and methods do not seem very different from theirs, but an uneasy feeling about Nechaev remains. Dostoevsky expressed it in his *Diary of a Writer,* when he said that he could conceive of himself as a Nechaevist in his youth, but could never have been Nechaev. Camus distinguished Nechaev from the revolutionary terrorists who followed him—*les assassins purs.*

> From their earliest days they were incapable of justifying what they nevertheless found necessary, and conceived the idea of offering themselves as a justification and of replying by personal sacrifice to the question they asked themselves. For them, as for all rebels before them, murder is identified with suicide. A life is paid for by another life, and from these two sacrifices springs the promise of a value.[107]

Yet at another point he seemed to find a way of joining Nechaev to the tradition of creative rebellion:

> Yes, the ancient value lives once more, at the culmination of nihilism, at the very foot of the gallows. It is the reflection, historic on this occasion, of the "we are" which we found at the termination of our analysis of the rebel mind. It is privation and at the same time enlightened conviction. It is this that shone with such mortal radiance on the agonized countenance of Doris Brilliant at the thought of him who died for himself and for tireless friendship; it is this that drives Sazonov to suicide in prison as a protest and "to earn respect for his comrades"; and this, again, which exonerates even Nechaev on the day when he is asked to denounce his comrades by a general, whom he knocks to the ground with a single blow. By means of this, the terrorists, while simultaneously affirming the world of men, place themselves above this world, thus demonstrating for the last time in our history that real rebellion is a creator of values.[108]

Nechaev's melodramatic gesture in 1875—the Potapov incident (somewhat exaggerated by Camus)—had little to do with a spirit of comradeship. It was, rather, an expression of Nechaev's pride, which he was as likely to express with violence against his own brothers—to use Camus's phrase—and which he would in any case justify in the name of the cause. But Nechaev undoubtedly had been preparing himself for martyrdom all the while. As we shall see, Nechaev's fascination with and final resort to symbolic rather than direct action places him within the tradition of Camus's *les assassins purs*. Camus was perhaps closest to the truth about them when he noted in passing their "nostalgia for the supreme sacrifice."[109]

Nechaev's appearance near the conclusion of Trifonov's *Impatience* may seem a somewhat contrived way of raising the fundamental issue of terrorism—whether one can justify taking another person's life in the name of some greater good. But although Nechaev's miraculous re-emergence into history by way of a message conveyed from the Peter and Paul Fortress is indeed an excellent opportunity for Trifonov, in fact the novelist was accurately reporting actual events. Nechaev had gradually won over his guards, and during much of his imprisonment lived a double life—an underground life, as it were, even while in the custody of the Third Section. He carried on a two-front struggle at first: against the higher officials—Korsakov, Maidel', and the successive chiefs of the Third Section—and against the watchdogs immediately around his cell. Eventually, Nechaev got from his guards what Mezentsev and Drentel'n refused—additional reading material, pen and ink, and even tidbits to augment his satisfactory but austere diet. The struggle against the higher officials also yielded results. As noted earlier, Drentel'n had given Maidel' permission to give Nechaev a monthly ration of books. Maidel', in fact, had argued that this was a better way to maintain security, for he had discovered that Nechaev had scribbled messages in library books, which circulated in the fortress. On October 14, 1878, Ol'ga Natanson, the wife of Mark Natanson, and like him a member of Land and Freedom, was imprisoned in the fortress—though not in the Alexeevskii ravelin—for two and one-half years. She found Nechaev's messages in prison library books.[110] It is not clear why she was not able or did not choose to get word of his presence to others, but it did not matter a great deal whether she did or not, for Nechaev got word out with the help of his guards seven months after she was removed from the fortress in May 1880.

In April 1880, Nechaev requested new books and a catalogue from which to select them. He received instead eight books of the authorities' choosing, and on April 12 returned all of them, saying that he had already read several and that the others were so insubstantial they were not worth reading. On April 13, he was deprived of the right to read new books and journals.[111] According to the prison bulletin, he broke into tears and fasted for an entire day. When given tea, he took the teaspoon and scratched a message in the ocher covering the walls of his cell. It was addressed to His Imperial Highness the Lord Emperor Aleksandr Nikolaevich. The message contained Nechaev's second known threat of suicide.

> Lord,
>
> At the end of eight years of solitary confinement, the Third Section without any grounds in my behavior deprived me of the last essential activity, the reading of *new* books and journals. Even General Mezentsev, my personal enemy, did not deprive me of this activity when he tormented me in chains for two years. In this way the Third Section condemns me to unnerving idleness, to inactivity which destroys reason. Taking advantage of the diminution of my strength after many years of suffering in prison, it pushes me directly onto the terrible path of madness or to suicide.
>
> Not desiring to suffer the horrible fate of my unhappy fellow prisoner, whose insane howls do not permit me to sleep at night—I inform You Lord that the Third Section, a Chancellery of Your Highness can deprive me of my reason only together with my life, and not otherwise.
>
> Palm Sunday, the year 1880 Sergei Nechaev[112]

Nechaev began a hunger strike on April 13 for the purpose of getting new books and journals but abandoned it on April 18, stating that his life was too precious to society. Evidently, the hunger strike worked. On April 19, Count Loris-Melikov visited the ravelin and promised Nechaev new books and journals.[113] On that day an order came through for ten books in French and German and a catalogue of French books. Having won this battle, Nechaev renewed his requests for writing material. Maidel' proposed that he be given a slate and slate pencil. When he received them early in May 1880, he immediately sent back a message to the commandant. The commandant had petitioned the Third Section only for permission for Nechaev to receive new books and catalogues. Nechaev now hoped to restore full writing privileges through Maidel' 's intercession. He wrote:

> In setting forth my request for permission to use new books and journals, I asked Your Excellency to petition about the possibility of granting me the opportunity to study seriously and to read systematically works in philosophy, history, and politics. But such reading

can only be fruitful if excerpts can be taken from scientific works and notes from the readings; if it does not please the Third Section to procure for me writing materials, which Count Levashev permitted me to use during the first years of solitary confinement, then I request, at the very least, permission to have a notebook, in which I could enter the briefest, most essential notes as references for the further study of serious literature.

A week ago I received the work of a philosopher, Professor Lange's *Histoire du materialisme* and other writings numbering five volumes—and yesterday, May 3, they sent me a slate and slate pencil!

While expressing sincere gratitude for the excellent works of Lange—permitting me to hope that in the future I will be able to use not only new books, but journals, about which I spoke with Count Loris-Melikov—I ask your excellency to inform the Third Section that I am returning the slate which was sent to me to the inspector of the ravelin, as something quite useless to a person in my position, which would remain in my possession without the slightest use.

Please be assured, general, of my deepest respect to you

Sergei N.

4 May 1880[114]

Maidel' did not encourage the higher authorities to yield to Nechaev's newest request, and Nechaev went back to writing with a spoon on the walls of his cell. Nechaev insisted that Loris-Melikov had promised him freedom to select books from the catalogues but that only three or four of his selections were sent each month—not enough to keep him occupied for more than a week. Nechaev described it as "unbearable torture" to remain idle during the long summer days, and asked General P. A. Cherevin, second in rank to N. K. Schmidt in the reformed security police (reorganized under Loris-Melikov's "dictatorship of the heart"), to send him the periodicals for 1879 that Cherevin had evidently promised him. The request was dated July 21, 1880. Despite Maidel' 's willingness to support Nechaev in his demand for new books, the prisoner remained discontented after a delivery at the end of July. On August 25, Nechaev, having been supplied with pen and paper for the purpose of listing selections from catalogues, once again complained, this time to Baron Johann Velho, director of the state police. In his letter he reiterated his complaints about the murderous idleness that threatened to ruin his physical condition and drive him mad and renewed his requests of April, May, and July. The authorities did not yield.[115]

Nechaev's campaign during the spring and summer of 1880 was evidently a smokescreen. It appears that all the while friendly guards had been smuggling newspapers and writing materials into his cell. All of

Nechaev's talk about isolation and idleness were evidently deceptions, as was the extreme humility of his communications in 1880. The story of Nechaev's proselytizing of his guards emerges from the investigations and trials of 1882. Behind it lay the surprising laxness of the inspector of the Alekseevskii ravelin, Colonel Filimonov, whose wife and eleven children received more of his time and attention than his duties did. Gradually, Nechaev broke down the guards' resistance to communication. Once having gotten both gendarme officers and common soldiers to break the rules, he found it possible to make them feel like accomplices in a conspiracy and even to threaten them. When he had gained a large enough following, the converted guards kept the others in line. Nechaev's skill as an actor and his talent at psychological manipulation served him well. He exploited religious and family feelings. He played upon his guards' sense of inferiority for their lack of education and development. The concept of martyrdom worked as well within the walls of the fortress as it did in the universities. Nechaev told his guards that he was suffering for them, for their fathers and brothers, for truth and justice. They were ignorant and, like obedient watchdogs, carried out the commands of their exploiters. But people like himself on the outside would lead a *bunt* which would overthrow all authority; the land would be taken away from the landlords and divided equally among the peasants; the factories and plants would be given to the workers; and Russia would have an elected Tsar, just as in more advanced nations, such as France.[116] In other words, Nechaev prophesied a communist republic.

The events of 1879 and 1880—Aleksandr Solov'ev's attempt on the life of Alexander II, the explosion on the Moscow-Kursk railway, the explosion in the Winter Palace—provided Nechaev with external evidence to support his contention that a revolution was near. Furthermore, he used every concession made to his welfare or comfort by the prison authorities and the Third Section and the occasional visits by high-ranking officials—especially that of Loris-Melikov in April 1880—to convince his guards that he was protected by persons within the court itself who sympathized with the revolution. Thus, he used not only arguments about social revolution, but appealed to the inside knowledge all capital dwellers had of a historical past of court intrigues. Nechaev's conspiratorial methods within the fortress very closely resembled his earlier modus operandi, although it was impossible to realize the organizational forms of 1869 in the fortress. He retained an extraordinary capacity to subject people to his will. He still adhered to the principle that tasks should be divided up among the conspirators and that each man should have limited contact with the others and limited knowledge of the others' roles. Having gathered piecemeal an enormous amount of information from each guard about the others in his organization, he used this information to impress them. The newspapers evidently provided him with enough knowledge of current events to permit him to make shrewd guesses about the trajectory of the revolutionary movement, which enhanced his mystique among the guards. Finally, the authorities inadvertently provided him with the opportunity to make contact with revolutionaries on the outside.

The first member of the revolutionary movement with whom he made contact was Leonid Mirskii. Mirskii had shot at Drentel'n, at the time chief of the Third Section, on March 13, 1879, and had been imprisoned in a different corridor of the Alekseevskii ravelin on November 28, 1879. Nechaev established ties with him through the guards.[117] But the turning point in Nechaev's career in prison did not occur until November 1880, when Stepan Shiriaev was imprisoned in cell No. 13 of the ravelin. Shiriaev was a member of the Executive Committee of The People's Will. On November 19, 1879, he had set off the eighty-pound charge of dynamite buried under the tracks of the Moscow-Kursk line in a southern suburb of Moscow, in hopes that the explosion would take the life of Alexander II, who was presumably aboard the train. He was not. Shiriaev had been tried in October 1880. Through him Nechaev learned how to contact the Executive Committee, which persisted in its efforts to assassinate the Tsar. The inside man was Andrei Grekhov, and his first outside contact was E. A. Dubrovin, a medical student who lived near the fortress. Although Dubrovin belonged to another revolutionary faction, *Chernyi Peredel* (Black Repartition), he contacted G. P. Isaev, a member of the Executive Committee. Vera Figner recorded the moment of Nechaev's resurrection in her memoirs:

> One January night, during a frigid spell, at 10:00 P.M. Isaev arrived home all covered with hoar-frost. Doffing his overcoat and hat he came over to the table where I and two members of the Committee sat, and having placed before us a little scroll of paper, unemotionally said, as if there was nothing extraordinary in it: "From Nechaev, from the ravelin." From Nechaev, from the ravelin!

Figner had been nineteen years old in 1871 when she had first heard of Nechaev, and in the intervening years his name had evoked mainly the indelible impression formed by the gruesome and tragic murder story. When N. A. Morozov had raised the question of a secret, central organization within Land and Freedom at the Voronezh meeting in

1879, she had opposed it because it resembled Nechaev's mode of behavior. But now, what impressed her most was the calm dignity of the letter before them. It was a straightforward request for help.

> This letter produced an astonishing impression: the entire black stain besmirching Nechaev's personality disappeared: the spilled blood of an innocent person, the extortions, the theft of compromising documents with the aim of blackmail—everything that had developed under the motto "the end justifies the means," all of the falsehood which had surrounded Nechaev's revolutionary image. There survived a rational faculty, undimmed by many years of solitary confinement; there survived a will, unbowed by all the weight of the penalty laid upon it; energy, still not exhausted despite all of the failures in his life. When Nechaev's request was read at a meeting of the Committee, with unusual emotion we all said: "He must be freed."[118]

During the next few months, Nechaev smuggled out a considerable quantity of information. He described the methods he had used to acquire his influence and transmitted detailed information about the fortress. He told the story of his imprisonment and sent copies of his pleas for judicial review to the authorities. He regaled the *narodovol'tsy* with lurid stories of brutality within the walls of the fortress. All of the old rhetoric, undiminished in intensity, reappeared—now inscribed in tiny hieroglyphs on little scrolls of paper about an inch wide.

Above all, Nechaev sent directions: how to handle the soldiers in his organization (keep them busy, don't let them drink too much, reward them moderately); where to set up conspiratorial nests on the outskirts of St. Petersburg near the factory districts; how to bring about and conduct the revolutionary dictatorship after Alexander II's death.[119] Nechaev's feverish revolutionary vision had survived nine years of imprisonment. He picked up where he had left off, but now there was a genuine Committee. Nechaev had armed soldiers under his command, and The People's Will had its own military organization. The Executive Committee had before it as the first order of the day the assassination of Alexander II. Under the circumstances, the question of Nechaev's liberation had to be put off. No matter! His escape from the fortress would be a relatively simple maneuver. At one point he had planned to seize the fortress during a visit of the royal family to the chapel on the island. Odd though it may seem, a short distance from the moldy walls of the ravelin rose the gilded spire of the chapel, which contained the marble sarcophagi of Peter the Great and the Russian rulers who had followed him. Nechaev would imprison the royal family and declare a coup d'état. He planned to revive the ancient Russian political tradition of pretendership. A. P. Korba-Pribyleva claimed that Nechaev had two additional plans: In the garden of the fortress there was a cast-iron cover to a drainpipe, which debouched on a bank of the Neva, just above the water. Nechaev would get into the pipe while guarded by his faithful. Zheliabov went to inspect the place where the pipe emerged; he feared that Nechaev would suffocate—the pipe was quite long—and the plan was abandoned. Alternatively, Nechaev's helpers would acquire a disguise for him with the help of the Executive Committee of The People's Will. The soldiers would escort him to the gate. Once outside, the Executive Committee would also supply transportation, a passport, money, and refuge.[120]

While these plans were being discussed, the Executive Committee was working on the tunnel from their shop on the Malaia Sadovaia. According to Lev Tikhomirov, one of the only members of the Executive Committee still at large in 1883, the Executive Committee told Nechaev that they could not arrange both his escape and the assassination of the Tsar and gave him the choice. He wrote back: "Forget about me for the time and get on with your business, which I will follow from afar with the greatest interest."[121]

Some, if not all, of Nechaev's last manifestoes and appeals—what one might call the unpublished proclamations campaign of 1881—have survived in the archives of The People's Will. Tikhomirov published long excerpts from some of Nechaev's appeals requesting a review of his case, shorter excerpts from other communications, and a brief summary of some of Nechaev's manifestoes in the first issue of the *Vestnik Narodnoi Voli* (*The Messenger of the People's Will*) in 1883, but the documents themselves were never published. They are undated and unsigned, and the original coded versions have disappeared, but they are unmistakably Nechaev's work.[122] Their contents reveal that most of them were written after March 1, 1881—that is, after the assassination of Alexander II—and at least one of them was written after Alexander III's famous proclamation of April 29, 1881, in which he reaffirmed the principle of autocracy. In his last proclamations, Nechaev expressed with singular ferocity his wholehearted devotion to the Jacobin tradition of revolutionary terror. Life in prison had only whetted his appetite for revenge. All of his earlier fraudulent claims about struggle with the dark forces and police brutality had come true. He had, as it were, earned his revenge. In addition to the proclamations and manifestoes Nechaev wrote several revolutionary songs or poems, most of them with the imprimatur of the

Executive Committee, but some with that of the Great National Assembly or the Committee of Public Safety (*Komitet Obshchestvennogo Spaseniia*).

Nechaev's plans for a revolutionary dictatorship and his unregenerate savagery are nowhere more clearly set forth than in these last bizarre proclamations, and they warrant lengthy quotation:

> For the greater success of the leadership of the cause of the great, holy struggle, a Council of Ten is chosen which in the name of the Committee of Public Safety will utilize the sovereign power of a revolutionary dictatorship for the decisive overthrow of the imperial yoke, until the complete liberation of the people. The new Committee will have one goal: the success of the revolution and victory over imperial despotism. It will pursue this goal by all paths and means, not showing scruples about the choice of means, not stopping because of the number of those sacrificed. It will answer for its activity before the court of its contemporaries and posterity.
>
> The Committee of Public Safety will transfer its terrible power only to the Constituent Assembly of the representatives of the liberated people at the decisive victory and triumph of the revolution and the complete destruction of the existing political structure.
>
> All of the remaining members of the Ex. Com. not belonging to the Council of Ten, equally with all members of the party—henceforth will be unconditionally subordinated to all of the instructions and directions of the Com. P. Saf. and its plenipotentiary commissars in the provinces. All the members of the party who have placed the interests of the general revolutionary cause higher than any other consideration, will provide the highest example of stern civic discipline and self-sacrifice.
>
> Long live the revolution![123]

The members of the Executive Committee of The People's Will who read Nechaev's proclamations in 1881 reprimanded him for his unscrupulousness about means, while he took them to task for their unwillingness to exploit the position they had won by their successful campaign of political terror. He called for deception—for exaggeration of the Committee's resources by two orders of magnitude.[124] Nechaev's fundamental technique of deception had always been exaggeration. His new colleagues, however, were in control of their conspiracy, and they resisted any resort to charlatanism.[125] Nor did they approve of Nechaev's penchant for elevating superheroes to dictatorial positions. Nechaev suggested that Zheliabov become revolutionary dictator,[126] though one wonders how long that improbable situation would have lasted with Nechaev at large. In a proclamation headed "The Executive Committee to Russian Society," Nechaev wrote:

> Citizens! During days of stormy social upheavals, when the people overthrow decrepit political forms and create a new political structure, it sends forth from its womb into the struggle the brilliant [but hitherto] hidden strength of giants, who leave behind themselves a brilliant, radiant path of history and whose activity surprises posterity.[127]

To paraphrase Trotsky's prophetic remarks about the Bonapartism inherent in the emerging Bolshevik faction of the Russian Social Democratic Labor Party, the party is replaced by the Executive Committee; the Executive Committee is replaced by the Council of Ten; and the Council of Ten is replaced by the Dictator. The last has at his disposal an all-powerful Committee of Public Safety—which seems to be nothing other than a new mechanism of political and social control similar to the dread security police of other systems. And what would the first Dictator's radiant measures be—what would be the first tasks of the Committee of Public Safety? Nechaev left little to the imagination in his proclamation "After the Major Act of Terror ("*Posle Krupnogo Fakta Terrora*")—from the Committee of Public Safety!" It is addressed to the inhabitants of St. Petersburg, Moscow, Odessa, Warsaw, Kiev, Khar'kov, Kazan', and the other great cities of the Russian land. Nechaev wanted to establish a secret revolutionary tribunal, which would be ready to go into action after a popular uprising. It would prepare for the "fatal night of decisive retribution." The tribunal would judge traitors to the revolution and would be responsible for summary retribution against all enemies of the people. It would hand down only two sentences: acquittal or death.

> For the execution of the decisions of the tribunal, there will be subordinated to it a *druzhina* [an armed body] of revolutionary avengers. The tribunal will issue its sentences in absentia [of the accused]; the execution will occur publicly and openly in especially important cases, when the political considerations of the Committee call for it. In the majority of cases for speed and ease the carrying out of retribution will occur secretly, and all of the signs of natural death will be arranged (the latter condition especially calls for the advice of medical experts and the officials making up the documents pertaining to the death, in order to avoid contradicting the wishes of the tribunal).

> All advance notice and warning will be abolished, the Tribunal will punish suddenly and unexpectedly.[128]

Who would be punished? All enemies of the people—traitors, spies, supporters of the Tsar, all who directly or indirectly helped the police uncover revolutionary activities or hunt revolutionaries. Special lists of all people hostile to the revolution would be read on public squares to the "agitated worker population." There they would be beaten by the enraged mob. Nechaev ended this singularly bloodthirsty proclamation with an exhortation to merciless revenge: "All of the inveterate enemies of the people are inevitably, implacably, unavoidably doomed to perish. The scythe will cut its swath of their heads and will not offer mercy for gray hairs or feebleness. Long live the revolution!"[129]

The central position of revenge in Nechaev's revolutionary vision is appallingly evident here, as is his chronic love of deception. The element of deception is, however, more vivid and direct in other proclamations and manifestoes. In the instructions accompanying "A Manifesto on Land and Freedom" issued by the Great National Assembly, Nechaev exhibits a plan to exploit the religious fears of the villagers. Messengers would be sent to the villages—undercover agents. Anyone who gives them away to the police or officials

> will be put to death cruelly, as a traitor to the Russian Land . . . and will be as accursed of the Lord God as a betrayer as Judas was, with all of his kind until the ninth generation, and such a traitor and informer will suffer great tortures on this earth, darkest hell, in fiery Gehenna and neither his children, nor his grandchildren, nor his great grandchildren will pray for his soul.[130]

Nechaev lavished great care upon the physical design of the "Manifesto," issuing the *narodvol'tsy* meticulous instructions about the printing of the text, the use of gold letters, and the kind of seal to affix to it. Localities where faith in the Tsar was still strong would receive in addition "A Secret Ukaz of the Most Holy Ruling Synod to the Priests of all the Churches in Russia." The ukaz would tell the priests that God had seen fit to subject Russia to a great trial. The new Tsar Alexander III had suffered a mental affliction and was reduced to imbecility. A statement in Alexander III's name (in accordance with the counsel of his beloved spouse, Maria Fedorovna and the insistence of his beloved brother Vladimir Aleksandrovich, and the princes, magnates, ministers, generals, and the entire gentry class) would order the reinstitution of serfdom, and where there were no landlords, the sale of peasants in the public market to the Jews, the proceeds going into the Tsar's treasury; extension of the term of military service to twenty-four years; the destruction of all Old Believer churches and places of prayer, the persecution of all sectarians, seizure of their property, their expulsion to distant monasteries or Siberia, or in the most extreme cases, execution.[131]

Nechaev had special proclamations for the armed forces whose fundamental message was that the Empress was in control and that Russian soldiers would be treated as they had been in the reign of Catherine II. He named prominent generals as Maria Fedorovna's lovers.[132] In an address to the Cossacks, Nechaev appealed to the tradition of Pugachev and Razin, and indeed to the Time of Troubles, when the Cossacks sat Tsars upon the throne and removed them at will.[133]

In these proclamations, Nechaev tried to evoke the historical memory of the Russian masses—memories of rumors about court intrigue, durable oral traditions about great historical upheavals, deep anxieties about the return of the bad old days, or stubbornly persisting hopes for a good Tsar who would give all the land to the people. There is almost a total absence of developed ideas in the manifestoes and proclamations. Only one, "To Russian Workers, Factory and Plant, Town Artisans and Craftsmen," refers to the International.[134] It is a genuine socialist agitational piece, with a six-point program for popular government and socialism, but Nechaev's radicalism is true to itself, one suspects, when it is at its most primitive. It is difficult to measure Nechaev's commitment to any positive program. Hatred for the existing order seemed to overwhelm all other motivations, and revenge to take precedence over reconstruction. As usual, Nechaev directed his agitation toward specific groups and designed it to evoke their most basic anxieties. This was especially true of the proclamations to the peasants and the armed forces—the groups most crucial to any foreseeable revolutionary upheaval in Russia. The gratuitous appeal to anti-Semitism in the proclamation to the peasants and the attempt to manipulate the soldiers' masculine pride by rumors of a return to the sissified uniforms and hair styles of the time of Catherine II (not to mention the attempt to cast Maria Fedorovna as Catherine) were Nechaev at his primitive worst. The Executive Committee, however, was in no position to further Nechaev's schemes, even if it had decided to yield to his Jesuitism.

Zheliabov was arrested on February 17, 1881, and Perovskaia on March 10, 1881. Both had in their possession coded notes from Nechaev. The note found among Zheliabov's papers contained character sketches of several of Nechaev's guards and suggestions about the best way to exploit their special talents. Yet the authorities did not connect the code names to the soldiers in the fortress. Even more extraordinary, the note found in Perovskaia's possession contained the real names of two of Nechaev's accomplices of 1868–1869—Aleksei Zubkov and Aleksei Kapatsinskii—yet the authorities did not connect them with Nechaev.[135] It is clear now that the arrests that began in March 1881, and the general paralysis of the revolutionaries which followed the assassination of Alexander II ended any possibility of realizing the plans for Nechaev's escape. There was nothing implausible about the plans, given Nechaev's organization within the fortress, his knowledge of the terrain, and the resources available to The People's Will (before the assassination of Alexander II). According to some accounts—accounts that inspired Trifonov to create a night visit by Zheliabov to Nechaev in the fortress—Zheliabov had actually spoken to Nechaev. Figner dismisses the idea in her memoirs.[136] In any event, as noted earlier, the Executive Committee had agreed to help Nechaev escape once they had assassinated Alexander II. Only the breakdown of The People's Will and the simultaneous change of regime within the fortress itself changed Nechaev's position.

After an interruption of communication in April 1881, Nechaev described the measures introduced in the fortress by General I. S. Ganetskii, the hero of Plevna in the Russo-Turkish War who had become commandant after the death of Baron Maidel' on March 20, 1881. Nechaev evidently wrote two letters—one to Alexander III and one to The People's Will, the second a copy of the first—complaining of Ganetskii's measures. The letter to Alexander III, according to Nechaev's testimony, was written by means of dipping a nail in his own blood. It should be noted that at the end of Maidel' 's regime Nechaev had enjoyed a good diet, books, and one-hour walks twice daily in the prison garden, in addition to the newspapers and journals, writing material, food and money smuggled to him by his organization within the prison and The People's Will. He had practiced a disciplined routine of reading, writing, and physical exercise. The letter to Alexander III—written before the collapse of Nechaev's organization—was therefore a subterfuge designed to dramatize what was presumably an intolerable situation. There can be no doubt that there was a decline in the quality of food. Ganetskii also deprived Nechaev of his walks for several months and cut down Nechaev's time in the garden to twenty minutes when the walks were restored. In addition, he had the windowpanes in the cell painted over to prevent any daylight from entering.[137] Nechaev complained bitterly about all these conditions, but the most interesting parts of the letter review the period before Ganetskii's arrival:

In 1875, when the government proposed that I state my views on the situation—in a detailed note to his majesty I announced to your most august parent, that absolutism had outlived its time, that all of the bases of an absolute monarchy had been decisively shattered, and that only by giving a constitution might the autocratic will preserve Russia from the horrors of revolution. I said that the immediate introduction of liberal, representative institutions in our dear fatherland could prevent the development of internal troubles and bold assassination attempts, which would stop at nothing. I said that after a few years it might be too late. The course of events during the recent period has confirmed my speculations. A reaction after the catastrophe of March 1 was inevitable. That is in the nature of things . . . but the dimensions of the reaction and its continuation can also only be inevitably fatal for the existing order, if the officials of the state during such a tense period spend their time hitting people who are already down. Already the victim of the greatest judicial injustice, I was judged by the Moscow district court in complete violation of the basic formalities of legal procedure. They not only refused me the defense attorney whom I had selected, they did not even give me a copy of the charges, so that when I entered the public courtroom, I did not know what the accusation against me was. In order to attain the sentence from the jurors (all commanded by the prosecutor) they literally did not permit me to speak—and no sooner did I open my mouth in order to give my explanation, then they dragged me from the courtroom at a signal from the judge and into the corridor, where the gendarme officers struck me in the head—until I lost consciousness. Having sentenced me to penal servitude for twenty years on the basis of the unsubstantiated accusations of the prosecutor, despite the real evidence known to all Russia, the court granted me, evidently, the right of appeal. In reality they deprived me of any possibility of exercising this right, not having given me a copy of the sentence and having forbidden me the pen and ink with which I might write a complaint. Having been conducted secretly during the night, straight from the scaffold [pillory] (in a roundabout way, having traveled all over half of Russia) to the Peter and Paul fortress, I was buried alive in the walls of the Alekseevskii ravelin, where, imprisoned in solitary confinement in such exceptional circumstances, I do not expect any mitigation of my fate on the part of the new government, and will not be surprised if this letter still further worsens my position. Louis XVI also only understood all of the horrible suffering of the prisoners of the Bastille when he himself ended up in the state prison. But since

> nowhere in the world has the arbitrary power of the representatives of the administration reached such dimensions as in Russia, and since in no other country is the will and desire of the head [of the government] distorted to such a degree as it is here . . . I considered it my duty to bring to the attention of your highness the aggravation of the conditions of my prison life, without any cause on my part. Now any further oppression will occur with your royal knowledge, by virtue of your royal will. I will endure without a murmur every kind of arbitrariness as soon as I know that I am subjected to them by the instructions of the higher authority. But, to be a victim of the inhuman arbitrariness of his excellency [Ganetskii] and remain silent . . . I cannot.[138]

The letter represents still another of Nechaev's attempts to rewrite the history of his case. For example, in his earlier descriptions of the beating outside the courtroom he had claimed only that he had been kicked and beaten in the back—not beaten senseless. Unless the government documents are falsifications, Nechaev had refused to examine the formal charges and had disdained the court's formal procedures. More interesting still was Nechaev's resort to a barely veiled threat—Alexander III could hardly avoid the implications of the reference to Louis XVI. In view of the fact that Nechaev was simultaneously writing proclamations and manifestoes that he assumed would bring down the Tsarist state, the letter must be seen mainly as a deception and partly as theatrical self-indulgence. There is no evidence that it ever reached Alexander III.

Nechaev smuggled his last communications out of the fortress between the late spring or summer of 1881 and October or November of the same year. Isaev, one of Nechaev's main links with the Executive Committee, had been arrested on April 1. After a break in communications, Savelii Zlatopol'skii became Nechaev's intermediary and, presumably, the person who would arrange his escape, but he himself left St. Petersburg for Moscow in October 1881.[139] The last writings, aside from the proclamations and manifestoes, were mainly descriptions of the horrors of prison life. He described the prison diet in a note smuggled out during the late spring or early summer:

> under the name of soup they give you plain water most of the time, slightly adulterated with a handful of flour without any kind of fat, and instead of the pound and a half of meat prescribed by the regulations, they throw in little pieces of horsemeat, as tough as shoe leather.[140]

In a number of stories, Nechaev dwelt on the depravity of the prison staff—not only the petty graft at the expense of the prisoners' diet—but outright sadism. Just as the last proclamations represented Nechaev's revelations of his real revolutionary plan, the last prison stories make explicit the masturbation phobia and other sexual messages in his earlier rhetoric. They had been veiled (sometimes thinly, as in the expression "mental onanism") in their earlier variations mainly under the guise of an appeal to the young to break out of their isolation, their fantasizing. Now the prison doctor, G. Vil'ms, joined the Tsar as the embodiment of depraved authority. The situation of the young prisoner, Nechaev implied, was only an extreme case of the position of the younger generation in an authoritarian society.

> One [of the prisoners] developed a disease of the testicles. The shamelessness and insolence of the doctor achieved repulsive, terrible dimensions. "For such ailments I'm not going to waste medicine. Take care of it yourself! Masturbate. D—— more often in the K——" The sick man was dumbfounded at this unexpected nastiness; but the doctor laughed contemptuously, and on the way out added: "You're afraid of softening of the brain or madness? Sooner or later that's what will happen—for you there's only one road."[141]

In another prison story, Nechaev returned to one of his favorite themes, Alexander II's unbridled sexual lust. His fellow inmate of the ravelin, a former officer, spent most of his days and nights insanely shrieking. According to Nechaev, the prisoner's beautiful sister had inspired lust in the Tsar:

> This illustrious liberator and martyr courted Shevich's sister and finally violated her. Then Shevich, at the next review, left the formation and addressing the Tsar, expressed his indignation and contempt publicly in the sharpest words to this crowned addlepate . . . For this, Shevich was buried forever in the ravelin, without any trial, at his majesty's personal command.[142]

Once again Nechaev's stories about the authorities look very much like projections: *They* are lustful; *they* want us to masturbate.

In what must have been one of his last messages to The People's Will, Nechaev related the tragic death of Stepan Shiriaev. Shiriaev had contracted tuberculosis soon after his imprisonment and died on August 18, 1881, presumably from the disease, although Nechaev suggested that he had been given a truth serum which poisoned him.[143]

Despite all of the horrors (real or fictitious) described above, Nechaev did not attempt to break out of prison. This seems all the odder in view of the fact that The People's Will had virtually disintegrated. Could he have failed to understand this by October 1881? One of the guards in his organization, Ivan Gubkin, was arrested in September 1881, for breaking the security regulations of the ravelin and having outside contacts. Although Gubkin had sealed his lips, and although the authorities did not know that he had been working for Nechaev, its seems unlikely that Nechaev did not understand that an organization of his sort could not endure much longer. Most of the guards loyal to him had entered service in the ravelin between 1878 and 1881.[144] Nechaev had been able to pay his accomplices during the period he had ties with The People's Will, and the loyalty of the guards cannot be questioned. Nechaev was their "Eagle." They respected and feared him.[145] They had been converted by him—so he had told The People's Will, and there is no reason to doubt his claim—to atheism, to revolutionary socialism, and to Tsaricide. The court that tried Nechaev's accomplices found twelve of them to be genuine accomplices, fully converted to his ideas. Another fourteen were found to be impressionable imitators.[146] With that many armed men at his command, and given the other resources available to him during most of 1881, it seems astonishing that Nechaev did not make an attempt to escape by November 1881. It may be that he still wanted to carry out his plan of capturing the entire royal family during a visit to the chapel near the fortress. It may be that the precise moment for the escape simply did not present itself. Perhaps after all he did fail to understand the gravity of the situation. More than three years of success and his optimism that The People's Will would liberate the Russian Bastille may have blinded him to the need to act quickly. But it is also possible that his judgment was affected by a deeper motive, and that he did not really want to escape. Perhaps his desire for martyrdom, all the more attractive once he knew that word of his suffering in the fortress was safely in the hands of posterity, won out. The final event in his biography, his death, suggests this last explanation.

On November 16 and 18, 1881, General Ganetskii sent detailed sets of instructions to one of the captains of the fortress guard and the inspector of the ravelin. The instructions reveal that Ganetskii expected disturbances in the Alekseevskii ravelin and wanted the troops of the garrison on other parts of the island to be prepared to suppress them and to secure all exits from the fortress. On November 19, he asked that a twenty-four-hour guard be placed at the outside wall under the window of cell No. 5 and tightened security on the inside. The orders accompanied requests to the minister of internal affairs for the arrest of thirty-four members of the fortress garrison and sweeping changes in personnel.[147] Eventually, sixty-nine people were arrested in connection with the plot, forty-four of them on December 29, 1881.[148] It is impossible to determine how the authorities uncovered the plot. Gubkin had been arrested again on November 15, 1881, but the most assiduous student of the plot in the ravelin, the Soviet historian P. Shchegolev, believed that his arrest was a symptom and not a cause of the conspiracy's discovery. Shchegolev believed that Mirskii, Nechaev's fellow prisoner in the ravelin, had given the secret away in return for a better diet, tobacco, and in general, more tolerable living conditions. The long delay between Gubkin's arrest, Ganetskii's orders, and the arrests of December 29 suggests either an elaborate intrigue by the director of the police, V. K. von Plehve, to cast as wide a net as possible or the simple fact that Gubkin was the key to the discovery of Nechaev's organization and that it took a while to extract the information from him. On December 4, 1881, Count N. P. Ignat'ev, Loris-Melikov's successor as minister of internal affairs, wrote to Alexander III that the coded note found in Zheliabov's possession had been deciphered and the plot in the ravelin uncovered.[149] It appears from Ignat'ev's note and von Plehve's correspondence that a secret informer had alerted them. Evidently, the police could not piece together the plot until Gubkin's arrest and Zheliabov's deciphered note gave them the key to the personnel involved, and even then the intricacy of Nechaev's precautions made it difficult for them. The investigation was completed on March 10, 1882, and Alexander III commented on Ignat'ev's report of that day: "I believe there has never been a more shameful affair involving the military command and its leadership."[150] The trials occurred in May and December 1882. Most of the soldiers tried for violation of military discipline were sent to disciplinary battalions for two to three years, while those tried mainly for political crimes were sent to Siberia.[151]

Meanwhile, Nechaev had been transferred to cell No. 1 on December 29, 1881. It is certain that he now experienced complete isolation. The new guards fulfilled the regulations meticulously under the ravelin's watchful, pedantic new supervisor, M. E. Sokolov. Although no communications from Nechaev survive for this period, several members of The People's Will who were imprisoned in the fortress in March

1882, have left vivid accounts of the diet, the prison regime, and Sokolov. P. G. Polivanov's description of Sokolov captures the terrifying impression made by the man:

> The first thing about him that struck me was the expression of his eyes. To this very moment I have not seen anything like it in any other person. They strikingly resembled the eyes of the large reptiles. The very same cold glitter, the very same absence of thought. The very same expression of dumb, pitiless malice. One could clearly read in these eyes that their possessor . . . would as coldbloodedly and systematically crush his victim, as a boa constrictor would a sheep. The repulsive impression made by this man was reinforced by a bristling, cropped mustache, a prominent, clean-shaven chin and his entire manner, which did not call forth the image of the butcher and executioner that he was, as singularly as did his thick, stocky physique with its heroically protruding chest and wide hands, whose fat fingers were in constant motion, as if looking for work.[152]

The Tsaricides were subjected to a twenty-four-kopeck diet and one-half hour walks per day in solitary—that is, single prisoners accompanied only by guards. Nechaev, however, remained on a seventy-kopeck-a-day diet until Ganetskii convinced von Plehve that Nechaev's special treatment might affect the new guards, just as it had those whom Nechaev had convinced of his high court connections. Von Plehve in turn dissuaded Count Ignat'ev from his previous position that they maintain Nechaev's situation as before. On June 2, 1882, word came to Ganetskii that Nechaev should be placed on the same diet as the *narodovols'ty;* that he should be dressed as a convict; and that he should be given no books other than the Bible.[153] The last information we have about Nechaev's actions comes from Ganetskii's report of July 1, 1882, in which he informed von Plehve that Nechaev had asked for a Bible and wanted to see a priest because of a "confused, unfamiliar desire to turn to faith." The request was fulfilled at the highest level, but Ganetskii evidently decided not to let Nechaev see a priest. (The regulations permitted unmonitored interviews with priests.) Did the odd request signify a real breakdown in Nechaev's resolve, or was it—as Ganetskii apparently thought—the prisoner's last, desperate attempt to establish contact with the outside? The latter seems more likely.

The last clear sign of Nechaev's indomitable will to rebel appears in one of Ganetskii's reports to von Plehve during the late summer of 1881. On September 6, 1881, when Nechaev was given a list of Russian books from which to choose (having been denied foreign language books), he wrote an insulting inscription instead, whereupon he was deprived of the right to order books until he apologized. There is no record of an apology, but in December 1881, von Plehve began ordering French books for Nechaev once again.[154] Evidently, then, he retained most of his old privileges, with interruptions, until June 1882, when the authorities imposed the new conditions described above. Between July and November 1882, there is complete silence about Nechaev, and then only one ominous report of November 8 signed by Dr. Vil'ms.

> The prisoner confined in No. 1 of the Alekseevskii ravelin has developed scurvy complicated by general edema [dropsy] to such a high degree that the prisoner's life is threatened, and therefore along with other medical means I consider it essential that the aforementioned prisoner be given a half bottle of milk daily and for the successful cure of the aforementioned disease I consider it also extremely essential that he take open-air walks daily.[155]

Similar expressions of solicitude for their health heralded the deaths of the members of The People's Will imprisoned in the ravelin. Nechaev had met his match in the reptilian Sokolov. On November 21, 1882, Dr. Vil'ms reported: "The prisoner confined in cell No. 1 this 21st day of November at approximately 2:00 P.M. died of general edema complicated by scurvy."[156] Ganetskii immediately reported the death to the Tsar, Ignat'ev, and von Plehve, with a request to the last for instructions about the disposal of the body. He received them the same day. Everything was carried out with a punctiliousness suggesting the observation of some primitive rite rather than mere bureaucratic efficiency. The body was transferred secretly to another part of the fortress and delivered at 1:00 A.M. to von Plehve's agent, who was not told the identity of the corpse. Three officials transported Nechaev's remains, by way of the Nikolaevskii railway, to an unidentified cemetery and buried him. Only Nechaev's clothes remained, and they too were scrupulously listed in the last official report about his imprisonment. On December 24, 1882, Sokolov, assisted by two junior officers, presided over the incineration of Nechaev's wardrobe. With his usual pedantry, Sokolov ended his report: "I should add, that there remained a pair of spectacles with a case which were broken and thrown into the furnace."[157]

A legend circulated in the revolutionary underground that Nechaev had committed suicide. Should we believe the medical report and

Dr. Vil'ms or the revolutionary underground? Nechaev's death follows the pattern of those of several other prisoners subjected to the regime of Ganetskii and Sokolov. But death from dropsy—an unpleasant death, to be sure—somehow lacks the elements of control and drama one expects of Nechaev. The revolutionary underground supplied these elements by supposing that he had committed suicide, and this too is not implausible, since Nechaev had threatened suicide more than once. Can it be pure accident that Nechaev died on November 21—the anniversary of Ivanov's murder? Perhaps, in the end, Nechaev did remain in control—the peculiar control of the martyr over his own death—and perhaps, in the end, the most unscrupulous revolutionary of his time proved himself a most scrupulous man. If so, the opening line of "The Catechism of a Revolutionary" at last unfolds its full personal meaning as Nechaev's self-fulfilling prophesy: "The revolutionary is a doomed man."

Chapter VII

The Problem of Nechaevism

The Politics of Revenge

Nechaev belonged to the left wing of the French revolutionary tradition in his strategies and to the utopian socialist tradition of the mid-nineteenth century in his aims. But the positive revolutionary socialist aspect of Nechaev's career contributed little to the meaning of "Nechaevism." It was rather his conduct of his conspiracy and his translation of utopian socialism into "barracks communism" that distinguished him from the socialists of his era and gave meaning to "Nechaevism." Perhaps he does not deserve to be elevated to the status of an "ism." Later Russian revolutionaries almost universally condemned Nechaev's methods, an attitude they expressed in typical Russian fashion by adding to his name the suffix "*shchina*." "*Nechaevshchina*" signified primitivism and unscrupulousness in revolutionary politics. But even in its negative sense, as a warning that centralized conspiracies might assume harmful forms, *Nechaevshchina* inhibited for only a brief period the development of Jacobin strategies in the Russian revolutionary movement. Nechaev's ruin of Bakunin, which some might argue had profound consequences for the history of socialism, was probably made possible because of Bakunin's lack of political acumen and his self-destructive tendencies. It seems unlikely that Bakunin's immediate or long-term impact on revolutionary politics in Europe or Russia would have been much different, had there been no Nechaev. At the very least, Nechaevism taught the Russian revolutionaries of the 1870s that noble ends do not justify the use of all means, and that progressive doctrines can be distorted into primitive forms. For a relatively small price, Nechaev gave his contemporaries a striking lesson in the disastrous possibilities of revolutionary politics. The ultimate failure of Russian revolutionaries to make use of that lesson and, indeed, the failure of twentieth-century revolutionary movements to heed it, suggest that the problem of Nechaevism is in miniature the expression of a vast human problem. In the end, it is the inner story of Nechaevism, the story Dostoevsky told best, not so much in *The Devils* as in the entire body of his work, that is of enduring historical interest. It is a story about pathologies of conscience.

From a distant vantage point, one can readily see how Nechaev's pathology might go undetected in the nihilist subculture of the 1860s. The revolutionaries were only part of a larger rebellion of educated youths who had drawn a sharp line between themselves and an abhorrent, backward, social and political order. The Tsar and his officials became screens upon which young rebels projected every form of human depravity. Rumors circulating in the capital about the Tsar's lechery and drunkenness, about debauchery at the court, about the obscene methods used by officials to advance themselves, about the sadism of the police, kindled the rage of youths like Nechaev. The nihilists' theoretical condemnations of the old order had small significance for Nechaev compared to stories of real abuses by real persons, upon whom he could focus his deep resentment of authority and power. On the other hand, the image of a new kind of person, a revolutionary hero, faintly sketched in the literature of nihilism, excited Nechaev's imagination. The first interpreters of the role of revolutionary hero proved deficient, although Karakozov's attempt and his martyrdom inspired Nechaev to take up the task. While Nechaev's sense of a calling and his decision to use "Jesuitical" methods in themselves do not necessarily imply pathology, the deceptions Nechaev employed to create a heroic image for himself, the grandiose quality of that image, and its sadistic and masochistic features leave little doubt that we are dealing with psychopathology. It is a testimony to the extreme rhetoric, the need for heroism, and the millenarian mood of the young revolutionaries that Nechaev's stories were not immediately recognized for what they were. Paranoid projections and abnormal power seeking could not be distinguished from exposés of the government and heroic commitment to the revolutionary cause.

After Nechaev's methods had been exposed, for a short time Russian revolutionaries shunned techniques of recruitment and conspiratorial organization that remotely resembled *Nechaevshchina*, but as Trifonov's novel *Impatience* vividly illustrates, the logic of commitment and revenge drove them into conspiratorial activities and "political" methods that, at least on the surface, were difficult to distinguish from Nechaev's. The *assassins purs* of The People's Will, with whom Nechaev established contact after eight years of imprisonment, believed in their own nobler motives. The *narodovol'tsy* condemned Nechaev's violence against brothers and his deceit, while Nechaev fretted within the walls of the fortress over their scrupulousness. Yet even the *narodovol'tsy* did not appreciate fully the dangers of recognizing in Nechaev a comrade—someone committed to the cause, who had used the wrong methods and principles in serving it. Furthermore, they saw Nechaev as a victim of the evil power they were trying to destroy. Nechaev's self-sacrifice and indomitable revolutionary will disarmed them. They had little or no understanding that Nechaev might have exacted a terrible, destructive revenge for his suffering had he escaped and that his rage might fall not only on the Tsar and his hirelings, but on comrades who opposed his will. Astute observers like Lopatin, who had earlier recognized in Nechaev the features of an aspiring tyrant, might warn others, but events proved that the revolutionaries had not found ways to protect themselves against their own comrades.

Nechaev's success depended upon his ability to "touch the most sensitive areas of a young conscience," as one of his acquaintances had put it to police interrogators. Nechaev probed for and found deep anxieties and feelings of guilt—some of them associated with adolescence and student life, others with privilege, and still others with the struggle of the younger generation to break out of traditional cultural and political patterns of behavior. To these he added naked fear. In his role of revolutionary man of action, Nechaev manipulated his followers' anxieties about dependence, passivity, lack of development, and lack of will, while in his role of popular avenger he exploited their guilt before the *narod*, their identification with the victim, and their fear of the people's revenge. Nechaev succeeded at least partly because he suffered himself from similar anxieties and feelings of guilt and offered his followers ideologically sanctified mechanisms of defense against them. Rarely have mechanisms of defense been translated so directly into political strategies as in Nechaevism, and rarely does one find political rhetoric that points so directly to its psychological sources.

In his own family, Nechaev had been the relatively privileged child, the intellectual, the drone. He too had suffered the anxieties of the uprooted adolescent. His rage against privilege may have been as much a function of the feelings of guilt he had experienced for abandoning his family and pursuing a career in St. Petersburg, as it was of the frustrations and humiliations he had encountered as a poor but talented and ambitious child and adolescent. One can only speculate about the deeper background of Nechaev's rage and lust for revenge. His inability to sustain normal personal relationships, his disappointments with the "Judases" who betrayed him at every stage in his life, suggest a repeating pattern originating in extremely early experiences. Otto Fenichel's succinct formulation perhaps comes closest to the heart of the matter: "Revenge is a special type of the old 'magical' undoing of frustrations or humiliations, based on an identification with the aggressor."[1] Nechaev felt that he had paid in advance for his right to kill and to assume supreme power. Vengeful power seeking and martyrdom were two sides of the same psychological coin.[2] In the end, however, Nechaev showed more kinship with Raskolnikov than with Verkhovenskii. He was but a pale criminal.

Nechaevism was not simply a random pathology in an otherwise healthy movement. It was an especially clear example of the psychology of revenge raised to the level of politics. Furthermore, the politics of revenge is not a uniquely Russian problem, although Russia and the Soviet Union have provided the world with particularly extreme versions of it. Nechaev arrived at a historical moment when a callow, romantic youth might nakedly display his conspiratorial ruthlessness in a setting that supported political theater rather than mass politics. But he was a genuine forerunner of twentieth-century dictators and a clear warning that archaic motives might transform new political and social ideas into atavistic expressions of power.

Like individuals, collectivities are burdened with historical memories of past humiliations. At times, both individuals and collectivities seem to need heroism, great leaps forward, and vast renewals. Political rhetoric and national symbols, whether religious or secular, reflect the psychology of individual humiliation and pride. During periods of crisis collectivities sometimes choose to be led by heroes, whose extreme rhetoric and all-or-nothing will to power promise escape from the misery of collective defeat and humiliation. The politics of crisis often promotes individuals who, in the name of an ideology of collective salvation or rejuvenation, pursue the politics of revenge; and the rhetoric of the politics of revenge, however cogent it may be in some historical contexts, may camouflage a paranoid syndrome. In Nechaev's case, it was identification with the aggressor.[3] Political heroes, desperately seeking personal revenge for humiliations long forgotten at a conscious level, during their rise to power may assume the features of archetypal avengers; and if they achieve power, they may take on the appearance of the most dread rulers in their political tradition. Orwell's *Animal Farm* is still the great political parable of our era, but ought we to abandon hope that understanding the past will unburden us of the necessity of repeating it?

Notes

Abbreviations Used in the Notes

TsGAOR Tsentral'nyi Gosudarstvennyi Arkhiv Oktiabr'skoi Revoliutsii. Numbers refer to fond, delo, chast', and list'.

TsGIAL Tsentral'nyi Gosudarstvennyi Istoricheskii Arkhiv v Leningrade.

IISH International Institute for Social History (Amsterdam).

Notes

Chapter I

1. P. M. Ekzempliarskii, "Selo Ivanovo v zhizni Sergeia Gennad'evicha Nechaeva," p. 9. Ekzempliarskii claims that the child was born in the home of his maternal grandparents. However, Nechaev's sister Fioniia in her memoirs (told to N. Bel'chikov in 1922) claims that he was born in the apartment of a peasant woman named Postnikova, whose son Fioniia later married. See N. Bel'chikov, "S. G. Nechaev v s. Ivanove v 60-e gody," p. 153.
2. Ekzempliarskii, "Selo Ivanovo," p. 8; Bel'chikov, "S. G. Nechaev," p. 153.
3. Zemliak, "Novoe o Nechaeve," p. 71.
4. Ekzempliarskii, "Selo Ivanovo," p. 11.
5. According to Ekzempliarskii, Praskov'ia Petrovna was twenty-two years old during the census of 1850 (ibid., p. 7), but this age does not follow from her birth date, July 25, 1826. Fioniia, Sergei's younger sister, was eight years old in 1858, and she claims that her mother died when she was seven. Assuming that Fioniia was indeed seven when her mother died, Sergei, who was about two years older than Fioniia, would have been about nine. (In her memoirs, Fioniia gives her birth year as 1848, but this would have made her one year or less younger than Sergei, whereas the census of 1858 lists her as two years younger.) But Ekzempliarskii claims that Praskov'ia Petrovna died in 1854 or 1855, when Sergei could have been at most seven or eight years old, and Fioniia about five or six. In any case, Sergei could not have been less than six or more than nine when his mother died.
6. Ekzempliarskii, "Selo Ivanovo," p. 9; Bel'chikov, "S. G. Nechaev," p. 153.

7. Ekzempliarskii, "Selo Ivanovo," p. 8.
8. Bel'chikov, "S. G. Nechaev," p. 153.
9. Ekzempliarskii, "Selo Ivanovo," p. 9; Bel'chikov, "S. G. Nechaev," p. 154.
10. Zemliak, "Novoe o Nechaeve," p. 71.
11. Bel'chikov, "S. G. Nechaev," p. 154.
12. Ibid.
13. N. Malitskii, "K biografii S. G. Nechaeva," p. 134.
14. Ekzempliarskii, "Selo Ivanovo," p. 10.
15. Nechaev's public sentence was never carried out, but the family could not have known this during the 1870s. His real sentence, life imprisonment in the Peter and Paul Fortress, was a carefully guarded secret.
16. According to a report from Captain Timofeev, the police official responsible for surveillance of Nechaev's family in 1870, Gennadii was given a letter from Sergei to Anna by Fioniia's husband, Ia. G. Postnikov. Without opening it, Gennadii delivered the letter to the district chief of police. (TsGAOR, 109.112.4.20.) In a deposition from one of Nechaev's coconspirators, the police learned that Gennadii "positively" refused to meet Sergei in Moscow, saying that he didn't have any kind of relationship with his son. (TsGAOR, 109.115.5(1869).41. Also, see Bel'chikov, "S. G. Nechaev," p. 155.)
17. Zemliak, "Novoe o Nechaeve," pp. 70–72; Bel'chikov, "S. G. Nechaev," p. 154.
18. Ekzempliarskii, "Selo Ivanovo," pp. 11–12.
19. Ekzempliarskii, "Selo Ivanovo," p. 11.
20. N. Bel'chikov, "Iz byta literaturnykh kruzhkov 60–70 godov," pp. 121–123; and *Narodnichestvo v literature i kritike*, pp. 198–237.
21. Ibid.
22. Ibid.
23. On Nefedov, see A. V. Smirnov, "F. D. Nefedov, ego zhizn' i deiatel'nost'," pp. 1–18; also, M. Goriachkina, *Khudozhestvennaia proza narodnichestva*; V. V. Bush, *Ocherki literaturnogo narodnichestva*.
24. P. M. Ekzempliarskii, *Istoriia goroda Ivanova*, p. 119.
25. A. F. Selivanov, "Ivanovo-Voznesensk," p. 756.
26. Ibid., p. 757.
27. This excerpt is taken from selections of Nefedov's work printed in *Pervoe stoletie: Ivanovo, 1871–1971* (Iaroslavl', 1971), pp. 15–17. The translation is mine.
28. Bel'chikov, "S. G. Nechaev," p. 155; Zemliak, p. 72.
29. Zemliak, "Novoe o Nechaeve," p. 72.
30. Bel'chikov, "S. G. Nechaev," p. 154.
31. Ibid., p. 155.
32. It is quite difficult to ascertain Nechaev's age. Fioniia was seventy-two

when she recounted her memoirs to Bel'chikov, and, as noted above, she erred about her age at her mother's death. In her earlier memoirs of 1910, the year 1861 is indicated for the mill incident (Zemliak, p. 71). In all probability, therefore, Sergei was at least eleven and perhaps as old as thirteen when he left Garelin's office.

33. Bel'chikov, "S. G. Nechaev," p. 153.
34. Zemliak, "Novoe o Nechaeve," p. 61.
35. Bel'chikov, "S. G. Nechaev," p. 153.
36. Ibid., p. 154.
37. Ekzempliarskii, "Selo Ivanovo," p. 12.
38. Ibid.
39. Ibid., pp. 19–20.
40. *Moskovskie vedomosti*, p. 1374.
41. Ekzempliarskii, "Selo Ivanovo," p. 21.
42. Fourteen letters, in Bel'chikov, "S. G. Nechaev," pp. 138–152.
43. From the original deposition given by A. Kapatsinskii to the Third Section on May 29, 1869, TsGAOR, 109.112.2.38.
44. Ekzempliarskii, *Istoriia*, p. 112.
45. Letter of March 6, 1864. In Bel'chikov, "S. G. Nechaev," p. 145.
46. Undated letter in ibid., p. 144.
47. Ibid., p. 151.
48. Ibid., p. 152.
49. *Obshchina* (London), September 1, 1870, part 3, p. 3.
50. Anna Freud, *The Ego and the Mechanisms of Defense*, chap. 9.
51. Rosa Luxemburg, *The Russian Revolution, and Leninism or Marxism?*, p. 107.
52. Ibid., p. 100.
53. Nicholas Berdiaev, *The Origin of Russian Communism*, p. 63.
54. Erik Erikson, *Childhood and Society*, chap. 10.
55. Michael Cherniavsky, *Tsar and People*, p. 127.
56. Ekzempliarskii, "Selo Ivanovo," p. 21.
57. A. Kapatsinskii, TsGAOR, 109.112.2.38.
58. Bel'chikov, "Iz byta literaturnykh," pp. 124–5; B. P. Koz'min, "Novoe o S. G. Nechaeve," no. 14, pp. 148–158.
59. Kapatsinskii, TsGAOR, 109.112.2.38; Koz'min, "Novoe o S. G. Nechaeve," no. 14, p. 151.
60. Bel'chikov, "S. G. Nechaev," p. 154. I have taken liberties by translating the expletive "ekh" as "my God."
61. Ibid., p. 153.
62. Kapatsinskii, TsGAOR, 109.112.2.38; Koz'min, "Novoe o S. G. Nechaeve," no. 14, p. 151.
63. TsGAOR, 109.112.2.34.
64. Koz'min, "Novoe o Nechaeve," no. 14, p. 151.
65. Kapatsinskii, TsGAOR, 109.112.2.38.
66. Ibid.

67. Putsykovich, TsGAOR, 109.112.2.63–66; also Koz'min, "Novoe o Nechaeve," no. 15, pp. 150–163.
68. Putsykovich, TsGAOR, 109.112.2.63.
69. Avvakum was the seventeenth-century rebel archpriest who led the struggle of hundreds of thousands of Old Believers against changes in Orthodox ritual. After numerous trials, he paid for his heresy in 1682, when the authorities burned him at the stake. Avvakum's autobiography became a literary classic.
70. Bel'chikov, "S. G. Nechaev," p. 148.
71. TsGAOR, 109.112.2.34.

Chapter II

1. TsGAOR, 109.112.1(1869).8; also published by B. P. Koz'min in "Novoe o S. G. Nechaeve," pp. 160–161.
2. B. P. Koz'min, *Nechaev i nechaevtsy sbornik materialov*, p. 62.
3. Koz'min, "Novoe o Nechaeve," pp. 160–161.
4. TsGAOR, 109.112.1(1869).10.
5. TsGAOR, 109.112.1(1869).11.
6. TsGAOR, 109.112.1(1869).10.
7. P. Pomper, "Nechaev and Tsaricide: The Conspiracy within the Conspiracy," pp. 123–138.
8. See V. I. Zasulich, *Vospominaniia*; A. I. Uspenskaia, "Vospominaniia shestidesiatnitsy," pp. 19–45.
9. My translation, based upon the version published by A. Shilov, "Katekhizis revoliutsionera," p. 268.
10. For good biographical material on Chernyshevskii and Dobroliubov see E. Lampert, *Sons Against Fathers*. Vladimir Nabokov has brilliantly satirized Chernyshevskii in *The Gift*.
11. The reference is, of course, to his novel, *Chto delat'?* (*What Is to Be Done?*), first published in 1863.
12. N. G. Chernyshevskii, *Chto delat'?*, p. 273. The translation is mine.
13. Ibid., p. 179.
14. I. S. Turgenev, *Fathers and Sons*, p. 185.
15. Ibid., p. 198.
16. Two articles by Patrick Dunn discuss this question. "Fathers and Sons Revisited: The Childhood of Vissarion Belinsky," pp. 389–407; " 'That Enemy is the Baby': Childhood in Imperial Russia," pp. 383–405. One should mention as well Marc Raeff, *Origins of the Russian Intelligentsia*, and Erik Erikson, *Childhood and Society*, pp. 359–402.
17. Quoted from the stenographic account of the trial of the Nechaevists published in *Pravitel'stvennyi vestnik*, July 22, 1871, p. 3.
18. A. P. Mal'shinskii, *Obzor sotsial'no-revoliutsionnogo dvizheniia v Rossii*, pp. 222–224.

19. See Franco Venturi, *Roots of Revolution*, chap. 8; Daniel Brower, *Training the Nihilists*, chap. 3.
20. See Brower, chap. 6.
21. Venturi.
22. Mal'shinskii, p. 226.
23. Venturi, pp. 226–231; P. Pomper, *The Russian Revolutionary Intelligentsia*, pp. 81–88.
24. On Zaichnevskii see: B. P. Koz'min, *Iz istorii revoliutsionnoi mysli v Rossii*, pp. 127–345; Venturi, pp. 285–298.
25. B. P. Koz'min, ed., *Istoriko-revoliutsionnaia khrestomatiia*, p. 55.
26. Ibid., p. 53.
27. Ibid., p. 59.
28. For a recent study of the revolutionary underground during the 1860s, see E. S. Vilenskaia, *Revoliutsionnoe podpol'e v Rossii 60-e gody XIX v.*
29. See ibid., pp. 183–465.
30. Quoted in Venturi, p. 377.
31. See Vilenskaia, pp. 394–398.
32. Ibid., pp. 414–416.
33. Ibid., pp. 437–440.
34. M. M. Klevenskii, ed., *Pokushenie Karakozova*, p. 16.
35. *Kolokol* (London), September 1, 1866, p. 1854.
36. Ibid., January 1, 1867, p. 1890.
37. Ibid.
38. Ibid.
39. Ibid., July 1, 1866, p. 1806.
40. Ibid., February 1, 1867, p. 1908.
41. Quoted in B. P. Koz'min, *Revoliutsionnoe pod'pole v epokhu "belogo terrora,"* p. 148.
42. See Pomper, "Nechaev and Tsaricide," pp. 124–126.
43. S. G. Sviatikov, "Studencheskoe dvizhenie 1869 goda (Bakunin i Nechaev)," p. 181.
44. Ibid.
45. Ibid., p. 182.
46. Brower, pp. 72, 139; Pomper, *The Russian Revolutionary Intelligentsia*, pp. 76, 113.
47. Sviatikov, p. 183ff.
48. S. S. Tatishchev, "Sotsial'no-revoliutsionnoe dvizhenie v Rossii. Sudebno-politseiskaia khronika, 1861–1871. Glava odinnadtsataia. Nechaevskoe delo, 1869–1871 gg." Typed ms. in TsGIAL, fond 878. opis' 1. ed. khr. 82. list' 94.
49. This information is taken from the stenographic account of the trial, published in *Pravitel'stvennyi vestnik* during the summer of 1871 in issues 155–206. Brief biographies of the persons named appear in

B. P. Koz'min, ed., *Deiateli revoliutsionnogo dvizheniia v Rossii,* vol. 1 (part 2).

50. Koz'min, *Deiateli,* vol. 1 (part 2).
51. For a time he was one of Orlov's students. Tatishchev, TsGIAL, fond 878. opis' 1. ed. khr. 82. list' 98.
52. Ibid. list' 129. Other evidence suggests that Zubkov was more deeply involved. He may have used his money to buy his freedom.
53. Florinskii's trial testimony, *Pravitel'stvennyi vestnik,* no. 158 (1871).
54. Zubkov's trial testimony. Ibid., no. 160 (1871).
55. Tomilova's trial testimony, ibid.
56. See Venturi, pp. 354–356.
57. Koz'min, *Deiateli* 2: 806.
58. First used by N. Pirumova, "M. Bakunin ili S. Nechaev?," pp. 168–181.
59. TsGAOR, 109.112.1(1869).180.
60. Ibid., list' 181.
61. Z. Ralli, "Sergei Gennad'evich Nechaev," pp. 40–41.
62. L. Nikiforov, "Moi tiur'my," pp. 189–191.
63. B. P. Koz'min, *Nechaev i nechaevtsy,* pp. 142–143.
64. Pirumova, "M. Bakunin ili S. Nechaev?"
65. Ibid., p. 178.
66. Ibid., p. 179.
67. Ibid., p. 180.
68. Tatishchev, TsGIAL, fond 878. opis' 1. ed. khr. 82. list' 95.
69. Pirumova, "M. Bakunin ili S. Nechaev?"
70. TsGAOR, 109.112.1(1869).88.
71. Koz'min, *Deiateli* 1 (part 2): 406.
72. Ralli, "Sergei Gennad'evich Nechaev," p. 137ff.
73. Koz'min, ed., *Khrestomatiia,* pp. 74–75.
74. *Pravitel'stvennyi vestnik,* no. 163 (1871), p. 2.
75. B. Bazilevskii (V. Ia. Iakovlev), *Gosudarstvennye prestupleniia v Rossii v XIX veke,* p. 312. Cf. B. P. Koz'min's analysis of Volkhovskii's circle in "Nechaev i ego protivniki," *Revoliutsionnoe dvizhenie 1860-kh godov,* ed. B. I. Gorev and B. P. Koz'min, pp. 190–198.
76. *Pravitel'stvennyi vestnik,* no. 156 (1871), p. 3.
77. A number of scholars have argued with some cogency that Tkachev had probably influenced Nechaev's vision of heroism through his article, "People of the Future and Heroes of the Meshchanstvo," which appeared in 1868. For a recent discussion of this issue and the issue of Tkachev's role in writing the "Program," see Deborah Hardy, *Peter Tkachev: The Critic as Jacobin,* pp. 120–123, 136.
78. See Venturi, chapter 16.
79. B. P. Koz'min, *P. N. Tkachev i revoliutsionnoe dvizhenie 1860-kh godov,* p. 145.

80. See Gorev and Koz'min, eds., *Revoliutsionnoe dvizhenie 1860-kh godov*, p. 174; Koz'min, *Iz istorii revoliutsionnoi*, p. 357.
81. *Pravitel'stvennyi vestnik*, no. 163 (1871), p. 3.
82. TsGAOR, 109.115.10(1869).30.
83. Koz'min, *Khrestomatiia*, pp. 81–85.
84. The fact that the original copy Volkhovskii received was in Orlov's handwriting (Bazilevskii, p. 312) and delivered by Orlov at least points in that direction. The testimony by Tomilova about Orlov, in which she refers to his interest in "cosmic, physiological and historical laws," gives us some clue to his intellectual bent, and the "Program" is certainly concerned with historical laws. Finally, if we assume that Volkhovskii's annotations were elicited by Orlov, then the peculiar character of the former's remarks (quoted below) makes a great deal of sense.
85. *Pravitel'stvennyi vestnik*, no. 163 (1871), p. 3.
86. TsGAOR, 109.112.3(1869).259.
87. Pomper, "Nechaev and Tsaricide," p. 133.
88. Ibid., p. 134.
89. Ibid.
90. TsGAOR, 109.112.3(1869).259. See Sviatikov, pp. 189–193; and the testimony of Ralli and Ezerskii in Koz'min, *Nechaev i nechaevtsy*.
91. Koz'min, *Nechaev i nechaevtsy*, p. 85.
92. Ibid., p. 79.
93. Sviatikov, pp. 190–191; Koz'min, *Nechaev i nechaevtsy*, p. 189, footnote 9.
94. TsGAOR, 109.115.10(1869).29. Also, see Gorev and Koz'min, eds., *Revoliutsionnoe dvizhenie 60-kh godov*, p. 175.
95. Koz'min, *Nechaev i nechaevtsy*, p. 136.
96. Zasulich, pp. 23–24.
97. Tatishchev, TsGIAL, fond 878. opis' 1. ed. khr. 82. list' 98.
98. Ibid.
99. This, at least, is claimed by Zasulich (p. 26) in her memoirs, but Nechaev evidently salvaged part of his library. Years later he begged prison authorities to contact his sister, Anna, to whom he'd given his French and German books.
100. A. I. Uspenskaia; and Zasulich, p. 19.
101. Zasulich, p. 60.
102. Ibid., p. 63.
103. Ibid., p. 25.
104. Ibid.
105. Although Zasulich portrays Anna in this light, one has to entertain the possibility of deception on Anna's part.
106. Ibid.
107. Tatishchev, TsGIAL, fond 878. opis' 1. ed. khr. 82. listi 98–100.
108. Sviatikov, p. 197ff.

109. TsGAOR, 109.44.1(1869).107; 152. In a report dated April 12, 1869, one agent described an incident in St. Petersburg in which a student named Sudakov was denied vodka by a tavern keeper and then told by a patron that rebellious students were a danger to society. Sudakov seized the patron, a crowd gathered (generally, sympathetic to the student), and the police were called. Similar scenes were probably not uncommon.
110. TsGAOR, 109.44.1(1869).74.
111. Ibid., list' 108 (a report of April 3, 1869).
112. TsGAOR, 109.144.1(1869).177.
113. See Zasulich, p. 30.
114. TsGAOR, 109.44.1(1869).67.
115. See Koz'min, *Nechaev i nechaevtsy*, p. 191, note 29.
116. Tatishchev, list' 129. This will be examined in chapter 4.

Chapter III

1. The story of the Herzen and Ogarev families, with vivid chapters on Ogarev's decline, is told in E. H. Carr, *The Romantic Exiles*.
2. Nechaev's arrival is heralded by Ogarev's letters to Herzen. See B. P. Koz'min, "Gertsen, Ogarev i molodaia emigratsiia," pp. 32–33.
3. TsGAOR, 109.110.1(1869).3.
4. A. I. Gertsen, *Polnoe sobranie sochinenii i pisem* 21:545. The double dates represent both Russian (twelve days behind) and European calendars.
5. Ibid., p. 546.
6. *Pravitel'stvennyi vestnik*, no. 163 (1871), p. 2.
7. B. P. Koz'min, "Gertsen, Ogarev," p. 33.
8. Ogarev's contributions to the pamphlet campaigns are examined in E. L. Rudnitskaia, *N. P. Ogarev v russkom revoliutsionnom dvizhenii*, p. 384ff. See also E. Kusheva, "Revoliutsionnye proklamatsii zhenevskoi tipografii 1869–1870 godov," pp. 121–150; Ia. Cherniak, "Neizdannye i nesobrannye proizvedeniia Ogareva," pp. 590–601; Stephen T. Cochrane, *The Collaboration of Nečaev, Ogarev and Bakunin in 1869: Nečaev's Early Years*, pp. 100–101.
9. Stephen Cochrane has provided a thorough and thoughtful study of Ogarev's contribution to Nechaev's output in the work cited in note 8.
10. Bakunin's influence on Nechaev can be derived from indirect as well as direct evidence. Ogarev's letter to Nechaev "Ot dedushki vnuchky" ("From a Grandfather to a Grandson"), written early in 1870 (that is, during Nechaev's second exile, but before the break with Bakunin) reveals that Nechaev, in conversation with Ogarev, had expressed typically Bakuninist ideas about a Razin or Pugachev type of rebellion. Ogarev was trying to dissuade Nechaev from his fascination with the

razboinik approach to revolution. (*Literaturnoe nasledstvo* 41–42 (1941): 65–66.)

11. TsGIAL, fond 878. opis' 1. ed. khr. 82. list' 100.
12. TsGAOR, 109.112.1(1869).19.
13. Ibid. The annotations by the police suggest this, and it is a plausible guess.
14. Bakunin bitterly complained about this to Louis Palix in Lyons during the disturbances of September 1870. (R. M. Kantor, *V pogone za Nechaevym*, p. 125.)
15. TsGAOR, 109.112.1(1869).30.
16. Zamperini remained one of Nechaev's contacts during his second exile as well. He is mentioned by several memoirists as Nechaev's accomplice.
17. TsGAOR, 109.112.1(1869).25.
18. Ibid., list' 90.
19. Tatishchev, TsGIAL, fond 878' 1. ed. khr. 82. list' 103.
20. In my opinion, Bakunin is the primary author of this pamphlet, and certainly wrote all of the first part. In the second part, however, there are a number of passages that are apparently inspired by Nechaev, if not written by him. (Arthur Lehning, ed., *Archives Bakounine* 4: 17–21.)
21. Ibid., p. 3.
22. Ibid., p. 4.
23. Ibid., p. 12.
24. Bakunin's letter of June 2, 1870, to Nechaev, in English translation in M. Confino, *Daughter of a Revolutionary*, p. 241.
25. See P. Dragomanov, ed., *Pis'ma Bakunina k A. I. Gertsenu i N. P. Ogarevu*, pp. 463–468.
26. Gertsen, *Polnoe sobranie sochinenii i pisem* 21: 365 (letter to Ogarev of April 4/16, 1869).
27. *Literaturnoe nasledstvo*, 41–42 (1941): 121–128.
28. Ibid., pp. 34, 48, n. 149.
29. Letter of June 10/22, 1869, to Natalie. A. I. Gertsen, *Sobranie sochinenii v tridtsatii tomakh*, vol. 30, kniga 1, p. 138.
30. A. I. Gertsen, "K staromu tovarishchu," ("To an Old Comrade") p. 172.
31. N. Pirumova, *Bakunin* pp. 291–295.
32. Dragomanov, *Pis'ma Bakunina* (Geneva, 1896), pp. 207–208.
33. Sviatikov, "Studencheskoe dvizhenie 1869 goda," p. 224.
34. To say that Bakunin willed his own humiliation is to infer unconscious motivation from the pattern of his actions. I believe this to be a legitimate inference in the case of Bakunin's relationship with Nechaev. The rumors circulating in the émigré community about Bakunin's use of the woman's name "Matrena" in a document given to Nechaev may be more significant than E. H. Carr, for example, believes (E. H. Carr,

Bakunin, pp. 392–393), although it is virtually certain that no open homosexual relationship existed. Bakunin probably anticipated that he was going to be abused by Nechaev. In his pamphlet "To the Officers of the Russian Army" he announced that he had "subordinated himself unconditionally to the power of the Committee"—that is, to Nechaev. (Lehning, ed., *Archives Bakounine* 4: 11.)

35. G. A. Kuklin, *Itogi revoliutsionnogo dvizheniia v Rossii za sorok let* p. 36. As noted above, Nechaev accepted wholeheartedly this aspect of Bakunin's teaching. One cannot rule out his collaboration on this pamphlet, although scholarly authority, including that of the most recent Soviet Bakunin scholar, Pirumova, supports Bakunin's authorship.
36. Dragomanov, *Pis'ma Bakunina* (Geneva, 1896), p. 481.
37. Ibid., p. 479.
38. Ibid., p. 478.
39. Ibid., pp. 478–479.
40. Ibid., p. 480.
41. Ibid., p. 481.
42. Ibid., p. 482.
43. V. Burtsev, *Za sto let* (1800–1896), p. 91.
44. V. G. Belinsky, *Polnoe sobraine sochinenii* 12: 31. Letter to Botkin of March 13, 1841.
45. Ibid., 11: 425.
46. Ibid.
47. Ibid., p. 544.
48. TsGAOR, 109.110.1(1869).41. Reports of the postal inspector.
49. TsGAOR, 109.110.1(1869).104.
50. TsGAOR, 109.110.2(1869).165.
51. Ibid., list' 262.
52. Ibid., list' 263.
53. Ibid.
54. TsGAOR, 109.110.1(1869).3ff.
55. Nechaev claimed in a footnote to his article "Glavnye osnovy budushchego obshchestvennogo stroia" ["The Primary Bases of the Social Edifice of the Future," *Narodnaia rasprava* (Geneva), no. 2 (1870), p. 10] that a "more detailed theoretical development of our views will be found by those who seek it in the article 'The Manifesto of the Communist Party,' edited by us." Lehning accepts Koz'min's conjecture that neither Bakunin nor Ogarev, but rather a member of the younger generation of émigrés translated it. I would guess that the conjecture is correct, but that Koz'min was wrong to ignore Nechaev's role. The translator was probably one of Nechaev's associates. (See Lehning, ed., *Archives Bakounine* 4: 28–29; *Literaturnoe nasledstvo*, 63 (1956): 700–701.)
56. TsGAOR, 109.110.2(1869).271.
57. Burtsev, pp. 93–94.

58. Ibid., p. 95.
59. *Narodnaia rasprava*, no. I (summer, 1869), p. 13.
60. Burtsev, p. 96.
61. A photocopy of this notebook with the names exists in the International Institute for Social History in Amsterdam.
62. Burtsev, p. 93.
63. Of course, Nechaev also wanted to confuse the Third Section and impress Russian youth by advertising an underground Russian revolutionary publication.
64. Burtsev, p. 92.
65. In *Narodnaia rasprava*, no. 1 (1869), Bakunin's "Postanovka revoliutsionnogo voprosa" is cited as "Postanovka revoliutsionnykh voprosov"—that is, in the plural.
66. Nechaev and Bakunin signed some proclamations and not others. I believe the unsigned proclamations represent some sort of collaboration—at the very least, mutual approval of the general line of the piece; at most, the injection of specific phrases and ideas by the minor author.
67. Paul Avrich, *Bakunin and Nechaev*, p. 11.
68. Bakunin understood this quite well. In his letter of June 2, 1870, he wrote: "Yes, dear friend, you are not a materialist like us sinners, but an idealist, a prophet like a monk of the Revolution, your hero should not be Babeuf, not even Marat, but some sort of Savonarola." (Confino, *Daughter of a Revolutionary*, p. 244.) But even while understanding Nechaev's fanaticism, Bakunin could not break away from him—Nechaev had too great a personal hold on him.
69. See A. Shilov, "Katekhizis revoliutsionera," pp. 262–272. The original was burned accidentally, and Shilov worked from a copy in the files of the Third Section.
70. Nechaev later claimed in a statement written to Count N. V. Levashev that the "absurd catechism" had not been read by the conspirators tried in 1871 and that they did not know the cipher. (TsGAOR, 109. 115.23[1869].105–107. Also, E. P. Shchegolev, *Krasnyi arkhiv* 4 (1923): 229. The communication is dated January 10, 1873. See also Iu. Steklov, *M. A. Bakunin* (3: 467)
71. Confino, Lehning, Pirumova, and Avrich have reversed an earlier tendency to attribute the "Catechism" to Bakunin. Steklov, Koz'min, and Nettlau believed Bakunin wrote it. Stephen Cochrane's recently published dissertation *The Collaboration of Nečaev* presents the most thorough and least biased analysis.
72. M. P. Sazhin, *Vospominaniia*, p. 14.
73. Confino, *Daughter of a Revolutionary*, p. 243.
74. See M. Confino, *Violence dans la violence: le débat Bakounine-Nečaev*, p. 41 n. 54.
75. For a more detailed analysis, see P. Pomper, "Bakunin, Nechaev, and

the 'Catechism of a Revolutionary': The Case for Joint Authorship," pp. 535–546; cf. Stephen Cochrane, *The Collaboration*, pp. 200–222.

76. The translation is mine. I did not find either Max Nomad's translation in *Apostles of Revolution*, pp. 228–233, or the one in Confino's *Daughter of a Revolutionary*, satisfactory. The former was not based upon Shilov's more accurate version; the latter was, but was awkward in places. I have not translated the "General Principles of the Organization" or the "General Principles of the Network of Sections." These can be found in *Daughter of a Revolutionary*, pp. 222–224.
77. This word is not in the Shilov version, but the only word that makes sense in context is "sloi," the word for strata, given the fragment "sle" in the text.
78. Confino, *Daughter of a Revolutionary*, pp. 222–224.
79. Bazilevskii, "Gosudarstvennye prestupleniia," p. 308. These words in French appeared in the seal: "alliance révolutionnaire europèene. Comité générale."
80. Those involved with Nechaev before his flight abroad—the radicals in the student movement who were trying to push it toward political goals—were the likely members. However, they tried to hide their intentions behind other publicly expressed purposes. Tkachev, Dement'eva, the Ametistov brothers, Orlov, Ralli, Enisherlov, Volkhovskii, Nikiforov, Vsevolod Lopatin, Vera and Aleksandra Zasulich, Kapatsinskii, Antonova, Kolachevskii, Tomilova, Nikolaev, Uspenskii, Florinskii, the Mavritskii brothers, Semen Serebrennikov, and probably several others included in a list drawn up by Nikolaev in his deposition formed a kind of organization. Precisely which members comprised the Committee is difficult to say. (See also Confino, *Violence dans la violence*, p. 43; Cochrane, p. 51.)
81. Steklov, *M. A. Bakunin* 3: 437.
82. Gertsen, *Sobranie sochinenii* 30: 186.
83. Ibid., p. 154, See also Lehning, ed., *Archives Bakounine* 4: xlii.
84. V. Ia. Grosul, *Rossiiskie revoliutsionery v iugo-vostochnoi evrope*, pp. 372–373. Grosul presents a thoughtful and intelligent assessment of the evidence for Nechaev's relationships with Bulgarian revolutionaries and his travels through the Balkans. Grosul reviews critically the literature on Nechaev's impact on the Bulgarian movement through his ties with Khristo Botev and Liuben Karavelov. Grosul doubts that Nechaev ever established direct ties with Botev (p. 383), although he believes that he met Karavelov in Odessa in connection with the Elizavetgrad affair (p. 387), to be discussed later. (Cf. K. A. Poglubko, *Ocherki istorii bolgaro-rossiiskikh revoliutsionnykh sviazei*, p. 142ff.

    If Grosul is correct, Nechaev was in Romania for two weeks beginning August 10. For Nechaev's itinerary, see Poglubko, *Ocherki istorii*, pp. 150–151; Koz'min, "K istorii Nechaevskogo protsessa," pp. 160–161. Poglubko has published a letter from Nechaev to Ralli relating to this period. See "Sviazi bolgarskikh i russkikh emigrantov," pp. 4–5.

85. From the deposition of Nikolai Sobeschchanskii, dated April 16, 1870: TsGAOR, 109.115.7(1869).239. It can hardly be doubted that Sobeshchanskii lied about his relationship to Nechaev, although some of the details presented in the text probably bear some relationship to what actually happened. On Sobeshchanskii, see Grosul, pp. 383–397.
86. TsGAOR, 109.115.7(1869).238–241.
87. Ibid., list' 241.
88. Pomper, "Nechaev and Tsaricide," p. 125.
89. Ibid.

Chapter IV

1. S. S. Tatishchev, TsGIAL, fond 878. opis' 1. ed. khr. 82. list' 120; B. Bazilevskii, *Gosudarstvennye prestupleniia*, p. 343.
2. *Pravitel'stvennyi vestnik*, no. 162 (1871), p. 2.
3. Ibid.
4. TsGAOR, 109.115.6(1869).146; also published in Koz'min, *Nechaev i nechaevtsy.*
5. *Pravitel'stvennyi vestnik*, no. 156 (1871), p. 6.
6. Ibid.
7. Ibid., no. 175 (1871), pp. 2–3.
8. Ibid., no. 163 (1871), p. 3; no. 157 (1871).
9. For a brief account of Pryzhov's career see F. Venturi, *Roots of Revolution*, pp. 375–378.
10. *Pravitel'stvennyi vestnik*, no. 163 (1871), p. 3.
11. Ibid., no. 168 (1871), p. 5.
12. Ibid., no. 176 (1871), p. 2; V. I. Zasulich, *Vospominaniia*, p. 31.
13. A plan of the organization was found on Uspenskii's person. (*Pravitel'stvennyi vestnik*, no. 179 (1871), p. 3.)
14. Ibid., no. 156 (1871), p. 5.
15. The organization's accounts were seized with other materials in Uspenskii's apartment. (Ibid., no. 162 (1871), p. 5.)
16. Ibid., no. 173 (1871), p. 3.
17. Ibid., no. 172 (1871), p. 2.
18. All of the above is gathered from the trial testimony.
19. For a description of the Moscow organization, see Bazilevskii, pp. 343–367.
20. *Pravitel'stvennyi vestnik*, no. 156 (1871), p. 5.
21. Bazilevskii, p. 384.
22. Ibid., pp. 384–385.
23. TsGAOR, 109.115.6(1869).92. See also *Pravitel'stvennyi vestnik*, no. 180 (1871), p. 2.
24. TsGAOR, 109.115.6(1869).90.

25. *Pravitel'stvennyi vestnik*, no. 180 (1871), p. 2.
26. M. Confino, *Daughter of a Revolutionary*, pp. 283–284. The phrase is in Bakunin's letter of June 10, 1870, to Ogarev, Natalie Herzen, Vladimir Ozerov, and Semen Serebrennikov.
27. *Pravitel'stvennyi vestnik*, no. 198 (1871), p, 2.
28. A. I. Uspenskaia, "Vospominaniia shestidesiatnitsy," p. 34.
29. *Pravitel'stvennyi vestnik*, no. 177 (1871), p. 2.
30. Ibid., no. 176 (1871), p. 3.
31. Ibid., no. 177 (1871), p. 2.
32. Ibid., no. 176 (1871), p. 4.
33. Ibid., no. 160 (1871), p. 2.
34. Ibid., no. 195 (1871), p. 4.
35. Ibid., no. 198 (1871), p. 3.
36. I have used the translation in Confino, *Daughter of a Revolutionary*, p. 327.
37. See Nikolaev's testimony in *Pravitel'stvennyi vestnik*, no. 157 (1871).
38. B. P. Koz'min, "S. G. Nechaev i Tul'skie oruzheiniki," *Krasnyi arkhiv*, no. 30 (1930), p. 186.
39. From a copy in TsGAOR, 109.115.4(1869).115.
40. Both versions were published by Koz'min in *Krasnyi arkhiv*, no 22 (1927), pp. 241–245; the second version by Lehning in *Archives Bakounine*, 4: 20–21.
41. *Pravitel'stvennyi vestnik*, no. 158 (1871).
42. Cherniak, "*Neizdannye*," pp. 590–592.
43. E. Kusheva, "*Revoliutsionnye proklamatsii*," pp. 129–138; Cherniak, p. 590.
44. Koz'min, *Khrestomatiia*, p. 84.
45. See Kuznetsov's testimony, *Pravitel'stvennyi vestnik*, no. 156 (1871), p. 5.
46. In a number of sessions during the trial Uspenskii explained Nechaev's decision and did everything possible to convince the court that Nechaev did not act from personal motives. (Ibid., no. 168 (1871), p. 5; no. 158 (1871).)
47. Kuznetsov's account of his role sounds suspicious. (Ibid., no. 156 (1871), p. 6.)
48. Ibid.
49. This account is pieced together from the testimony of the accomplices ibid., nos. 156–160 (1871) and the information in the stenographic account of Nechaev's own trial, published in Bazilevskii, pp. 415–456.
50. *Pravitel'stvennyi vestnik*, no. 197 (1871), p. 2.
51. Ibid., no. 205 (1871), p. 2.
52. Ibid.
53. See Koz'min, "Nechaev i ego protivniki."
54. *Pravitel'stvennyi vestnik*, no. 199 (1871), pp. 1–2; no. 198 (1871), p. 2.

55. The police had searched the apartment of V. Evdokimov, an employee in Cherkesov's bookstore in St. Petersburg. They were seeking information about illegal travel abroad and decided to search Uspenskii's apartment in Moscow as well. Tatishchev, TsGIAL, fond 878. opis' 1. ed. khr. 82. list' 140.
56. Bazilevskii, pp. 294–295.
57. Tatishchev, TsGIAL, fond. 878. opis' 1. ed. khr. 82. list' 141.
58. TsGAOR, 109.115.24(1869).34–36.
59. Koz'min, "S. G. Nechaev i Tul'skie oruzheiniki."
60. See Nikolaev's testimony, *Pravitel'stvennyi vestnik*, no. 157 (1871).
61. She also carried copies of Pryzhov and Nechaev's leaflet "Until the Storm," Ogarev's "To the Peasants and all Plain Workers," Nechaev's newest appeal to the students, and copies of Bakunin's leaflet to "his young brothers," written during the first proclamations campaign. (Bazilevskii, p. 389.)
62. *Pravitel'stvennyi vestnik*, no. 198 (1871), p. 3.
63. TsGAOR, 109.115.2(1869).108.
64. The investigative commission began its work on December 29, 1869. (Tatishchev, TsGIAL, fond 878. opis' 1. ed. khr. 82. list' 143.) For the Third Section's investigation, see B. P. Koz'min, "K istorii Nechaevskogo protsessa," pp. 116–165.
65. Tatishchev, TsGIAL, fond 878. opis' 1. ed. khr. 82. list' 144.
66. TsGAOR, 109.115.12(1869).166 (a report of September 3, 1870, signed by Count Pahlen).
67. TsGAOR, 109.115.13(1869).34–35.
68. Ibid., list' 35.
69. M. F. Frolenko, *Sobranie sochinenii* 1:169.
70. Koz'min, *Nechaev i nechaevtsy*, p. 169ff.
71. Frolenko, *Sobranie sochinenii* 1:169–170.
72. B. S. Itenberg, *Dvizhenie revoliutsionnogo narodnichestva* p. 136.
73. Bazilevskii, pp. 341–342.
74. TsGAOR, 109.115.20(1869).158.
75. Koz'min, *Deiateli* 1 (part 2): 418.
76. Ibid., p. 194.
77. TsGAOR, 109.115.15(1869).7–17.
78. All of the above information is taken from Bazilevskii and Koz'min, ed., *Deiateli*.
79. Bazilevskii, p. 342.
80. TsGIAL, fond 1016. opis' 1. delo 193. Alexander's message is from Saratov and dated August 31, 1871.
81. Bazilevskii, pp. 381–382.
82. See the relevant articles in Koz'min, *Deiateli* 1 (part 2).
83. Bazilevskii, pp. 402–403.
84. Ibid., p. 411.
85. Based upon those actually tried—sixty-four people.

86. This is based on information in the stenographic accounts of the trial and in Koz'min, ed., *Deiateli*. There were occasional discrepancies between birth dates and age at the time of the trial but not enough to affect the figures significantly. Also, some of the information about social background was vague. Nonetheless, the figures roughly confirm what other researchers have found. For comparative data, see Brower, *Training the Nihilists*, p. 42; Itenberg, pp. 374–377.
87. The figures upon which the comparison is based are from Itenberg, p. 377. The latest study, by Mironov, of the composition of the revolutionary movement confirms the view that not only Nechaev's conspiracy, but the revolutionary movement as a whole during the 1860s and 1870s, was largely comprised of the educated young and that the experience of student life probably radicalized many youths. It also confirms the high degree of participation of the more privileged strata, although it emphasizes their access to education—rather than their social position—as the significant factor. Unfortunately, the author does not provide the absolute number of revolutionaries studied—only the percentages of revolutionaries from each social and age group and their educational background; and he only indicates that the percentages apply to revolutionaries of the 1870s but does not say precisely which years. In addition, he uses different social categories than the other authors cited—a common problem in Russian and Soviet historiography. But the results do not seriously conflict with the conclusions presented in the text; the most significant difference is in the figures for age of participation. The figures in Mironov show 37 percent of the revolutionaries of the 1870s were below the age of twenty and only 5.3 percent above the age of thirty, with 45 percent in the twenty-one-to-twenty-five-year-old group. See B. N. Mironov, *Istorik i matematika* p. 124ff.
88. Quoted in Koz'min, "Nechaev i ego protivniki," p. 209.
89. From the single surviving issue of *Obshchina*, published in London, September 1, 1870. The journal is reproduced in Lehning, ed., *Archives Bakounine* 4: 435–442.
90. *Pravitel'stvenyi vestnik*, no. 157 (1871).
91. Confino, *Daughter of a Revolutionary*, pp. 176–177.
92. Ibid.
93. TsGAOR, 109.115.7(1869).207.
94. "K ofitseram Russkoi armii," in Lehning, ed., *Archives Bakounine* 4: 17.
95. *Obshchina*, p. 3 (Lehning, ed., *Archives Bakounine* 4: 437).
96. *Kolokol* (Geneva), no. 1 (April 2, 1870), p. 6 (12). I have used the Soviet reprint of the journal *Kolokol*, V. I. Nevskii and E. A. Morokhovets, eds. The number in parentheses following the page number here and in subsequent citations indicates the page of the Soviet reprint.

97. Quoted in Venturi, p. 373.
98. *Kolokol* (Geneva), no. 1 (April 2, 1870), p. 5 (11).
99. *Kolokol* (Geneva), no. 4 (April 25, 1870), p. 4 (40). The article is signed by "an inhabitant of Lifland." This suggests that Vladimir Serebrennikov collaborated. I believe that the imagery is inspired, if not authored, by Nechaev.
100. From *Narodnaia rasprava*, no. 1 (1869). Quoted in Burtsev, *Za sto let*, p. 95.
101. Lehning, ed., *Archives Bakounine* 4: 309.
102. *Kolokol* (Geneva), no. 6 (May 9, 1870), p. 5 (59). The article is signed "Zh." I assume Nechaev's collaboration and approval, although Nikolai Zhukovskii was the primary author.

Chapter V

1. Z. Ralli, "M. A. Bakunin. Iz moikh vospominaniia," p. 160. Ralli implies that Nechaev's plans to organize bands of brigands from among his followers and the Swiss mountaineers was a major reason for Bakunin's break with him.
2. M. P. Sazhin, *Vospominaniia*, p. 66. In addition to memoirs, we have the reports of a Russian agent in Zurich who tried to keep track of Nechaev. They are summarized in N. N. Golitsyn, *Istoriia sotsial'no-revoliutsionnogo dvizheniia v Rossii, 1861–1881, glava desiataia*, pp. 8–10, 38–40. The reports sometimes contradict the other sources and mention trips to France, England, and Italy that cannot be verified. It is certain that Geneva was Nechaev's home base between January and July 1870, but there are only short periods for which we can be certain about his whereabouts. It is therefore difficult to dismiss the agent's reports, however implausible they sometimes seem. Nonetheless, one can say with certainty that Nechaev was not in Locarno with Bakunin in August 1870, as was reported by the agent.
3. A. I. Gertsen, *Sobranie sochinenii* 30: 297, 299.
4. Ibid., p. 299.
5. M. P. Dragomanov, *Pis'ma Bakunina k A. I. Gertsenu i N. P. Ogarevu* (Geneva), p. 255.
6. "To Russian Students," "The Noble Russian Gentry!," "To the Russian Meshchanstvo," and "To the Russian Merchants" were probably all written by Nechaev, although he signed only "To Russian Students." I believe that he composed sections of "From the Russian Revolutionary Society to Women," and there are passages in "To the Officers of the Russian Army," written by Bakunin, which I believe were either dictated by Nechaev or composed by him. Nechaev's contributions appear in roughly the second half of the article. Cf. Arthur Lehning, ed., *Archives Bakounine* 4: xxv–xxvi; Kusheva, "Revoliutsionnye proklamatsii," pp. 141–142.

7. "To the Village Clergy," "What Now Brothers!," and a leaflet dedicated to Herzen, "The Future." Kusheva, pp. 139–140, 142–147.
8. "To the Officers of the Russian Army," "Science and the Vital Revolutionary Cause," and "To Russian Youth." For the history of the last two brochures see Lehning, ed., *Archives Bakounine,* Vol. 5, Introduction. They are reproduced in the same volume.
9. TsGAOR, 109.110.3(1869).183.
10. Lehning, ed., *Archives Bakounine* 4: 308–309.
11. Ibid., p. 309.
12. Ibid.
13. Ibid.
14. Ibid.
15. Ibid., p. 320. The statement is italicized in the proclamation. One should note that while the proclamation describes women as victims of a repulsive system, it nonetheless expresses considerable hostility toward them as products of the system, suggesting that they are all prostitutes and deceivers, who give false love and care to husbands and children.
16. *Narodnaia rasprava* (Geneva), no. 2 (January 1, 1870), p. 11.
17. Ibid.
18. Ibid., p. 12.
19. Ibid.
20. Ibid., pp. 12–13.
21. Ibid., p. 14.
22. *Obshchina* (London), no. 1 (September 1, 1870), p. 5 (439). The number in parentheses is the page number in Lehning, ed., *Archives Bakounine,* Vol. 4.
23. Ibid., p. 4 (438).
24. *Narodnaia rasprava,* no. 2, (January 1, 1870), p. 1.
25. Ibid., p. 5 (419).
26. *Kolokol* (Geneva), no. 1 (April 2, 1870), p. 5 (11).
27. Ibid., p. 7 (13).
28. Lehning, ed., *Archives Bakounine* 4: 44–47.
29. Ibid., pp. 51–75.
30. K. Marx and F. Engels, *Sochineniia* 32: 426.
31. Ibid., p. 434.
32. Lehning, ed., *Archives Bakounine* 4: 55.
33. Ibid., p. 56.
34. *Obshchina,* no. 1, p. 6 (440).
35. V. D. Bonch-Bruevich, *Izbrannye sochineniia* 2: 314.
36. There is a photocopy of a ledger that sheds some light on expenditures and the transfer of funds in the B. I. Nicolaevsky Archive, Hoover Institution for War, Revolution, and Peace, Stanford, California, No. 161, 4: 11. The largest entry is for the transfer of 7,000 francs from the representative of the Committee of the Russian Society, N° 2664

to N°N° F_{12} and A[42]. The next largest entry is for 4,900 francs "received through Leipzig." There is an entry for a disbursement of 240 francs to Bakunin during the month of March and another for 100 francs on April 17 [1870]. A note in the ledger states that 3,840 francs had been set aside by the Committee for the publication of its organ (*Kolokol*), brochures, and leaflets. The ledger ends on May 13 [1870]. Most of the other entries deal with running expenses associated with the shipment of proclamations and brochures. Some of them are for travel expenses, and one of these is for over 1,000 francs. Among the notes there is an imperiously scrawled demand for 300 francs, signed with a flourish "Barsov," and dated June 19, 1870.

A fragment of a letter among the Nechaev documents in the Herzen collection contains Nechaev's excuse for refusing to give Ogarev a receipt for the money in the name of the Committee. The receipt would be tantamount to a confession that a secret society still existed in Russia, and this would endanger those who were still at large. It would be better to act as if the organization had been destroyed. Ogarev could fend off questions by saying that the disposition of the fund was entirely in his hands after Herzen's death and that it was to be used for propaganda in Russia. (Nicolaevsky Collection, No. 161, 4.) The fragment is in Nechaev's handwriting (photocopy). (See also Lehning, ed., *Archives Bakounine* 4: xliii–xliv.)

37. *Literaturnoe nasledstvo,* 41–42 (1941): 163.
38. For a good account of the Liubavin affair, see M. Confino, *Violence dans la violence,* pp. 77–82.
39. *Literaturnoe nasledstvo,* 41–42 (1941): 157–158.
40. Ibid., pp. 155–156.
41. A. K. Vorob'eva, ed., *K. Marks, F. Engel's i revoliutsionnaia Rossia,* p. 174.
42. Sazhin, pp. 63–64.
43. See Confino, *Daughter of a Revolutionary,* pp. 14–20.
44. Dragomanov, *Pis'ma Bakunina* (Geneva), pp. 262–264.
45. Confino, *Daughter of a Revolutionary,* p. 187.
46. Ibid., p. 189.
47. Ibid.
48. The correspondence is published in English translation in Confino, *Daughter of a Revolutionary.*
49. See ibid., pp. 163–164.
50. Ibid., pp. 201–207, 376–381.
51. One wonders why Natalie did not include this fact in her diary. Ordinarily, one would expect to find more details in an account written (presumably) three months after the events than in reminiscences written many years later.
52. Ibid., p. 207.
53. Ibid., pp. 211–216.

54. Ibid., p. 219.
55. Ibid., p. 170.
56. "Splotimtes' druzhno" [Unite in a Friendly Way].
57. *Kolokol* (Geneva), no. 2 (April 9, 1870), p. 4 (20).
58. Ibid., no. 4 (April 25, 1870). pp. 3–5 (39–41).
59. Ibid., no. 6, p. 5 (59).
60. Ibid., no. 1 (April 2, 1870), p. 4 (10).
61. Ibid., no. 3 (April 16, 1870), p. 7 (33).
62. Ibid., no. 4 (April 25, 1870), p. 4 (40).
63. E. L. N. P. Rudnitskaia, *Ogarev v russkon*, pp. 390–398.
64. *Literaturnoe nasledstvo*, 63 (1956): 711–712.
65. See J. M. Meijer, *Knowledge and Revolution*, pp. 63–64; Golitsyn, p. 7.
66. Serebrennikov's account of his arrest appeared in *Narodnoe delo* (Geneva), nos. 4 and 5 (June 30 and July 31, 1870); a separate brochure, *L'Arrestation de S. Serebrenikoff par la police de Genève* (Geneva, 1870), reprinted in Lehning, *Archives Bakounine* 4: 339–345. Not all of the émigrés believed his stories of Swiss police brutality.
67. These actions are described in N. A. Tuchkova-Ogareva, *Vospominaniia*, pp. 450–457; Confino, *Daughter of a Revolutionary*, pp. 381–384 (Natalie Herzen's version of the same episode). According to Tuchkova-Ogareva, Nechaev stayed with them for about eight days.
68. These facts are reconstructed from the correspondence between Lopatin and Natalie Herzen; Lopatin and Bakunin; and Bakunin and Nechaev. See *Literaturnoe nasledstvo* 63 (1956): 497–498; Confino, "Autour de l'affaire Nečaev," pp. 460–491; Confino, "Bakunin et Nečaev," pp. 624–696.
69. Confino, "Autour de l'affaire Nečaev," p. 470.
70. Ibid.
71. Ibid., p. 480.
72. Ibid., p. 486.
73. Lehning, ed., *Archives Bakounine* 4: 134–135.
74. See, K. Marx and F. Engels, *Sochineniia*, 32: 430–431; Confino, *Daughter of a Revolutionary*, pp. 314–315.
75. In the letter of August 1, 1870, Lopatin wrote that they had all attacked Ivanov with stones and had all beaten and strangled him. Also, Lopatin described how Nechaev had seized Uspenskii by mistake. According to the trial testimony, it was Nikolaev who had been seized in the dark. Finally, Uspenskii had not accompanied Ivanov on the way to the grotto, as claimed by Lopatin.
76. Lehning, ed., *Archives Bakounine* 5: 40–41.
77. For an English translation see Confino, *Daughter of a Revolutionary*, pp. 238–280.
78. Ibid., pp. 239–240.
79. Ibid., p. 244.

80. Ibid., p. 249.
81. Ibid., p. 274.
82. Lehning, ed., *Archives Bakounine* 4: 132. This is my own translation from the Russian.
83. Ibid., p. 191.
84. Ibid., pp. 142–148; English version, Confino, *Daughter of a Revolutionary*, pp. 291–300.
85. See Natalie Herzen's diary: Confino, *Daughter of a Revolutionary*, p. 303.
86. See Bakunin's letter of July 24, 1870, to Alfred Talandier in Dragomanov, *Pis'ma Bakunina* (Geneva), p. 286ff.
87. Ibid., p. 285. Bakunin and Natalie Herzen, with the aid of Ozerov, tried to get the letters and other documents back from Nechaev before he left for England but failed. Nechaev had stayed with James Guillaume shortly before his departure for England in July, and he evidently had the papers with him in a trunk, which Vladimir Serebrennikov took from Guillaume after Nechaev left. Somehow, the others found out that Nechaev had stayed with Guillaume and left his trunk there. They arrived too late. (James Guillaume, *L'Internationale* 2: 63.)
88. S. Serebrennikov, "Zapiska o Nechaeve," p. 13.
89. Confino, *Daughter of a Revolutionary*, p. 311.
90. *Obshchina* (London), no. 1 (September 1, 1870), p. 8 (442). For Nechaev's calculations, as reported by Sazhin, see Sazhin, pp. 68–70.
91. Marx and Engels, *Sochineniia* 17: 440.
92. Lehning, ed., *Archives Bakounine* 4: 167.
93. Letters in the Staatsarchiv in Zurich reveal that Nechaev had a girlfriend in Paris named Albertine Hottin. Bills for his room at rue du Jardinet indicate that he lived there between December 1 and December 19 [1870]; between December 15, 1871 and January 19, 1872; and again between May 9 and June 20, 1872. (Staatsarchiv P191b, "Auslieferung des Sergius Netschaieff, 56: 13, 14, and 40; letters from Albertine Hottin, 56: 25 and 42; drafts of two letters from Nechaev to her in a notebook.) In his deposition to the Zurich police Nechaev claimed that he had left Paris during the Commune, which would mean sometime after March 18, 1871, and had traveled to Brussels, where he had lived on the rue des Sables. He claimed to have returned to Paris after the Commune—that is, sometime after May 29, 1871.

    Material on Nechaev's life in London is even scantier. A Soviet scholar published a brief summary of the reports of a Russian police agent in London during 1870 and 1871. A. Balashevich-Pototskii reported that Nechaev was in London in May 1870, and had been seen by him in 1871 in a London restaurant. Unfortunately, I have not seen the documents upon which the article is based. (See V. A. D'iakov, "Glazami tsarskogo agenta," pp. 327–339.)

The Russian agent in Switzerland (as reported in Golitsyn) places Nechaev in Geneva in June 1871; in Annecy in July; in La Drire in August; in Vevey in October; and, in the same month, in Austrian Galicia under the name Tsekhanovskii. (The agent in this instance may have confused Nechaev with N. A. Tikhanov, a Nechaevist whose activities are examined in Grosul, *Rossiiskie revoliutsionery*, pp. 416–418, 459–464. Tikhanov used the name R. Tsekhanovskii.) There he was pursued by the Austrian police but escaped with the help of a Galician Jew named Weber, who gave him money and whose son accompanied Nechaev to London. In November, Nechaev and Weber's son traveled to Zurich. Nechaev now carried an English passport under the name Braunschweig. The agent has Nechaev in Zurich until the end of January 1872, except for a trip to Italy. Then, he reports that Nechaev has moved to Paris and in March to Heidelberg to agitate among the students there. In May, he is reported to be in Geneva; in June, in Paris, Vienna, and Munich until June 15, when he is in Zurich discussing Serbian revolutionary matters; in July, he arranges a truce with Bakunin; and in August 1872, he travels to Geneva. (In the absence of the complete set of reports, it is impossible to verify Golitsyn's accuracy in summarizing them.)

The agent credits Nechaev with a central role in the émigré colony in Zurich, especially in organizing the Russian women and the library there. The most scholarly account of the Russian colony in Zurich (J. M. Meijer, *Knowledge and Revolution*) does not accord Nechaev such a role. The agent also describes Nechaev's dress and habits: He wears his hair long; dresses in pleated trousers, a red shirt, a tall hat, and an outer jacket drawn back like a frock coat. Despite warnings, he moves about boldly, visits meetings of the International, and dines in restaurants. He lives at the Hotel du Cygne and works as a sign painter. Nechaev tells everyone what they want to hear, does not adhere to any party line, and presents himself as a lover of the people, a patriot, and a simple humanitarian.

The agent's account confirms what memoirists and other sources suggest—that during most of 1871 and for several weeks in 1872 Nechaev used Zurich as his main base but that he ranged far and wide. Both Grosul and Poglubko believe that he visited Romania during his second exile, and Poglubko claims that Nechaev left Russia in December 1869, through the southern route. Grosul believes that Nechaev took the northern route described above, but that he spent some time in the Balkans in January for conspiratorial purposes (Grosul, *Rossiiskie revoliutsionery*, p. 400) and believes he might have been in Romania in June 1871 (ibid., p. 410–418), as well.

94. Kantor, *V pogone za Nechaevym*, pp. 120–124. In Lyons Nechaev evidently relied upon Bakunin's ally Louis Palix. He met Bakunin's companion, a young Pole named V. Lankiewicz, sometime after September 14, 1870, in Lyons. Lankiewicz had left for Lyons in the company of Bakunin and Ozerov on that date. The conversation is reported by Bakunin's colleague and a police agent, Karl-Arvid Roman.
95. Ibid., p. 124.
96. Boris Sapir, ed., *Lavrov, gody emigratsii*, 1: 24.
97. Ibid., p. 17.
98. Ibid., p. 30.
99. Staatsarchiv, "Auslieferung des Sergius Netschaieff," nos. 50a and 50b.
100. Staatsarchiv, no. 47. Letter dated May 15, 1872.
101. Sazhin, p. 66. Although I have consulted *Nedelia* for 1871 and 1872, I have not been able to confirm Sazhin's claim that several of Nechaev's letters were published. Most of the correspondence about events in France was signed Mikh. Tar——ts', which was the pseudonym of M. V. Dal'mert.
102. Sazhin, pp. 64–66; cf. Grosul, pp. 413–414.
103. Sazhin, p. 66. One wonders if Sazhin is correct about this. Presumably it was A. Stempkowski who got Nechaev the job as sign painter in the summer of 1872.
104. Sazhin, p. 67.
105. Ibid.
106. He showed Sazhin and Smirnov a "memorandum" about the fund. Ibid., p. 68ff.
107. Ibid., p. 171.
108. On Turskii and his group, see B. P. Koz'min, *Russkaia sektsiia pervogo internatsionala*, pp. 242–243; T. G. Snytko, *Russkoe narodnichestvo i pol'skoe obshchestvennoe dvizhenie, 1865–1881 gg.*, pp. 90–91; Lehning, *Archives Bakounine* 4: 530; R. Theen, "The Russian Blanquists and the Hague Congress," pp. 347–376.
109. B. Nikolaevskii, "Pamiati poslednego 'iakobintsa'-semidesiatnika," p. 216ff.
110. For a recent study emphasizing not only Nechaev's influence on Turskii but his influence on Tkachev by way of Turskii during Tkachev's exile as well, see Deborah Hardy, *Peter Tkachev*, pp. 250–277.
111. Koz'min, *Russkaia sektsiia*, p. 243.
112. Ibid.
113. Meijer, pp. 90–91.
114. For one of Nechaev's projects—a draft of a program for Slavic socialist unity—see W. McClellan, "Nechaevshchina: An Unknown Chapter," pp. 546–553. McClellan has also written about Nechaev's Serbian ties in "Rusi, Srbi i revolutsija, 1870–1872."

115. Sazhin, pp. 72–74.
116. Ralli, "Sergei Gennad'evich Nechaev," p. 146.

Chapter VI

1. TsGAOR, 109.115.2(1869).108.
2. See R. Theen, "Nečaevs Auslieferung 1872. Der diplomatische Hintergrund," p. 576; Kantor, V *pogone za Nechaevym*, pp. 11–12.
3. The sometimes amusing story of Roman's relationship to the émigrés is told in Kantor, V *pogone*.
4. Ibid., pp. 91–92.
5. Ibid., p. 105.
6. Roman learned this from V. Lankiewicz, as noted in Chapter 6.
7. TsGAOR, 109. appendix to 112(1869).–.1.
8. Ibid.
9. TsGAOR, 109.115.8(1869).243.
10. TsGAOR, 109.115.9(1869).9.
11. Archives of the Préfecture de Police (Paris), $B\frac{9}{92H}$, Netchaieff. French agents in Zurich inform Monsieur Lombard on July 11, 1872, that they have no information about Nechaev.
12. TsGAOR, 109.112.5.203.
13. Evidence in the Staatsarchiv in Zurich suggests that he also might have lived with two Serbian students, Hrvachanin, mentioned above, and Tasa Stoianovich. Envelopes bearing letters to him (Monsieur Étienne) were addressed to both of them. (Staatsarchiv, "Auslieferung des Sergius Netschaieff," no. 56, pp. 37, 38. See also Ralli, "Sergei Gennad'evich Nechaev," pp. 143–146; and Kantor, V *pogone*, p. 130.)
14. Préfecture de Police, Letters to Monsieur Lombard dated August 1–8, 1872.
15. Préfecture de Police, Telegram from Gorchakov, August 8, 1872.
16. Kantor, V *pogone*, p. 130.
17. Ibid., pp. 130–133.
18. Ibid., p. 133.
19. Ibid., p. 134; TsGAOR, 109.112.5.60; Leonhard Haas, "Njetschajew und die Schweizer Behörden," p. 361; Hermann Greulich, *Das grüne Husli*, pp. 64–65.
20. Haas, p. 361.
21. Kantor, V *pogone*, p. 134.
22. Ibid., p. 135.
23. TsGAOR, 109.115.23(1869).168; Kantor, V *pogone*, p. 135.
24. TsGAOR, 109.115.23(1869).168.
25. TsGAOR, 109.115.7(1869).140.
26. Ibid.

27. Haas, p. 317.
28. TsGAOR, 109.115.7(1869).–. in a letter from Giers to Gorchakov of March 21/9, 1870.
29. Haas, p. 317.
30. Ibid., p. 321.
31. Ibid., p. 322.
32. Ibid., pp. 322–323; see also Theen, "Nečaevs Auslieferung," p. 578. The decision of the Bundesrat gave the Russian ambassador little cause for celebration, for he had no confidence in the Swiss political system. Giers believed that pressure from the Russian government on the Bundesrat might yield little, given the vigilance with which the cantons guarded their rights. (Giers to Shuvalov, dispatch of June 1/May 20, 1870, in TsGAOR, 109.115.8(1869).12.)
33. Haas, p. 326.
34. Theen, "Nečaevs Auslieferung," p. 579.
35. Haas, p. 329.
36. Staatsarchiv, "Auslieferung des Sergius Netschaieff," no. 26.
37. Ibid., no. 28.
38. Haas, pp. 332–334; Staatsarchiv, "Auslieferung des Sergius Netschaieff," nos. 33–41; TsGAOR, 109.112.5.158.
39. Staatsarchiv, "Auslieferung des Sergius Netschaieff," no. 49.
40. Ibid., no. 50.
41. Ibid., no. 48.
42. Ibid., no. 54.
43. TsGAOR, 109.112.5.66.
44. TsGAOR, 109.112.6.86.
45. Ibid.
46. TsGAOR, 109.112.5.98–99.
47. Staatsarchiv, "Auslieferung des Sergius Netschaieff," no. 46. The émigrés Alexander El'snits, Zemfri Ralli, Valerian Smirnov, Vladimir Gol'shtein, and Kaspar Turskii sent the Swiss authorities a copy of their pamphlet, "Is Nechaev a Political Criminal or Not?" For excerpts, see Arthur Lehning, ed., *Archives Bakounine* 4: 389–392.
48. Haas, pp. 339–341; Staatsarchiv, "Auslieferung des Sergius Netschaieff," no. 79.
49. TsGAOR, 109.112.5.98–99.
50. Haas, pp. 342–343. Pfenninger, who was a strong advocate of extradition, had lost patience with the Russian and Polish émigrés in Zurich. On October 20, 1872, Gorchakov had written in a secret dispatch to de Westmann that an agent had informed him that Pfenninger had said: "We have here an assassin, we have all of the Russian legal materials in perfect order. We must extradite. This will be done soon. The Russian and Polish émigrés are far too influential in Zurich. They must be given a real lesson." (TsGAOR, 109.112.5. 135.)

51. Published in full in Haas, pp. 362–363; Lehning, ed., *Archives Bakounine* 4: 398–399. The document is in French, as are all of Nechaev's Swiss prison writings. Staatsarchiv, "Auslieferung des Sergius Netschaieff," no. 94.
52. TsGAOR, 109.112.5.159–161.
53. The vote was close—four in favor of and three against extradition. See Haas, p. 344.
54. TsGAOR, 109.112.5.155.
55. TsGAOR, 109.112.5.175.
56. Emil Szymanowski, "Zapiska E. Shimanovskogo," in Nicolaevsky Collection, no. 161, 3, pp. 14–15. Also see N. G. Kuliabko-Koretskii, *Iz davnikh let*, pp. 50–52; Meijer, *Knowledge and Revolution*, pp. 104–109; and Ralli, "Sergei Gennad'evich Nechaev," p. 146.
57. The Russian agent's report is at complete variance with Szymanowski's account, and since Szymanowski was a participant in the events, it appears that the agent's report was based on rumors. He claimed that two groups of émigrés were involved. One group was armed with clubs and revolvers. The other group, unarmed, was supposed to throw sand in the eyes of the gendarmes, but failed to fulfill its commission. Although the firearms did not come into play, the police were forced to use their swords. Several of the attackers were wounded and six of their leaders arrested. These events came to pass only after the sum of 50,000 francs had been offered to unnamed Swiss officials (evidently in vain) and another 3,000 francs had been given to one Brüner, a Swiss official who accepted the bribe and provided information about the time when Nechaev would be taken to the railroad station (TsGAOR, 109.115.23(1869).35–36).
58. TsGAOR, 109.112.6.152–154.
59. TsGAOR, 109.115.23(1869).24–27, 63–71.
60. P. Shchegolev, 4 (1923): 222.
61. TsGAOR, 109.115.23(1869).72.
62. Ibid., list' 76.
63. Ibid., list' 82.
64. Ibid., list' 93.
65. Bazilevskii, *Gosudarstvennye prestupleniia*, p. 415.
66. Ibid.
67. TsGAOR, 109.115.23(1869).105.
68. Ibid., listi 98–103.
69. Quoted in Shchegolev, *Krasnyi arkhiv* 4 (1923): 227.
70. Bazilevskii, p. 416.
71. Ibid.
72. Ibid., p. 422.
73. Ibid., p. 424; TsGAOR, 109.115.23(1869).93.
74. Bazilevskii, pp. 449–451.
75. Ibid., p. 453.

76. Ibid., p. 451.
77. Ibid., p. 454.
78. Ibid., p. 451.
79. TsGAOR, 109.115.23(1869).93.
80. Bazilevskii, p. 455.
81. TsGAOR, 109.115.23(1869).93.
82. Printed in full in Shchegolev, *Krasnyi arkhiv* 4 (1923): 229–231.
83. TsGAOR, 109.115.23(1869).110–111.
84. Ibid., list' 113.
85. Shchegolev, *Krasnyi arkhiv* 4 (1923): 235; TsGAOR, 109.115.23 (1869).130.
86. Shchegolev, *Krasnyi arkhiv* 4 (1923): 236.
87. Ibid., p. 237.
88. Ibid., pp. 242–247.
89. Ibid., p. 247.
90. TsGIAL, fond 1280. opis' 5. delo 158.
91. Shchegolev, *Krasnyi arkhiv* 4 (1923): 249.
92. The original is in TsGAOR, 109. appendix to 112(1869).–.61aff. It is published in full in Shchegolev, *Krasnyi arkhiv* 4 (1923): 252–257.
93. Shchegolev, *Krasnyi arkhiv* 4 (1923): 256.
94. Ibid., p. 257.
95. Ibid.
96. TsGAOR, 109. appendix to 112.–.39–43. The report is dated April 24, 1876. Published in full in Shchegolev, *Krasnyi arkhiv* 4 (1923): 259–262; in English translation in Confino, *Daughter of a Revolutionary*, pp. 325–329.
97. Confino, *Daughter of a Revolutionary*, p. 329.
98. Shchegolev, *Krasnyi arkhiv* 4 (1923): 257.
99. Ibid.
100. *Vestnik Narodnoi Voli* (Geneva), no. 1 (1883), p. 143.
101. Shchegolev, *Krasnyi arkhiv* 4 (1923): 258.
102. Ibid., p. 262.
103. Ibid., pp. 263–264.
104. Iurii Trifonov, *Neterpenie*, p. 203.
105. Ibid., pp. 307–308.
106. Ibid., pp. 468–469.
107. A. Camus, *The Rebel*, p. 169.
108. Ibid., p. 172.
109. Ibid., p. 168.
110. Before this, Solomon Chudnovskii, who had been imprisoned in another area of the fortress in 1876, had found a "letter" from Nechaev in one of the prison journals. Nechaev had evidently used a nail to underline individual letters on the pages of the books and journals given to him. When read consecutively, the letters formed words. In the message found by Chudnovskii, evidently in the late autumn of

1876, Nechaev described his enchainment. This confirms the fact that the authorities permitted Nechaev to read books from the prison library while he was still in chains. Chudnovskii claims in his memoirs that he told the story to other prisoners in the fortress, and Katherine Breshkovskaiia's memoirs confirm this. (Prisoners also communicated by tapping out messages to those in nearby cells.) Given that Nechaev had been discovered as early as 1876, it is difficult to understand why word of his imprisonment did not spread to the revolutionary underground before 1880, when he himself made contact with The People's Will. Chudnovskii's account, if accurate, is also valuable for its description of the prison diet and the treatment of the prisoners. (S. L. Chudnovskii, *Iz davnikh let*, pp. 125–128. For the story of Ol'ga Natanson's discovery, see TsGAOR, 109.112.5(1869).278–279.)

111. TsGAOR, 109.112.5(1869).280.
112. Ibid., list' 281. This is a copy. The original is in TsGIAL, fond 1280. opis' 5. delo 158. list' 48.
113. Shchegolev, *Krasnyi arkhiv* 4 (1923): 267.
114. The original copy from the slate is in TsGIAL, fond 1280. opis' 5. delo 158. list' 55.
115. Shchegolev, *Krasnyi arkhiv* 4 (1923): 267–.
116. Ibid., 5 (1924): 173–175; see also *Vestnik Narodnoi Voli* (Geneva), no. 1 (1883), pp. 187–203.
117. Vera Figner, *Zapechatlennyi trud* 1: 249.
118. Ibid., p. 252.
119. Shchegolev, *Krasnyi arkhiv* 5 (1924): 185–186; *Vestnik Narodnoi Voli* (Geneva), no. 1 (1883), pp. 150–151.
120. *Vestnik Narodnoi Voli* (Geneva), no. 1 (1883), p. 148; Shchegolev, *Krasnyi arkhiv* 5 (1924): 185–187. In an anonymous article (probably written by L. Tikhomirov) "S. G. Nechaev v Alekseevskom raveline v 1873–1883 [*sic*] gg.," it is claimed that Shiriaev opposed Nechaev's plan to seize the fortress and establish a pretender (*Byloe* 7 [1906]: 157).
121. Shchegolev, *Krasnyi arkhiv* 5 (1924): 187; cf. Figner, *Zapechatlennyi trud* 1: 254–255.
122. They are preserved in typed manuscript in the International Institute for Social History (Amsterdam), Archive of *Vestnik Narodnoi Voli*.
123. IISH, Archive of *Vestnik Narodnoi Voli*, 834/4/a–5.
124. [L. Tikhomirov?], "S. G. Nechaev v Alekseevskom raveline," pp. 157–158.
125. Ibid., p. 159.
126. Ibid.
127. IISH, Archive of *Vestnik Narodnoi Voli*, 834/6, p. 6.
128. Ibid., 834/4/b.
129. Ibid.

130. IISH, Archive of *Vestnik Narodnoi Voli*, 834/7.
131. Ibid., 834/8/a–b.
132. Ibid., 834/10/a.
133. Ibid., 834/11/a.
134. Ibid., 834/5.
135. Shchegolev, *Krasnyi arkhiv* 5 (1924): 191.
136. [L. Tikhomirov?], "Nechaev v Alekseevskom raveline," p. 157; Figner, *Zapechatlennyi trud* 1: 254–255; cf. Shchegolev, *Krasnyi arkhiv* 5 (1924): 187.
137. Shchegolev, *Krasnyi arkhiv* 5 (1924): 192.
138. Ibid., pp. 194–195.
139. Figner, *Zapechatlennyi trud* 1: 255–256; [L. Tikhomirov?], "Nechaev v Alekseevskom raveline," p. 160.
140. [L. Tikhomirov?], "Nechaev v Alekseevskom raveline," p. 163.
141. *Vestnik Narodnoi Voli* (Geneva), no. 1 (1883), p. 152.
142. Ibid., p. 143. The Shevich referred to by Nechaev was in reality a man named Beideman. For an explanation of Nechaev's erroneous identification, see P. Shchegolev, *Alekseevskii ravelin*, p. 173.
143. Shchegolev, *Krasnyi arkhiv* 5 (1924): 197.
144. From information provided in *Vestnik Narodnoi Voli* (Geneva), no. 1 (1883), pp. 187–203.
145. Figner claims in her memoirs that some of Nechaev's helpers in the ravelin met other revolutionaries in Siberia. Not one of them ever reproached Nechaev. Some of them still seemed to be in awe of him. They would not even pronounce his name—he had forbidden it—and referred to Nechaev as "he." Figner wrote: "The power (*avtoritet*) of his personality still dazzled them. It was suggestion, hypnosis destroyed neither by trials, nor time, nor space." (Figner, *Zapechatlennyi trud* 1: 258.)
146. Shchegolev, *Krasnyi arkhiv* 5 (1924): 184. Most of his accomplices came from the northwestern provinces of Russia—Arkhangel, Vologda, Novgorod, Pskov—and a few from Vladimir in the northeastern part of European Russia, Nechaev's own province of origin.
147. Ibid., pp. 199–202.
148. Ibid., p. 211.
149. Ibid., p. 209.
150. Ibid., p. 211.
151. Ibid., p. 212.
152. Quoted in Shchegolev, *Krasnyi arkhiv* 6 (1924): 92–93.
153. Ibid., pp. 82–84.
154. TsGIAL, fond 1280. opis' 5. ed. khr. 213. listi 36, 38.
155. Ibid., fond 1280. ed. khr. 213. list' 67.
156. Ibid., list' 68.
157. Ibid., list' 79.

Chapter VII

1. Otto Fenichel, *The Psychoanalytic Theory of Neurosis*, pp. 511–512.
2. Ibid., p. 500.
3. I have tried to show how this applies to Stalin as well as to Nechaev in "Nečaev, Lenin, and Stalin: The Psychology of Leadership," *Jahrbücher für Geschichte Osteuropas* 26 (1978): 11–30.

Bibliography

Primary Sources

Unpublished Materials

Amsterdam. International Institute for Social History. Archive of *Vestnik Narodnoi Voli*. 834.

Leningrad. Tsentral'nyi Gosudarstvennyi Istoricheskii Arkhiv v Leningrade. Fond 878. opis' 1. ed. khr. 82: Tatishchev, S. S. "Sotsial'no-revoliutsionnoe dvizhenie v Rossii. Sudebno-politseiskaia khronika, 1861–1871. Glava odinnadtsataia. Nechaevskoe delo, 1869–1871 gg."; fond 1280.

Moscow. Tsentral'nyi Gosudarstvennyi Arkhiv Oktiabr'skoi Revoliutsii. Fond 109. dela 110, 112, 115.

Paris. Archives of the Préfecture de Police. B$\frac{9}{92H}$, Netchaieff.

Stanford, California. The Hoover Institution Archives. The Nicolaevsky Collection, nos. 161, 183.

Zurich. Staatsarchiv, P191b. "Auslieferung des Sergius Netschaieff."

Published Materials

Antisferov, N. P. "Starshaia doch' Gertsena (Tata). Pis'ma, avtobiograficheskie nabroski, vospominaniia." *Literaturnoe nasledstvo* 63 (1956).

Bakounine, T. and Catteau, J. "Contribution à la biographie de Serge Nečaev; Correspondance avec Natalie Herzen." *Cahiers du monde russe et soviétique*, no. 2 (1966).

Bazilevskii, B. [Iakovlev, V. Ia.]. *Gosudarstvennye prestupleniia v Rossii v XIX veke*. Vol. 1. Stuttgart: Dietz, 1903.

Bel'chikov, N. "S. G. Nechaev v s. Ivanove v 60-e gody." *Katorga i ssylka*, no. 14 (1925).

Belinsky, V. G. *Polnoe sobranie sochinenii.* 13 vols. Moscow: Akademii nauk, 1953–1959.

Bonch-Bruevich, V. D. *Izbrannye sochineniia.* 3 vols. Moscow: Izd. Akademii nauk SSSR, 1959–1963.

Breshkovskaia, Katerina. *Hidden Springs of the Russian Revolution.* Edited by Lincoln Hutchinson. Palo Alto, Ca.: Stanford University Press, 1931.

Burtsev, V. *Za sto let (1800–1896).* Chast' pervaia. London: Russian Free Press Fund, 1897.

Cherniak, Ia. "Neizdannye i nesobrannye proizvedeniia Ogareva." *Literaturnoe nasledstvo* 61 (1953).

Chernyshevskii, N. G. *Chto delat'.* Moscow: Gos. izd. khudozh. lit-ry, 1960.

Chudnovskii, S. L. *Iz davnikh let.* Moscow: Izd. vses. ob-vo. politakatorzhan i ssyl'no-poselentsev, 1934.

Confino, Michael. "Autour de l'affaire Nečaev," *Cahiers du monde russe et soviétique,*" no. 3 (1967).

———. "Bakunin et Nečaev. Les débuts de la rupture," *Cahiers du monde russe et soviétique,* no. 4 (1966).

———. "Bakunin et Nečaev. La rupture. Letters inédites de Michel Bakunin et de German Lopatin," *Cahiers du monde russe et soviétique,* no. 1 (1967).

———. *Daughter of a Revolutionary.* La Salle, Ill: Library Press, 1973.

———. "Un document inédit: Le journal de Natalie Herzen 1869–1870." *Cahiers du monde russe et soviétique,* no. 1 (1969).

———. "Nečaev et le meurtre de l'étudiant I. Ivanov." *Cahiers du monde russe et soviétique,* no. 4 (1967).

———. *Violence dans le violence: le débat Bakounine-Nečaev.* Paris: F. Maspero, 1973.

Dostoevsky, F. M. *The Notebooks for the Possessed.* Edited by Edward Wasiolek. Translated by Victor Terras. Chicago: The University of Chicago Press, 1968.

———. *Pis'ma.* Edited by A. S. Dolinin. 4 vols. Moscow-Leningrad: Academia, 1928–1959.

Dragomanov, M. P., ed. *Pis'ma Bakunina k A. I. Gertsenu i N. P. Ogarevu.* Geneva. Ukrainskaia tipografia, 1896.

———. *Pis'ma Bakunina k A. I. Gertsenu i N. P. Ogarevu.* St. Petersburg: Izd. V. Vrublevskago, 1906.

Figner, Vera. *Zapechatlennyi trud.* 2 vols. Moscow: Mysl', 1964.

Frolenko, M. F. *Sobranie sochinenii.* 2 vols. Moscow: Izd. vses. ob-vo politkatorzhan i ssyl'no-poselentsev, 1930–1931.

Gertsen, A. I. "K staromu tovarishchu." *Literaturnoe nasledstvo* 61 (1953).

———. *Polnoe sobranie sochinenii i pisem.* Edited by M. K. Lemke. 22 vols. Moscow: Gosudarstvennoe izd., 1919–1925.

———. *Sobranie sochinenii v tridtsati tomakh,* 30 vols. in 34. Moscow: Nauka, 1954–1965.

Greulich, Hermann. *Das grüne Husli.* Zurich: Genossenschaftdruckerei, 1942.

Guillaume, James. *L'Internationale: documents et souvenirs (1864–1878).* 2 vols. Paris: Société nouvelle de libraire et d'édition, 1905–1907.

"Iz istorii vozobnovlennogo 'Kolokola' 1870g." *Literaturnoe nasledstvo* 63 (1956).

Klevenskii, M. M., ed. *Pokushenie Karakozova.* Vol. 1. Moscow: Izd. Tsentrarkhiva, 1928.

Kolokol. Geneva, 1870. Reprint edited by V. I. Nevskii and E. A. Morokhovets. Moscow: Izd. Vsesoiuznogo obshchestva politkatorzhan i ssyl'noposelentsev, 1933.

Kolokol. London, 1866–1867. Facsimile edition. Moscow: Nauka, 1964.

Kovalenskii, M. *Russkaia revoliutsiia v sudebnykh protsessakh i memuarakh.* Kniga 1. Moscow: Izd. Mir, 1923.

Koz'min, B. P., ed. *Istoriki-revoliutsionnaia khrestomatiia.* Vol. 1. Moscow: Novaia Moskva, 1923.

———. "K istorii 'Nechaevshchiny' (Dve proklamatsii k russkomu dvorianstvu)." *Krasnyi arkhiv,* no. 22 (1927).

———. "K istorii Nechaevskogo protsessa." *Krasnyi arkhiv,* no. 43 (1930).

———. "Kto byl pervym perevodchikom na russkii iazyk 'Manifesta Kommunisticheskoi Partii'?" *Literaturnoe nasledstvo* 63 (1956).

———. *Nechaev i nechaevtsy, sbornik materialov.* Moscow: Gosudarstvennoe sotsial'noekonomicheskoe izd., 1931.

———. "Novoe o S. G. Nechaeve." *Krasnyi arkhiv,* nos. 14–15 (1926).

Koz'min, B. P. and Pereselenikov, S. "K istorii Nechaevshchiny." *Literaturnoe nasledstvo* 41–42 (1941).

Kuklin, G. A. *Itogi revoliutsionnogo dvizheniia v Rossii za sorok let (1862–1902 gg.).* Geneva: Izd. G. A. Kuklina, 1903.

Kuliabko-Koretskii, N. G. *Iz davnikh let.* Moscow: Politkatorzhan, 1931.

Kusheva, E. "Revoliutsionnye proklamatsii zhenevskoi tipografii 1869–1870 godov." *Literaturnoe nasledstvo* 41–42 (1941).

Lehning, Arthur, ed. *Michel Bakounine, Étatisme et Anarchie, 1873. Archives Bakounine,* vol. 1. Leiden: E. J. Brill, 1967.

———. *Michel Bakounine et ses relations avec Sergei Nečaev. Archives Bakounine,* vol. 4. Leiden: E. J. Brill, 1971.

———. *Michel Bakounine et ses relations slaves, 1870–1875. Archives Bakounine,* vol. 5. Leiden: E. J. Brill, 1974.

Luxemburg, Rosa. *The Russian Revolution, and Leninism or Marxism.* Edited by Bertram D. Wolfe. Ann Arbor: University of Michigan Press, 1961.

McClellan, Woodford. "Nechaevishchina: An Unknown Chapter." *Slavic Review,* no. 3. (1973).

Marx, K. and Engels, F. *Sochineniia.* 2d ed. 39 vols. in 42. Moscow: Gospolitizdat, 1955–1966.

———. *Werke.* 39 vols. in 41. Berlin: Dietz Verlag, 1959–1971.

Moskovskie vedomosti, no. 172 (1862).
Narodnoe delo. Geneva, no. 1 (1868); no. 4 (1870).
Narodnaia rasprava, nos. 1 and 2 (1869–1870).
Nikiforov, L. "Moi tiur'my." *Golos minuvshego*, no. 5 (1914).
Obshchina. No. 1. London, 1870.
Pirumova, N. "M. Bakunin ili S. Nechaev?" *Prometei*, no. 5 (1968).
Poglubko, K. A. "Sviazi bolgarskikh i russkikh emigrantov." *Izvestiia Akademii Nauk Moldavskoi SSSR. seriia obshchestvennykh nauk*, no. 1 (1968).
Pravitel'stvennyi vestnik, nos. 155–206 (1871); no. 10 (1873).
Pryzhov, I. G. "Ispoved'." *Minuvshye gody*, no. 2 (1908).
———. "Nechaevets I. G. Pryzhov v ego pis'makh." *Katorga i ssylka*, no. 33 (1927).
Rakitnikova, I. "Pamiati F. A. Borisova." *Katorga i ssylka*, no. 53 (1929).
Ralli, Z. "M. A. Bakunin. Iz moikh vospominaniia." *Minuvshie gody*, no. 10 (1908).
———. "Sergei Gennad'evich Nechaev." *Byloe*, no. 7 (1906).
Sapir, Boris, ed. *Lavrov, gody emigratsii*. Russian Series on Social History, vol. 1. Dordrecht: D. Reidel Publishing Co., 1974.
Sazhin, M. P. *Vospominaniia*. Moscow: Vsesoiuznoe obshchestvo politicheskikh katorzhan i ssyl'no-poselentsev, 1925.
Serebrennikov, Semen. "Zapiska o Nechaeve." *Katorga i ssylka*, no. 112 (1934).
Shilov, A. "Katekhizis revoliutsionera." *Bor'ba klassov*, nos. 1–2 (1924).
Tikhomirov, L. "Materialy dlia biografii S. G. Nechaeva." *Vestnik Narodnoi Voli*, no. 1 (1883).
Tkachev, P. N. *Izbrannye sochineniia na sotsial'no-politicheskii temy*. Edited by B. P. Koz'min. 6 vols. Moscow: Obshchestvo politkatorzhan, 1932–1937.
Tuchkova-Ogareva, N. A. *Vospominaniia*. Leningrad: Akademiia, 1929.
Turgenev, Ivan S. *Fathers and Sons*. Edited by Ralph Matlaw. New York: Norton, 1966.
Uspenskaia, A. I. "Vospominaniia shestidestiatnitsy." *Byloe*, no. 18 (1922).
Vorob'eva, A. K., ed. *K. Marks, F. Engel's i revoliutsionnaia Rossiia*. Moscow: Institut Marksizma-Leninizma pri TsKKPSS. Izd. politicheskoi literatury, 1967.
Zasulich, V. I. *Vospominaniia*. Moscow: Izd. Politikatorzhan, 1931.
Zemliak, "Novoe o Nechaeve." *Byloe* [Paris], no. 14 (1912).

Secondary Sources

Al'tman, M. "Ivan Gavrilovich Pryzhov." *Katorga i ssylka*, no. 91 (1932).
Arnold, David O., ed. *The Sociology of Subcultures*. Berkeley: The Glendessary Press, 1970.

Bibliography

Avrich, Paul. *Bakunin and Nechaev*. London: Freedom Press, 1974.

Barrué, J. *Bakounine et Netchaiev*. Paris: Spartacus, 1971.

Bel'chikov, N. "Iz byta literaturnikh kruzhkov 60–70 godov," *Literatura i Marksizm*, kniga 3 (1928).

———. *Narodnichestvo v literature i kritike*. Moscow: Sovetskaia literatura, 1934.

Berdiaev, Nicholas. *The Origin of Russian Communism*. Ann Arbor, Michigan: University of Michigan Press, 1960.

Brower, Daniel. *Training the Nihilists*. Ithaca: Cornell University Press, 1975.

Bush, V. V. *Ocherki literaturnogo narodnichestva*. Moscow-Leningrad: Gos. Izd. Khudozhestvennoi literatury, 1931.

Camus, Albert. *The Rebel*. Translated by Anthony Bower. New York: Vintage, 1956.

Cannac, René. *Netchaiev: du nihilisme au terrorisme*. Paris: Payot, 1961.

Carr, E. H. *Michael Bakunin*. London: Macmillan, 1937.

———. *The Romantic Exiles*. London: Victor Gollancz, Ltd., 1933.

Cherniavsky, Michael. *Tsar and People*. New Haven and London: Yale University Press, 1961.

Cochrane, Stephen T. *The Collaboration of Nečaev, Ogarev and Bakunin in 1869: Nečaev's Early Years*. Giessen: W. Schmitz Verlag, 1977.

Deich, L. "Byl li Nechaev genialen?" *Gruppa "osvobozhdenie truda,"* Sbornik, no. 2. Moscow: Gosudarstvennoe izd., 1924.

D'iakov, V. A. "Glazami tsarskogo agenta." *Prometei*, no. 7 (1969).

Dunn, Patrick. "Fathers and Sons Revisited: The Childhood of Vissarion Belinsky." *History of Childhood Quarterly*, no. 3 (1974).

———. " 'That Enemy is the Baby'." In *The History of Childhood*, edited by Lloyd deMause. New York: The Psychohistory Press, 1974.

Ekzempliarskii, P. M. *Istoriia goroda Ivanova*. Chast' pervaia. Ivanovo: Ivanovskoe knizhnoe izd., 1958.

———. "Selo Ivanovo v zhizni Sergeia Gennad'evicha Nechaeva." In *Trudy Ivanovo-Voznesenskogo gubernskogo nauchnogo obshchestva kraevedeniia*, vypusk 4. Ivanovo-Voznesensk, 1926.

Erikson, Erik. *Childhood and Society*. 2d rev. ed. New York: W. W. Norton, 1963.

———. "The Legend of Maxim Gorky's Childhood." In *Childhood and Society*. 2d ed., rev. New York: W. W. Norton & Co., 1963.

Fenichel, Otto. *The Psychoanalytic Theory of Neurosis*. New York: W. W. Norton & Co., 1945.

Filippov, R. V. *Iz istorii narodnicheskogo dvizheniia na pervom etape "khozhdenie v narod"* (1863–1874). Petrozavodsk: Karel'skoe knizhnoe izd., 1967.

———. *Iz istorii revoliutsionno-demokraticheskogo dvizheniia v Rossii v kontse 60–kh, nachale 70–kh godov XIX veka*. Petrozavodsk: Gos. izd. Karel'skoe ASSR, 1962.

Firstova, V. N. "Tsarskaia diplomaticheskaia missiia v Berne i russkaia emigratsiia." *Voprosy istorii*, no. 6 (1973).

Footman, David. *Red Prelude*. New Haven: Yale University Press, 1945.

Frankel, Jonathan. "Party Genealogy and the Soviet Historians." *Slavic Review*, no. 4 (1966).

Freud, Anna. *The Ego and the Mechanisms of Defense*. Rev. ed. The Writings of Anna Freud, vol. 2. New York: International Universities Press, 1966.

Gambarov, A. *V sporakh o Nechaeve*. Moscow: Moskovskii rabochii, 1926.

Giliarov, F. A. *15 Let Kramoly, 4 aprel' 1866–1 mart 1881 g*. Vol. I, pt. 1. Moscow, 1883.

Golitsyn, N. N. *Istoriia sotsial'no-revoliutsionnogo dvizheniia v Rossii, 1861–1881, glava desiataia*. St. Petersburg, 1887.

Gorev, B. I. and Koz'min, B. P., eds. *Revoliutsionnoe dvizhenie 1860–kh godov*. Moscow: Izd. vses. ob-vo politkatorzhan i ssyl'no-poselentsev, 1932.

Goriachkina, M. *Khudozhestvennaia proza narodnichestva*. Moscow: Nauka, 1970.

Greenstein, Fred. *Personality and Politics*. Chicago: Markham Publishing Co., 1969.

Grosul, V. Ia. *Rossiiskie revoliutsionery v iugo-vostochnoi evrope*. Kishinev: Shtiintsa, 1973.

Haas, Leonhard. "Njetschajew und die Schweizer Behörden." *Schweitzerische Zeitschrift für Geschichte* 17 (1967).

Hardy, Deborah. *Peter Tkachev: the Critic as Jacobin*. Seattle and London: University of Washington Press, 1977.

Hingley, Ronald. *Nihilists: Russian Radicals and Revolutionaries in the Reign of Alexander II*. New York: Delacorte Press, 1969.

Itenberg, B. S. *Dvizhenie revoliutsionnogo narodnichestva*. Moscow: Nauka, 1965.

Kantor, R. M. *V pogone za Nechaevym*. 2d ed., rev. Leningrad: Gos. izd., 1925.

Kariakin, Iu. F., Plimak, E. G. and Volodin, I. A. *Chernyshevskii ili Nechaev?* Moscow: Mysl', 1976.

Kariakin, Iu. F., and Plimak, E. G. "Nechaevshchina i ee sovremennye burzhuaznye 'issledovateli'." *Istoriia SSSR*, no. 6 (1960).

Klevenskii, M., Koz'min, B. P., and Volk, S. N., eds. *Russkaia podpol'naia i zarubezhnaia pechat'*. Vol. 1. Moscow: Izd. politkatorzhan, 1935.

Koz'min, B. P. "Gertsen, Ogarev, i molodaia emigratsiia." *Literaturnoe nasledstvo* 41–42 1941.

———. "Istoriia ili fantastika?" *Pechat' i revoliutsiia*, no. 6 (1926).

———. *Iz istorii revoliutsionnoi mysli v Rossii*. Moscow: Izd. Akademii nauk, 1961.

———. *P. N. Tkachev i revoliutsionnoe dvizhenie 1860–kh godov*. Moscow: Novyi mir, 1922.

———. *Revoliutsionnoe pod'pole v epokhu "belogo terrora."* Moscow: Politkatorzhan, 1929.

———. *Russkaia sektsiia pervogo internatsionala.* Moscow: Izd. Akademii nauk SSSR, 1957.

———. "S. G. Nechaev i Tul'skie oruzheiniki." *Krasnyi arkhiv*, no. 30 (1930).

Koz'min, B. P., Kon, F., Shilov, A. A., Nevskii, V. I., and Teodorovich, I. A., eds. *Deiateli revoliutsionnogo dvizheniia v Rossii. Bio-bibliograficheskii slovar'.* 5 vols. Moscow, 1927–1934.

Kulczycki, Ludwik. *Geschichte der russischen Revolution.* 3 vols. Gotha: Friedrich Andreas Perthes A.-G., 1910–1914.

Kunkl', A. A. *Nechaev.* Moscow: Vses. ob-vo politkatorzhan i ssyl'no-poselentsev, 1929.

———. *Dolgushintsy.* Moscow: Izd. vses. ob-vo politkatorzhan i ssyl'no-poselentsev, 1931.

Lampert, Evgenii. *Sons Against Fathers.* Oxford: Clarendon Press, 1965.

Levin, Sh. M. *Obshchestvenno dvizhenie v Rossii v 60–70–e gody XIX veka.* Moscow: Izd. sotsial'no-ekonomicheskoi literatury, 1958.

Linkov, Ia I. *Revoliutsionnaia bor'ba A. O. Gertsena i N. P. Ogarev i "Zemlia i Volia" 1860–kh godov.* Moscow: Nauka, 1964.

McClellan, Woodford. "Rusi, Srbi i revolutsija, 1870–1872." In *Ujedin'ena omladina srpska. Zbornik radova*, Zhivan Milislavats, ed. Novi Sad: Matitsa srpska; Beograd: Istorijski institut, 1968.

Malitskii, N. "K biografii S. G. Nechaeva." In *Trudy vladimirskogo gubernskogo nauchnogo obshchestva*, vypusk 3. Vladimir, 1922.

Mal'shinskii, A. P. *Obzor sotsial'no-revoliutsionnogo dvizheniia v Rossii.* St. Petersburg: Tipografiia V. Demakov, 1880.

Masanov, I. F. *Slovar' psevdonymov russkikh pisateli, uchenykh, i obshchestvennykh deiateli.* 4 vols. Moscow: Izd. vsesoizunoi knizhnoi palaty, 1956–1960.

Mazlish, Bruce. *The Revolutionary Ascetic.* New York: Basic Books, 1976.

Meijer, Jan M. *Knowledge and Revolution.* Assen: Van Gorcum, 1955.

Mironov, B. N. *Istorik i matematika, matematicheskie metody v istoricheskikh issledovanii.* Leningrad: Nauka, 1975.

Nabokov, Vladimir. *The Gift.* Translated by Michael Scammel. New York: Capricorn Books, 1963.

Nettlau, Max. "Bakunin und die russische revolutionäre Bewegung in den Jahren 1868–1873." Arkhiv für die Geschichte des Sozializmus und der Arbeiterbewegung, edited by Carl Grünberg, vol. 5. 1915.

———. *The Life of Michael Bakounine. Michael Bakunin, Eine Biographie.* 3 vols. London, 1896–1900.

Nikolaevskii, B. "Pamiati poslednego 'iakobintsa'-semidesiatnika." *Katorga i ssylka*, no. 23 (1926).

———. "Varlaam Nikolaevich Cherkezov." *Katorga i ssylka*, no. 25 (1926).

Nomad, Max. *Apostles of Revolution*. Boston: Little Brown & Co., 1939.

Payne, Robert. *The Fortress*. New York: Simon and Schuster, 1967.

Pirumova, N. *Bakunin*. Moscow: Molodaia gvardiia, 1970.

Poglubko, K. A. *Ocherki istorii bolgaro-rossiiskikh revoliutsionnykh sviazei*. Kishinev: Stiintsa, 1972.

Pomper, Philip. "Bakunin, Nechaev and the 'Catechism of a Revolutionary': The Case for Joint Authorship." *Canadian-American Slavic Studies*, no. 4 (1976).

———. "Nečaev, Lenin, and Stalin: The Psychology of Leadership," *Jährbucher für Geschichte Osteuropas* 26, no. 1 (1978).

———. "Nechaev and Tsaricide: The Conspiracy within the Conspiracy." *The Russian Review*, no. 2 (1974).

———. *The Russian Revolutionary Intelligentsia*. New York: Thomas Y. Crowell Co., 1970.

Prawdin, Michael [Charol, M.]. *The Unmentionable Nechaev, a Key to Bolshevism*. New York: Roy Publishers Inc., 1961.

Raeff, Marc. *Origins of the Russian Intelligentsia*. New York: Harcourt, Brace & World, Inc., 1966.

Rudnitskaia, E. L. *N. P. Ogarev v russkom revoliutsionnom dvizhenii*. Moscow: Nauka, 1969.

Selivanov, A. F. "Ivanovo-Vosnesensk." *Entsiklopedicheskii slovar'*. edited by F. A. Brokgauz and I. A. Efron, vol. 24. St. Petersburg: Tip-Lit. I. A. Efrona, 1894.

Seth, Ronald. *The Russian Terrorists: The Story of the Narodniki*. London: Barrie & Rockliff, 1966.

Shchegolev, P. *Alekseevkii ravelin*. Moscow: Federatsia, 1929.

———. "S. G. Nechaev v Aleekseevskom raveline," *Krasnyi arkhiv*. no. 4 (1923); nos. 5–6 (1924).

Smirnov, A. V. "F. D. Nefodov, ego zhizn' i deiatel'nost'." In *Trudy vladimirskoi uchenoi arkhivnoi komissii*, kniga 18. Vladimir, 1917–1918.

Snytko, T. G. *Russkoe narodnichestvo i pol'skoe obshchestvennoe dvizhenie, 1865–1881 gg*. Moscow: Nauka, 1969.

Steklov, Iu. *Mikhail Aleksandrovich Bakunin, ego zhizn' i deiatel'nost' 1814–1876*. 2d ed. 3 vols. in 4. Moscow: Izd. Kommunisticheskoi akademii, 1926–1927.

Sviatikov, S. G. "Studencheskoe dvizhenie 1869 goda (Bakunin i Nechaev)." *Nasha Strana* [St. Petersburg], no. 1. (1907).

Theen, Rolf. "Nečaevs Auslieferung 1872. Der diplomatische Hintergrund." *Jahrbücher für Geschichte Osteuropas*, no. 4 (1973).

———. "The Russian Blanquists and the Hague Congress." *Canadian Slavic Studies*, no. 2 (1969).

[Tikhomirov, L. ?] "S. G. Nechaev v Alekseevskom raveline v 1873–1883[sic!]gg." *Byloe*, no. 7 (1906).

Trifonov, Iu. *Neterpenie*. Moscow: Izd. politicheskoi literatury, 1973.

Troitskii, N. *Bol'shoe obshchestvo propagandy, 1871–1874*. Saratov: Izd. saratovskogo universiteta, 1963.

Tucker, Robert C. *The Soviet Political Mind*. Rev. ed. New York: W. W. Norton & Co., 1971.

Varlamov, V. "Bakunin and the Russian Jacobins and Blanquists." *Rewriting Russian History*, edited by Cyril E. Black. 2d ed. rev. New York: Vintage Books, 1962.

Venturi, Franco. *Roots of Revolution*. New York: Alfred A. Knopf, 1960.

Vilenskaia, E. S. *Revoliutsionnoe podpol'e v Rossii 60–e gody XIX v*. Moscow: Nauka, 1965.

Volk, S. S. *Narodnaia volia 1879–1882*. Moscow: Nauka, 1966.

Von Borcke, A. *Die Ursprünge des Bolschewismus*. Munich: Johannes Berchmans Verlag, 1977.

Weinstein, Fred and Platt, Gerald H. *The Wish to Be Free*. Berkeley and Los Angeles: University of California Press, 1969.

Yarmolinsky, Avrahm. *Road to Revolution*. New York: Collier Books, 1962.

Index

Index

G

H

I

J

K

M

N